Lincoln Christian College

D0916746

The Land of Israel

The Land of Israel

*National Home
or Land of Destiny*

Eliezer Schweid

*Translated from the Hebrew
by Deborah Greniman*

A Herzl Press Publication
Rutherford ● Madison ● Teaneck
Fairleigh Dickinson University Press
London and Toronto: Associated University Presses

© 1985 by Associated University Presses, Inc.

Associated University Presses
440 Forsgate Drive
Cranbury, NJ 08512

Associated University Presses
25 Sicilian Avenue
London WC1A 2QH, England

Associated University Presses
2133 Royal Windsor Drive
Unit 1
Mississauga, Ontario
Canada L5J 1K5

Herzl Press
515 Park Avenue
New York, NY
10022

Library of Congress Cataloging in Publication Data

Schweid, Eliezer.
  The land of Israel.

  Translation of: Moledet ve-eretz ye'udah.
  "A Herzl Press publication."
  Bibliography: p.
  1. Jews—Restoration—History of doctrines.
2. Zionism—History. 3. Palestine in Judaism—History
of doctrines. I. Title.
BS649.J5S3813 1985   956.94'001   84-45015
ISBN 0-8386-3234-3

Printed in the United States of America

Contents

Introduction

Introduction

This book is about the meaning of the land of Israel to the Jewish people, as it is reflected in Jewish thought. The relationship of the people of Israel to its land, and its right to return to that land, have been subjected to incisive debate at various times in the course of Zionist history. That debate has arisen anew, with even greater intensity, in the wake of the Six Day and Yom Kippur wars, no longer primarily as a dispute between us and other nations, but rather as an internal controversy. The book were written after many discussions with young people—high school students and soldiers—and with their teachers. It aims to respond to an urgent need.

The fact that these questions are now being asked primarily from within, by the archetypal "four sons" of the Passover Haggadah, each in accordance with his character and temperament, shows that we have not fulfilled the commandment to "tell it to your son" (Ex. 13:8) as and when we should have. We are facing the painful result of a process whose onset can be discerned in the very earliest days of the secular Hibbat Zion movement. These early Zionists' understanding of the land of Israel, an innocent conception which doubted neither the vital relationship between the people and its land nor the people's right to return to it, derived from their traditional Jewish education. However, their awakening desire to realize this relationship and act on this right by settling the land and through political activity—testified to changes in the prevelant concept of Jewish nationhood and in the traditional image of the land of Israel. No longer was it seen as the land of destiny, the holy land; rather, it was a land to be possessed, a foundation upon which the national might of the people could stand; no longer an exalted religious symbol, it was a homeland, a "national home." Elements of traditional thought provided historical justification for the new secular outlook, which progressively obscured the traditional view. The process of realizing the Zionist ideal obscured it even further, and transformed the image of the land in accordance with modern material culture and of the complex web of modern socio-political life. We must admit that the correlation between the traditional image of the land of Israel, with all of its shadings, and its current image of a country in the process of being built up as a modern state is, at the very least, problematic.

This problematic correlation was made even more difficult by the assumption that education in the land of Israel could be based solely upon the existing reality. It was taken for granted that anyone born and raised in the land would automatically feel tied to it. There was no need for directed historical study or for the amassing of national memories. It was all obvious, immediate. One had only to live in the present, merge with the environment, participate in the enterprise, be in the land of Israel consciously. This, indeed, was the direction taken in educating toward love of the homeland. It is no wonder, then, that the historical dimension—both the distant past and more recent events—largely disappeared from the consciousness of those born in the land, and that this lack has been revealed in times of moral and spiritual trial.

The relationship of a people to its land is essentially historical. The homeland is not simply the plot of land upon which we tread, from which we bring forth our bread, and upon which we build our economy, our society and our state. It is of course all of these as well, but essentially, the word homeland denotes the overall environment which surrounds the individual and provides the framework for a life shared with his people. The image of the homeland is shaped in the hearts of the people by its material and spiritual/intellectual culture, and the wealth of meanings attached to its symbols is formed within this image. But culture is a product of history. One cannot arrive at it without living the national memories of the people. Happy are those peoples that have passed all of their history in their own lands. They dwell within the existing testimony concretized in the creations of their forebears, forming a stable historical environment for growth. Their environment is saturated with memories, and a person raised and educated within it absorbs them from the realism of everyday life. The people of Israel has not dwelt in its land throughout all of its history, nor did it fully develop its relationship with the land even when it did dwell therein. A person raised and educated in the land of Israel does not have the full testimony of his people's past around him. He very quickly discovers a stunning gap between a destroyed past, whose remains are buried in the earth, and a very different present. From where has this present grown? If it does have its own continuity, and if it is indeed related to the distant past, this continuity has left no tangible residue in the ambient material environment. It is to be found in memories alone. These memories are rich, awesome in their clarity and wealth, saturated with powerful feelings and a profound logic of their own. It is from these that the image of the Jewish homeland was formed and its significance interpreted.

A Jew who has come to live in his land, or even one born and raised in it, has still not yet entered the land of Israel until he has erected a palace of memories there and lives in it through the symbols around which a way of life can take shape. If he relies for support upon his concrete, tangible surroundings alone, adding but little from the treasures that have been stored up for him within his soul, he will remain outside, on the threshold.

The structure of this book and its content were determined by its educational goal, which seemed to demand a brief, succinct work that would delineate the overall picture, both the principal sources—the Bible, the Oral Teachings, philosophical and kabbalistic thought and modern Hebrew literature—and the sequence of historical transformations that have molded the people's perspectives on the subject. These range from the people's understanding of its land in ancient times, when it dwelt there, through its views of it from exile; from the conceptions that developed when it rose up to return to the land, through the ideas that are taking shape now that the people is once again living upon its own soil. There is both conformity and contradiction between the people's view of the land as a homeland and their conception of it as a land of destiny, and this vital tension serves as the focus of our discussion. The difficulties that have appeared throughout Jewish history arose from this tension and are entwined in it, and they are the same, with some slight change of appearance, as those we must still confront today as we attempt to realize the goals of Zionism.

Of course, the overall process can be presented only through outstanding examples. We are thus faced with a difficult methodological problem. We are dealing with a broad and very rich literature, both in the diversity of ideas that it comprehends and in the multitude of literary forms that express its various layers of thought, which include story, poetry and imperative in the Bible, the midrashic tales of the sages, the interpretive, philosophical and mystical literature of the Middle Ages, and the ideological essays, poetry and fiction of modern times. We could, of course, make do with very broad generalizations, but the influential power of a way of thinking or an emotional experience is to be found in its individual, unique expression. We have therefore preferred, as far as possible, to present each group of sources and each transformation through individual works that may be considered significant in terms of their fame and influence among the people, such as those of Judah Halevi, Maimonides, Joseph Gikatilla, Rabbi Nachman of Bratslav and others. The advantage of this approach is that it enables us in each instance to offer a detailed, in-depth presentation of a complete body of teaching or ideas, or to treat of a personal experience of *aliyah* to the land of Israel. It is clear, however, that we have had to forgo discussing a wide variety of other works. We have assumed that one person's ideas in general represent an entire stream, and that we have at least succeeded in presenting the most influential approaches.

The above remarks relate to the later sources. One book of the Bible, or just one of all the collections of *midrashim,* however, cannot serve to illustrate the significance attributed to the land of Israel throughout the Bible or in all the works of the sages. In dealing with these sources, it was thus necessary to draw material from all parts of them, despite our knowledge that each citation has a context which determines the way in which it should be understood. There appears to be no satisfactory solution to this methodological difficulty. The dimensions of the work have been kept within bounds, at any rate, by limiting the topics to be discussed within the broader subject matter. As for the problem of the removal of the citations from their context, we have done our best to isolate ideological motifs which may be shown to reappear throughout these bodies of literature and thus may be considered representative.

The reader of this book will certainly become aware of the fact that the style and form of the discussion change from section to section. The chapter on the Bible is theoretical and interpretive; that on the Middle Ages philosophical, and the section on modern Hebrew literature is literary and ideological. These transitions from one style or form to another may be disturbing, but they are necessitated by the character of the literary material with which we are dealing. The principal realms in which the Jewish people expressed its relationship to its land changed with every age, and these transformations were also evident in the literary forms dominant in the thought of each period. Not by chance, it would seem, were different literary forms preferred in every age, for these reflect the people's experience and modes of emotional and intellectual response, and their adaptation to different cultural environments. The historical story is characteristic of a people that dwells in its land; the philosophical essay is more fitting in a time when it must accept a state of dispersion and distance; while the expressive forms of the modern age are appropriate to its awakening to a change in its situation. The image and meanings of the land of Israel were thus formulated in different realms of thought and experience, which cannot always be dealt with in the same way. On the contrary, the instrument of study and research must be adapted individually to each of these different layers. The reader who is willing from the outset to accept these stylistic transformations may learn from them, too, something of the richness of the subject, so that what was originally perceived as a blemish may ultimately prove a blessing.

It is certainly difficult to succeed equally well in dealing with all aspects of so complex a discussion. The author is aware of the flaws in this book that have resulted from the impossibility of dealing exhaustively with all the necessary material, especially in the sections on the Bible and the works of the sages. The importance of the issue, however, has overruled all doubts. If this work should aid educators and their pupils to come closer to an understanding of the sources and to draw upon them directly—this will be my reward.

PART I

National Home or Land of Destiny

1

The Biblical View

In a study that sets out to trace a historical process, there is no need to explain why we should begin at the beginning—that is, with the Bible. We must, however, stress the fundamental role of biblical literature in shaping Jewish thought concerning the Land of Israel. The Bible is more than simply the collection of ideas, concepts and symbols that the Jewish people has drawn upon, directly or indirectly, in every generation; it is in itself the spiritual link between the people and its land. This is a fact upon which people of differing and even opposing views are in agreement, though they interpret its significance in widely different ways.

The Bible considers itself, as do those who accept it as a sacred document, the book of the covenants, ever-renewed, between God and His people Israel. The inheritance of the land of Israel is one of the terms of this covenant.[1] That is to say, the Bible bears witness to the Divine promise which predestined the land for this people, and to the terms by which the promise was to be fulfilled. This understanding gives form not only to the bond between land and people, but also to the image of the land and its significance for them: it is the Holy Land, the Promised Land.

For Jews who no longer acknowledge the covenant and the promise in their literal sense, the Bible is, at any rate, the most important creative work produced by the people of Israel in its land. Viewed in this way, the Bible is seen to mirror the scenery and nature of the land, the people's ideological and emotional relationship to it and the course of their history within its borders.[2] Scripture bears witness to the fact that the land of Israel was the birthplace of the people, and it deciphers the historical traces of those who remain there. For this approach, too, it is the Bible that interprets and formulates the image of the land in the people's memory and its significance in their thought. We may thus state with assurance that the importance of the concept of the land of Israel in biblical thought is more than historical in the technical sense of the word. This concept directly shapes and reshapes the relationship of the people with its land in every generation, including our own.

In using the phrase "biblical thought" we are not overlooking the premise of modern biblical research that the Bible is not all of a piece, literarily or

ideologically. Had we been undertaking a more detailed study, it would have
been desirable to present in chronological sequence the manner in which
each book of the Bible, in accordance with its own particular background
and context, views the land of Israel. Even were we to do this, however, we
still would find an underlying unity. This is, however, no simple unity, for it
comprehends the tension between the priestly view, which stresses the motif
of the Temple, site of God's indwelling among his people, and that of the
prophets, which emphasizes living in holiness in the ethical/social sense; and
this tension is understood in different ways in the context of various events
and processes in the life of the people. Even so, both this tension and the
multiple perspectives in the Bible form one overall outlook, albeit rich and
complex, to which all of the future generations had recourse, each in accordance with its place in the history of the Jewish people.

In a general study such as this, it is permissible for us to disregard the
inner divisions among the books of the Bible and sketch a panorama of the
principal ideas involved, their content and their relationships with one
another. There is also a historical justification for this kind of presentation: It
is in this way that later generations—including our own, despite its knowledge of biblical research—have related to the Bible when they have had
recourse to it as a source to guide them in formulating their own views.[3] We
too, then, shall take this course, which unites the perspectives of generations of teachers, interpreters and thinkers, and ask: what is the image of the
land of Israel that is to be drawn from all parts of the Bible, taken as a
whole?

In order to bring together the relevant "literary material," let us begin by
examining the kinds of assertions about the land of Israel that we encounter
in persuing the books of the Bible. These include, first of all, assertions
about the borders of the country and its position in relation to other lands.
Since we do not intend to go into the issue of borders, we shall note only one
general characteristic that has had a great deal of significance in shaping the
image of the land and endowing it with its various meanings. The land of
Israel is a land in the middle, in two respects.[4] It is a mountainous land
situated between the great lands of the rivers (the Tigris and Euphrates and
the land of the Nile) and between the desert and the sea, and it also a bridge
between the two great powers, Egypt on the one hand, and Assyria and
Babylonia on the other. We shall see that the significance attached by the
Bible to this midway location transcends both geography and politics.

The second group of assertions concerns the nature of the country: its
beauty, its abundant fruits, and the wealth that lies in its soil. Statements of
this kind show Israel to be a bountiful land capable of sustaining an independent national entity. It can provide its inhabitants abundantly with all that
they need to maintain themselves.[5] To this, however, we must add another
geographical-meteorological characteristic to which especial significance
was attached, as we shall see. Israel is described as a mountainous land that

"drinks water by the rain from heaven."[6] Considering the comparison of Israel to the lands of the rivers on the one hand and to the desert on the other, its mountainous character and its need for water to enable it to bring forth its bounty are very important indeed in the biblical conception.

A third kind of assertion deals with the history of the land of Israel. Before its settlement by the Israelite tribes, it is called "the land of Canaan"[7], "the land of the Amorites"[8], "the place of the Canaanites, the Hittites and the Amorites" or the land of the seven peoples.[9] The forefathers of the people walked it as strangers,[10] but their relationship to the land was determined by their anticipation of the future,[11] and they stamped it with the marks of deeds that were, to them, of consecratory significance. Later, there are the detailed descriptions of settlement of the land,[12] of the many wars with their enemies,[13] of their establishment within the land's borders, and then of the loss of their independence, and subsequent exile.[14] If we are to understand the significance of all these historical facts in relation to Israel's character as a homeland, we must emphasize the Bible's view that the previous inhabitants of the land were deeply sunk, perhaps even more than other peoples, in the sin of idolatry and the moral corruption that accompanies it.[15] True, at the time of the patriarchs this sin was "not yet complete."[16] However, the story of Ham, the son of Noah, who brought down a curse upon the descendants of his son Canaan,[17] shows that the Bible viewed idolatrous sin as being ingrained in the very essence of these peoples' national existence, and it justified their dispossession. We learn just how significant this historical motif is from the gravity of the biblical exhortation to destroy every trace of the idolatrous rites of the previous inhabitants.[18] Moreover, throughout the entire period of the Israelite settlement and establishment in the land, the prophets waged war against the idolatrous Canaanite interpretation of the nature of the land and championed the view laid down in the Torah of Moses. They warned the people that their fate would be that of the Canaanites and the Amorites if they followed in the ways of these peoples: they would not be able to remain in the land.[19] The image of the land and the way its symbolic significance was understood took shape in the course of this great struggle waged by the prophets, which left a powerful historical mark upon the land's cultural scenery.

A fourth set of assertions concerns the promise of the land to the people of Israel, a promise that is made over and over again, to the patriarchs, to Moses, and to all of the people of Israel.[20] Even when they were dwelling upon their own soil, however, the land never stopped being promised, not only because the borders framed by the promise were always wider than those of the areas in which the people actually settled, but also because throughout all their years in the land the people knew only brief periods of peace. Holding on to the land was a never-ending task, and living there in peace no more than a vision—a promise. Moreover, the prophets saw the people's dwelling in the land as conditional. The promise depended upon the fulfilment of certain conditions, and the fact that the people were actually living there did not make it absolute.[21]

We shall consider as a fifth type of assertion the commandments relating to the conquest of the land and its division among the tribes. The people was ordered to destroy the land's previous inhabitants, or at least to eradicate all traces of their idolatrous rites.[22] The stratum of idolatrous culture that had in a certain sense shaped the image of the land had to be wiped out, and a new cultural stratum, which would mold a different image, had to be created. This was not merely a new people coming to take the place of its predecessors: it was an opposing culture. And it stands to reason that the special nature of this culture should find expression in the way the people related to the land as their national home.

This last statement leads us to the sixth group of assertions: the commandments relating to the way in which the people of Israel was to live in the land—that is, the commandments that were to guide and form the new, anti-idolatrous culture. Of these, it makes sense to treat first the commandments relating to worship. A new kind of worship, different in both quality and form, was to take the place of the idolatrous rites, and its formation was to culminate in its centralization in the Temple in Jerusalem.[23] But the sixth group of assertions encompasses far more than this. It relates to the entire way of life of the people living on the promised soil, and first and foremost to the formation of their conception of possession of the land, as a people and as individuals. We are referring in particular to the commandments regarding the seventh and jubilee years,[24] the tithes and the offering of the first fruits in the Temple, the portions of dough that were set aside for the priests and the crops that were to be left over in the fields at harvest-time to be collected by the poor.[25] As we shall see, these commandments were to shape the way in which the people related to the land, and it is through them that the image of Israel as the Holy Land was understood and interpreted. The seventh and final group of assertions about the land of Israel consists of the descriptions found in the prophetic visions of redemption. These do not really add anything to the content of the assertions listed above, except for their idealization. In the visions of the prophets the real, physical land, whose image the people are commanded to mold, through their actions and way of life, reaches the height for which it was intended. They portray it as it will be in time to come, as it was meant to be according to the Torah.

2

One further issue remains to be clarified before we attempt to draw conclusions from these assertions and develop them into a comprehensive view. This is the ethico-religious and political matter of a people's right to its land, particularly where this involves the dispossession of peoples who had lived there previously. This matter would appear to have been dealt with thoroughly in the Bible's clear-cut, articulate statements concerning the promise, and claims to that effect are, indeed, put forward by modern orthodox thinkers.[26] Closer examination, however, will show this argument to be an oversimplification which takes the idea of the promise out of context. The issue of our right to the land must be dealt with on its own, not only with respect to the people of Israel but also in terms of the relationship between peoples and their lands in general. Discussion of the latter issue must, in fact, come first, as it will provide us with a broad conceptual framework for discussing the particular issue of the relationship of the Jewish people to its land.

Let us note briefly some of the fundamental ideas that are first expressed in the book of Genesis and go on to compromise a firm and consistent conceptual basis for all of the books of the Bible: God is the Creator of the Universe.[27] The world and all that is in it are created beings—that is, they exist by the will and the grace of God. Man, too, is created, but he has a unique status: he was made in the image of God.[28] His preeminence is shown by the fact that the world was created especially for him—but only because he is to settle it.[29] He is commanded to be fruitful and multiply and fill the land; to settle it, to work it and to preserve it. Man fulfills this obligation through the development of his progeny—that is, he does not live alone. Living together with others in society is essential to him.[30] Society comes into being and develops through the relational bonds of birth, which bring about the family, the tribe and the people:[31] the family is that association of individuals that conceives and raises the young; the tribe is an affiliation of related families, and the people an association of related tribes. All of the peoples have a single origin.[32] A new people comes into being when a tribe or group of tribes breaks away, settles in a different place and begins keeping its offspring within its own borders.[33] In this way, man carries out the commandment incumbent upon him to be fruitful and multiply and fill the land. The family, the tribe and the people are thus the social units that Scripture deems appropriate to man. It is within them that he can find his place and live as a human being—that he can fulfil his destiny and keep the commandments given him by his God. Tribes and peoples can thus maintain themselves only by living in a land of their own. From this land they draw their bread, and upon it they organize their society and lay down their patterns of law and leadership. God therefore designates a specific land for each people to hold as its own.[34] Along with the command to settle throughout the world, then, God divides up the land among the peoples and gives each one its share. Settlement, then, is both by the command of God and as a matter of national right. Let us stress once more that this holds true for all the peoples of the world. The designation of the land of Israel for the people of Israel and the commandment to settle it are not at all exceptional. They are particular applications of a general principle—though they involve a particular people and a particular land.[35]

The combination of the commandment of settlement and the right of possession frames the way in which a people's ownership of its land is realized. God designates a particular place for each people, and this creates a general right. A people actually comes into possession of its land, however, only when it fulfills the commandment to settle it. It is thus the settling in the land that secures possession, and this is therefore significant in its own right. A story from the book of Judges, that of the war between Yiftah of Gilead and the King of the Ammonites,[36] can teach us several useful things about the role of this relationship between divine designation and settlement in creating the right of possession. In the story, the King of the Ammonites demands that a tract of land which, he claims, belonged to his people before the Israelite conquest, be returned to him. Yiftah denies the claim. Underlying the dispute, however, there appears to be agreement on two basic principles. First of all, each people has a land that God has designated for it, and this is recognized as its rightful property: "Will you not possess what Chemosh your god gives you to possess? And all that the Lord our God has dispossessed before us, we will possess."[37] On this basis, Yiftah claims that the Israelites have respected the lands set apart for other peoples and refrained from injuring them, and they have taken only that land that God has designated for them. Secondly, a claim to ownership based on prior possession carries weight, and it is not invalidated by another people's conquest. If the people protests the conquest of its land, its claim is valid. On the basis of this principle, Yiftah claims that the Ammonites had never demanded the return of the disputed tract since its conquest, some three hundred years earlier.

How, then, do these two principles work together? The answer would appear to be this: God's designation of a land for a particular people is a promise of a standing right, which only He can withdraw; this right, however, must be realized through settlement. If the land involved is inhabited by another people, this realization depends upon a further condition which does not follow from the promise, since living in a land in itself constitutes possession. It is not enough for a people that would dispossess another to do so on the strength of a divine promise or divine designation alone; it must prove that the dispossessed people's ownership of the land is invalid, either because the conquering people had itself dwelt there before a previous conquest, or because the people to be dispossessed has relinquished its right. This much can be learned from the legal argument between Yiftah and the King of the Ammonites. By drawing upon other stories appearing in the Pentateuch, however, we can add another factor of great significance. The land of Israel was designated by God for the people of Israel. Furthermore, at the Covenant between the pieces,[38] God granted Abraham possession of the land: from that time on it is already his property. Even so, he had to wander through it as a stranger and to pay in full for the burial plot of the Cave of Machpela in Hebron. Other peoples held the land, and he had as yet no claim that could undermine their right. According to the same covenant, such a claim would come into being only several generations later, when the sin of the Amorites was complete. We may learn several things from this. First, a people's possession of a land by settlement has validity, and is not invalidated by Divine promise alone; secondly, there is an ethical/religious condition to possession by right of settlement. As long as a people dwells in a land and observes this condition, it retains ownership of the land. Whensoever it violates the condition, and its sin is "ripe", its right of possession is abrogated. Only then is the people for whom the land was designated permitted to conquer it for itself. Moreover, this ethical/religious condition applies to the people to whom the land was promised as well. The promise is, indeed, eternal, but its realization depends upon the condition being observed. If the people sin, as did the Amorites, it is driven from its land.[39]

In concluding our discussion of this issue, then, there would appear to be an instructive parallel between the biblical conceptualization and that which sees the justification for a people's possession of its land in "historical right."[40] Both recognize that every people has a "right" to live in a land of its own. Both also recognize that this right is realized in relation to a particular land through the historical fact of settlement, and settlement involves a physical act, so that a people's right to a particular tract of land comes in force only after settlement has taken place. The biblical conception does not contradict the argument of "historical right," which attributes a people's right of possession to its having dwelt in a particular land for generations, but it adds two further ideas: It is God Who designates a particular land for each people, and specifically for the people of Israel, and He attaches an ethical/religious condition, which follows from man's purpose in the world, to a people's possession of its land. This condition applies both to the realization of the right and to its continuing validity. We shall see that these two ideas play a very important role in molding Israel's image both as a national homeland and as a holy land, according to the Bible.

3

God designated a land of its own for each and every people, and the land of Israel was given to the people of Israel. But why this particular land? This question does not necessarily arise in connection with every people. But Israel was selected, by virtue of the merits of the patriarchs, as God's chosen people,[41] and this special relationship between God and His people is also expressed in the choice of its land. The fact that the country had previously belonged to the Canaanites, and that it is, moreover, called by their name, makes the question all the more urgent.

Why the land of Israel? According to the assertions discussed above, the land of Israel is especially beautiful and bountiful. It provides those who work its soil with abundance of excellent fruits, and its soil contains great wealth. If the people behave as they should, they can live there in peace and plenty. From the point of view of God's relationship with His people, of course, this is, an expression of love: For His chosen people God has designated the choicest of lands.

We have seen, too, that the land of Israel stands midway between all the ancient lands and, as a mountainous land, it is perhaps raised above the lands of the rivers, the desert and the sea. Its image in Scripture, then, is that of a central and lofty land: one must ascend to reach it and descend to depart. Needless to say, this image of centrality and elevation signifies its importance. All turn toward this land, and especially toward Jerusalem, the heart of Israel.[43]

However, the Bible gives the facts that the land is central and mountainous in contrast to the bordering riverlands an additional interpretation that is of great importance. As a mountainous land, its fertility depends upon rainfall, which is not as reliable as the waters of the great rivers that irrigate the lands of the Nile, the Tigris and the Euphrates. Sometimes it rains—but sometimes it doesn't. Does this not give the advantage to the riverlands, where water and crops are always abundant? The Torah's brief statements on this point hint at a boon enjoyed by a land that is watered by rainfall: the soil of the riverlands enslaves those who work it,[44] for they must carry the water to the fields, while rain-water reaches them all by itself. This intimation, however, can properly be understood only in a wider context. According to the Torah, as cited above, the rains express God's continual providence. The riverlands are bound by their natural cyclicity, and anyone who learns to exploit this can take his sustenance from them; but a land irrigated by precipitation is in the direct care of God. Rain falls by divine grace, which is intended, of course, for those who are worthy of it, and the abundance of the harvest is always seen as a gift of God. When it is given to those who are worthy of it, they are able to sustain themselves as free men.

This does not yet exhaust the distinction between the riverlands and the land of mountains. For it is clear that the riverlands more closely approximate the image of the Garden of Eden, which brings forth its fruits by itself. Even if irrigation demands an effort, the continual abundance of soil that is fertile and easy to work, and of water, gives man a feeling of complete security. It is as though he holds the guarantee of his future sustenance in his own hands. He can ensure himself against want. This is not so, however, of a land watered by rain. There nature gives no guarantees. All depends upon the grace of rain, over which man has no control. In the riverlands there can thus develop a culture based upon man's aspiration for complete mastery over the primary factors that condition his existence and his well-being.[45] In a mountainous country, however, this is not so. There, even the illusion of mastery cannot survive. One who lives in that land knows that he is dependent upon a force over which he has no control for the provision of his daily needs. True, it is not a desert. It is capable of providing generous bounty— but this bounty is uncertain. It depends upon a higher will. But is this not the very opposite of what we have said above? The land of mountains, it would seem, enslaves those who work it, in contrast to the mastery and freedom of those who dwell in the riverlands. The Bible, however, sees things differently: it is the very illusion of mastery, in contrast to an awareness of dependence, that enslaves. It is precisely the desire for sovereignty over the conditions of human existence that produces an idolatrous culture, and the essence of such a culture is that ambition for complete human mastery which turns these lands into giant tyrannies and houses of bondage.[46] On the other hand, awareness of the dependence that limits human sovereignty is the foundation for a culture of faith, the culture of free men. It is precisely on this account that the land of Israel is appropriate to the chosen people, which is subject to continual divine supervision and is always aware of being commanded by God. It is this awareness that guarantees its freedom.

These things will become clearer in the following paragraphs. At this point, however, we must ward off a possible misunderstanding. The Bible does not present this as the only possible interpretation of the mountainous, rain-watered character of the land of Israel. It does not *necessarily* follow from the qualities of the land that all its inhabitants will arrive of their own accord at that consciousness of dependence that ensures human freedom. On the contrary, those who dwelt there before the settlement of the Israelite tribes gave the qualities of the land quite a different interpretation, on the basis of which they created the idolatrous culture that Scripture condemns more than any other. This culture was based on the worship of Baal which, according to the prophets, is characterized by terrible moral degeneration. The purpose of the rites of Baal is to guarantee, by means of magic, enticement and appeasement, rainfall and the fertility of the soil.[47] Is it not, in fact, only to be expected that man's illusory effort to gain mastery over the means of sustenance should show itself in its most violent and corrupt forms precisely in that land where the maintenance of such an illusion is so very difficult? In any event, this perspective does enable us to gain a deeper understanding of the war of the prophets against the idolatry of the Canaanites, and its attendant dangers. Throughout the entire period of their settlement of the land the Israelites were drawn to the worship of Baal. They were attracted by the idolatrous aspiration for mastery over the basic factors of existence, and it was against this desire that the prophets struggled. We may view this conflict, which reached its climax and attained its clearest expression in the stand of the prophet Elijah against the priests of Baal on Mt. Carmel, as having been fought over the truth of the character of the land of Israel.[48] Who is it that brings the rain—God or Baal? What is it that ensures prosperity and freedom in the land of Israel—observing the commandments of the Torah in awareness of man's subjection to God, or the magical and carnal rites ensuing from the ambition for mastery? Elijah, and the prophets who came before and after him, sought to prove that their interpretation was the true one. In any case, it is clearly not the qualities of the land alone that determine its image and significance. These depend upon the spiritual attitude of its inhabitants as well. It is a particular spiritual and ideological way of relating to the qualities of the chosen land that creates its unique image.

We may now proceed to examine what may be learned from the demographic history of the land. The fact that other peoples dwelt there before the Israelite tribes, but were driven out because of their sins, is highly significant in this context. The land of Israel will not tolerate peoples that pollute it by their iniquities. It vomits them out, and this is what happened to the Canaanites and the Amorites.[49] The promise made to the people of Israel by virtue of the merits of their forefathers is, indeed, eternal, but when they misinterpret the qualities of their land they are enslaved by the surrounding peoples, and they, too, must ultimately go into exile. Only faithfulness to the commandments of their God, which reveal the way of life approporiate to the land of Israel, ensures them both freedom and peace.

Another motif emerges from these statements, in addition to that of the mountainous country watered by rain. As we recall, the land of Israel has a central location, and this, too, is both an advantage and at the same time—and for the same reasons—a disadvantage. The land of Israel is situated between great powers that have developed enormous military strength, based on their natural wealth. These idolatrous nations battle each other for ultimate sovereignty, and the tiny state in the land of Israel is in constant danger of conquest. There is a temptation for the kings of Judah and Israel to take part in this war over idolatrous sovereignty, either by joining one of the belligerent sides in order to tip the scales in its favor, or by making pacts with other, smaller states to create a third force.[50] The prophets struggle against the parallel tendency to pattern the governments of Israel and of Judah upon that of an idolatrous kingdom. They know that the people of Israel cannot retain its hold on its land if it does not ensure social justice by subjecting the sovereignty of the government to the law of the Torah, and display political humility towards its neighbors.[51]

The history of the people of Israel in its land thus shows that the character and location of the land constitute a condition upon which the people's existence there depends. This condition is religious, political and moral. If the people understand and live by it, they dwell in peace and dignity in their land; if they do not, the land, as it were, rejects them. May we not see in this the basis for the idea of the holiness of the land of Israel? Indeed, according to Scripture it is because it is holy, different from other lands and chosen by God, that the land of Israel is especially marked for the people of Israel. Even if we understand how its character and location are interpreted by the Bible, however, we still have not understood the nature of the land's holiness, and how it is expressed. After all, the facts that Israel is a mountainous country irrigated by rainfall, and that it is located midway between other lands, do not embody an essential difference between it and any other land. These distinctions are no more than relative. Should we, then understand the idea of holiness as having its source in the people's consciousness and behavior, or does the Bible view the land itself as having some exceptional quality? In later Jewish thought two views clash on this issue. One attributes an intrinsic holiness to the land of Israel[52], while the other, following the assumption that holiness cannot be attributed to things but only symbolized by them, stresses that it is behavior that sanctifies.[53] Despite their disagreement, however, these two streams are not entirely at odds with one another, for even the second does not deny that the Temple and Jerusalem do have, at least, an element of intrinsic holiness to them. This understanding appears to be drawn from the Bible, which is the common source for both streams.

The idea that the land of Israel is intrinsicly holy is based on the priestly rites, based, in turn, on the idea that God chose to dwell among His people precisely in the land of Israel, in Jerusalem, on Mt. Moriah, and nowhere else.[54] While it is true that before the settlement God did appear to them and dwell in their midst in various places outside of the land of Israel, and later, in Israel but outside of Jerusalem, these were temporary dwellings in transient abodes. None of these places, including Mt. Sinai, where the people received the Torah, was considered holy for any longer than the limited period in which the Israelites remained in its vicinity, while the holiness of the land of Israel, or at least that of Jerusalem and the Temple Mount, abides forever. After the settlement of the land is completed, God dwells among His people only in Israel, only in Jerusalem, only in the Temple. It is only in the Temple that God can be worshipped properly, and only in the land of Israel that the Divine Presence is permanently made manifest. The Temple is thus seen as the "House of God" in the primary, simple sense of the term.[55] It is the permanent Divine Presence in a place that sanctifies it, and it is therefore natural to assume that this divine "contact" imbues the things connected with it, the vessels, the stones, even the dust, with some special quality that makes them different. The fact that entrance to the Temple involved danger and required that a person sanctify himself through a special ritual testifies to this. Anyone who had not sanctified himself by means of the ritual—not spiritual or moral actions—risked his life if he entered the Temple. Holiness in the same sense may be applied to the land as a whole, and there are indeed allusions to this effect in several scriptural verses.[56]

Along with the concept of holiness associated with the priestly rites, however, and in continual tension with it, we find the interpretation of the prophets, who saw holiness as stemming from the sanctifying behavior of the people. The holiness of the land of Israel in this context is the sanctity of the commandments, and its essential uniqueness is moral rather than ritual.[57] The distinction between the idolatrous ambition to complete mastery and the monotheistic faith that considers man responsible before his Creator is fundamental to this concept of holiness. We find allusions to this in the attribution of religious significance to the difference between the mountainous country and the riverlands, between the worship of God and the rites of Baal, and between the ambition for political sovereignty and the subjection of governmental authority to divine law. The inheritance of the land of Israel is conditional, and the condition upon which it depends, and which makes Israel a promised land even when the Israelites dwell within its borders, is seen by the prophets as the source of its holiness.

In this connection we must take cognizance of the fact that this religio-ethical condition is not merely a fine idea to be studied and given symbolic expression in ritual form. The prophets demand that it be fulfilled as a way of life. Moreover, we are not speaking of their general vigorous insistence that the people distance themselves from the impurity and corrupt rituals of other nations and pursue righteousness and mercy in their interpersonal relations. The demand refers, too, to certain commandments related to the very act of settling and dwelling in the land, that is, to the commandments that can only be carried out in the land of Israel: the laws of the seventh year and the jubilee, the tithes, and the leaving of *leket, shikchah* and *pe'ah* in the fields for the poor. The condition is embodied in all of these commandments: one must give concrete expression to the understanding that man can never have absolute possession of the land. Absolute possession belongs only to God, Who in His grace makes man a gift of the land in order to enable him thereby to fulfill his destiny. In the seventh and jubilee years the land is, in fact, withdrawn from human ownership and returns to its primary state, as it was when it was brought forth by its Creator. This serves to remind man that the land is never completely his, and at the same time it provides him with a new beginning. The land will be divided justly, and the domination of the inheritance of the poor and the weak by the rich and powerful will be prevented. The same is true of the commandments that involve helping the poor. The significance of tithing, of *leket, shikchah,* and *pe'ah* is that helping the poor is not a matter of "generosity" but an absolute obligation. The poor have a share in the crops of the rich, for these are given by God to their owners only on condition, and they are never possessed outright. If the rich does not give the poor his due, he is a thief. The way in which they live in the land thus testifies directly to the people's faithfulness to the Torah, and they may remain in the land only insofar as they have the right attitude toward the land and its produce. In this way the land becomes a national possession upon which the relationship between the people and its God is founded, for by the manner in which it dwells in the land the people establishes its national way of life. If it acts in accordance with the Torah the land becomes both its national homeland in the usual sense as well as a holy land. The land's holiness stems from the sanctifying attitude, for it is the people who impart holiness to it by their mode of dwelling in the land, and by the significance they give to the land's image by their behavior.

This kind of sanctificatory attitude is possible in any country. Why, then, should the land of Israel have been chosen particularly? A priestly conception can help here. Just as a builder creates a building in which each part has a particular use, so the Creator of the Universe appointed a special role for each land. The land of Israel was designated from its very creation to be a sanctuary for all the lands, and its intrinsic, unique quality of holiness is innate in it. This is not entirely explicit in the Bible, but is intimated, as we noted above, in several passages, and these were seized upon in later thought. The prophetic conception, by contrast, can state initially only that God designated the land of Israel for the people of Israel for them to live there in consonance with the Torah, and the Will that so designated it is the Will that sanctified it. Its holiness abides because of the persistence of the sanctifying Will established in the covenant. In the land of Israel, the people of Israel are commanded to live a full national life in accordance with the Torah. This is a national obligation that cannot be cancelled. The land of Israel symbolizes this obligation in that it is a necessary base for its fulfilment, and its holiness thus can never cease.

The Divine Presence among the people can also be interpreted along the same lines: A life of holiness is life in the presence of God; it is proximity to God. When the people sanctifies itself to God, God dwells in its midst. This much can be said at the outset. Living in the land, however, shows how the sanctificatory attitude can reveal the significance of the special qualities of the land of Israel, shape its image in accordance with them and invest this image with meaning. The land of Israel becomes a sanctuary by the way in which the people lives in it; and the life of a people shapes the image of its land not only in its imagination but in reality as well. In accordance with this image and its significance the people builds its cities and villages and works its land. It is by way of the idea of holiness, therefore, that the people comes to understand the character of its land, as explained above: its qualities of beauty and abundance, expressing the love of God for his people; its centrality and elevation; its being a land subject to continual divine care; a land whose history testifies to its unique situation. À posteriori, then, the land of Israel appears marked for sancitity, so that prophecy can adopt and adapt for itself the priestly, ritual conception of holiness. The prophets, at any rate, did not negate the priestly approach. It is also clear, however, that they limited it and gave it a secondary status.[58] To them, ethical/religious holiness was primary. That is, it is the people's sanctificatory attitude, rooted in its ethical obligation before God, that gives meaning to the land's character and shapes its image as a holy land. The holiness of the land of Israel, then, stems from the divine will that appointed the land and from the will of the people to live there in obedience to the Torah.

4

In the Bible's view, then, the land of Israel is the national homeland of the people of Israel, a homeland like that of any other people. At the same time, however, it is set aside for the chosen people as a holy land. The unique relationship between people and land is comprehended at the outset in the undertaking of the people to live in the land in the presence of God and by His commandments. They are to dwell in Israel perceiving it as a promised land whose inheritance is conditional. The land's special character is understood and interpreted, and its symbolic quality perceived, through the people's life upon its soil, and this symbolic understanding continues to shape the image of the land through the living memory of its history.

This is a key statement: The special character of the land is understood, interpreted and perceived as symbolic, and this symbolic understanding continues to shape the image of the land through the living memory of its history. That is, insofar as the people is instructed by the words of the Torah and the prophets, it learns to view its land in accordance with the image that has its source in the historical events that took place between them and the land, and whose marks remain engraved in the scenery of the country. History accumulates in the culture that molds the land's present image, and memory gives life to the signs that remain and endows them with context and significance. This is true of every people living in its own country. Here, however, we must again call attention to the unique nature of the scriptural conception of history: history in the Bible is directed toward destiny. Historical memory is more than a recollection of past events. It is primarily a continual tension of anticipation directed toward the future, as each generation passes on to the next its expectations and hopes, its faith and its aims. All that we recall of the history of the people involves a constant readiness for the future destined for them, both as commandments and as reward. This orientation is also embodied in the people's perception of the land as being promised, a land of destiny—that is, a land in which one ought to live in a certain way and whose suitability for a particular people is determined by the way they act in it. That is to say: the image of the land of Israel reflects the vision of its future more than it reflects its past and present. In this sense, too, it is a promised land, a land that one day will fully become what it was destined to be by the will of God. This, indeed, is the form taken by the ideal image of the land of Israel described in the visions of redemption.

How does the land of Israel appear in these visions? They seem not to add anything to the motifs enumerated above, but rather to dramatize them and elevate them to the highest utopian level. First of all there is the great bounty that bursts forth from the inward recesses of the land as though from springs of love. The land will bear the people in its bosom and sustain them like a mother embracing her young and giving them suck. There will be a great abundance of food and fruit. The gladness of free people who are not oppressed by concern for their future will prevail, and there will be a feeling of gratitude over all.[59] Peace will reign in the land, and it will be founded upon righteousness and justice, not only among men, but even among animals.[60] The land itself will bestow peace on its very foundations. This will be the basis of the kingdom of God in the land. He will reign directly, for He will dwell in His sanctuary in Zion, in the midst of the people living according to His commandments.[61] Then, too, the status of the land, in the center of the world and raised on high, will become clear. The land of Israel will be a sanctuary for all peoples, and the teaching of God will go forth from Jerusalem.[62]

The biblical conception of the Land of Israel was captured in this vision of the redemption, and passed on to the following generations. He who would understand the image depicted in the words of the Tannaim and Amoraim, and those who appeared later in the writings of the medieval scholars, of the hasidim and their opponents, and even in those of the Zionists, must keep in mind that despite all the many and great differences between them, all of these had before them the same basic vision of the land of Israel as it is to be: the promised land as the prophets described it in their visions of redemption. Even when the physical land of Israel faded from sight in the darkness of the exile, the land to which the people related from afar—and this sense of distance, from the land of Israel as it was meant to be could be felt even within the land itself—was that of the visions. At times, in fact, the darkness of the exile added a further dimension of idealization, to the point where the relationship between the actual, physical land and its symbolic significance was almost severed. And then, with an abrupt change of direction, the people's devotion to the physical land, where it would dwell on its own soil amid great abundance, free and secure, returned. Through all of these transformations, this single basic vision remains evident—the vision of the land of Israel, the homeland of the people and its holy land, as the prophets foresaw it would be when all the promises concerning it should be fulfilled. The land, then, always symbolized its future as the chosen land destined for the chosen people.

PART II

From the Exile: Memories and Visions of the Destined Land

ritual, but also some relating to daily life in accordance with the Torah, which can only be carried out in the Temple or as long as the Temple exists. The people's vital link to the Temple and Jerusalem must not be relinquished. They are unique, and there can be no substitutes for them. Yet a substitute had to be found or else the people of Israel would cease to exist as a people.

This is the dilemma that confronted Rabban Yohanan ben Zakkai and his disciples in Yavne, and what they said then about Jerusalem and the Temple was applied later—when most of the people had gone into exile leaving behind them only an impoverished remnant—to the whole land of Israel. On the one hand, no people can long exist without a bond with its land, and it is all the more difficult for the people of Israel, the people of the Torah, to exist without the land of Israel, for only there can it live fully in accordance with the Torah's commandments. On the other hand, if no suitable substitute for the land were to be found for the diaspora, the destruction of the land would also mean the destruction of the people. It was the task of the sages, then, to cope with these two dangers: first, that Jerusalem and the Temple, and the land of Israel, not be forgotten, and second, that the people not despair of the possibility of maintaining Jewish life abroad. The eternal uniqueness of the land of Israel, for which there could be no alternative, had to be preserved, yet an alternative had nevertheless to be created, one that would consciously and emphatically be no more than a substitute, never competing with the original but constantly maintaining the tension of the people's anticipation that they would yet return to their true home.

This was a complex and difficult task, and not surprisingly, it gave rise to strong differences of opinion and clashing goals. Not all the sages were in agreement with what Rabban Yohanan ben Zakkai undertook in Yavne, proposing a substitute for what had been wrested from the people by the destruction of Jerusalem and the Temple. Nor did all assent to the actions of the Palestinian sages after the failure of the Bar Kochba revolt, when they persisted in going in the same direction. Discord arose from changes of situation, from conflicts of interest among Jewish communities in Israel and in the diaspora, and from differences of opinion and belief. Up until modern times, however, general agreement on one basic point seems to have remained unshaken: since the people of Israel is sentenced to live in exile for an indefinite period, it must establish itself there as well as it can and carry on a way of life whose tone is set by the sanctity of the commandments, so that something of the ways of the land will be reflected in their life in exile. Even the best of exilic abodes, however, may never become a homeland, neither in the national-political-legal sense nor in the sense of truly fulfilling the holiness of the commandments. The diaspora can provide substitutes for the land of Israel, but can never equal it. This was true even of the most comfortable of diasporas, that of Babylonia, where the Jews succeeded in

1

The Homeland Destroyed

From the point of view of historical scientific methodology, it would be appropriate to precede our discussion of rabbinic thought, which flourished primarily in the period following the destruction of the Second Temple, with a consideration of the ideas that prevailed at the time of the fifth century B.C.E. return to Zion, during the Hasmonean period, and at the beginning of the Roman conquest. We shall, however, omit these periods and procede directly to the broad and admittedly not very well defined concept of rabbinic thought because we are interested in the continuity of the Jewish people's cultural consciousness—in the national memories that have collected in its consciousness and shaped its relationship to the land in recent generations. From this point of view, the period of the return to Zion is the conclusion of the scriptural stratum in Jewish thought; the rabbinic thought that preceded the destruction of the Second Temple is included in the broad category of the Oral Law; and the ideas to be found in the Apocrypha have, indeed, remained external to the tradition. The sequence we follow thus reflects the later stratification of the source literature into the two primary layers of Scripture and Oral Law. It also reflects a later conception of the course of Jewish history, which sees the critical dividing line in the destruction of the Second Temple. Before this destruction, the people of Israel could be considered (despite the brief and highly significant interval of the Babylonian Exile), a people dwelling in its land; after the destruction, it was a people in exile. More precisely: as long as the people of Israel had some kind of proximity to its land, and even those who dwelt in the diaspora maintained their ties to it and could make their pilgrimages to the Temple, which stood during most of this period, the dispersion did not assume its full spiritual and religious significance. Once the Second Temple was destroyed, however, and it became clear that it would not speedily be rebuilt, even the land of Israel was transformed more and more into a place of exile.

It seems, indeed, that this view of the fateful turn taken by the course of Jewish history with the destruction of the Second Temple provides the key to understanding the unique quality of the concept of the land of Israel in rabbinic thought. It almost goes without saying that discussing "rabbinic thought" as a unified whole is no less problematic than was dealing with "biblical thought" in the same way. We are dealing with a literature created over the course of hundreds of years, two groupings distinguished by different intellectual disciplines: halakhah and aggadah (law and legend). There are, indeed, great differences among the sages, which stem from differences in outlook and in historical circumstance. But the common element, underlying and unifying their ideology, is decisive: it is the authoritative/interpretative form of expression that they employed, which is rooted in the Bible and draws on its store of ideas and images; and in their common goal—to cope with the realities of the exile and preserve the unity of the people, its faith and its way of life, and maintain a clear continuity despite the profound transformation they had undergone.

If we wish to understand what distinguishes rabbinic thought as a whole with regard to the land of Israel, we must first of all define the basic problem that confronted the sages. We have already seen in the first chapter that the land's image was shaped by the people's historical relationship to it. It was fixed in their consciousness that the land of Israel had been promised to them, first as the country that they were to inherit; later as a land where they must establish themselves and of which they must be worthy; and later still, as a land that at some future time would become fully what it was meant to be for them, the people that would dwell upon its soil and there order their lives in accordance with the word of God. This latter way of relating to the land of Israel persisted even after the return to Zion of those exile to Babylon. The struggle to resettle the land was protracted, and its progress was halted by retreats, by the Greek conquest, by internal conflicts over the choice of a way of life that would be proper from a political and religio-cultural point of view, and by the Roman conquest. Living in exile, meanwhile, outside of the homeland, came to be a permanent way of life for many.

The return to Zion did not, in fact, eliminate this phenomenon for even the briefest of historical periods. On the contrary, the diaspora phenomenon grew progressively broader with the reestablishment of Jewish settlement in the land of Israel. After the Roman conquest a retreat began, which gradually transformed the land of Israel itself into a place of exile while at the same time the Jews were successfully striking root in other countries. They were even able to develop a sense of homeland in their new lands that was closer, in the national, social, economic and political sense to that of free peoples than they might then have felt in the land of Israel.

Reminders that they were, in fact, in exile were embodied in several dramatic events, such as the destruction of the Second Temple and the failure of the Bar-Kochba revolt, but the symbolism of these events developed only in the course of a prolonged historical process that had begun even before they took place and ended only long after. Initially there was a large Jewish community in the land of Israel, surrounded by a Jewish diaspora. The diaspora was also large, rich and well integrated, but it also had a close territorial continuity with the land of Israel, was involved in the Tem-

ple service and subject to the leadership of the sages. Then the center in Israel began to decline: internal quarrels, foreign conquest, the destruction of the Temple, the growing exodus from the land, the failure of the Bar-Kochba revolt and the terrible slaughter in its wake all took their toll. The center in Babylonia was now clearly stronger than that in the land of Israel, and a struggle over the leadership developed.

The sages in Israel had to cope with the problems produced by each stage of the process we have just described: How was the bond to be maintained between the Jews of the diaspora, who were becoming more and more established and assimilated in the lands of their exile, with the land of Israel? How were they to stay the dwindling of the Jewish community in the land of Israel and the desertion of its soil? How was the authority of the Palestinian leadership to be preserved? This was a very long "rearguard" struggle. When it ended, several hundred years later, the land of Israel had ceased to be an active center of Jewish life. Although Jews continued to live there even after the Arab conquest, apart from periods during which they were utterly barred from its borders, they comprised no more than a small, weak community, representing the diaspora centers and relying upon them for support. What the land of Israel actually symbolized at that time and under those conditions was, more than anything else, the experience of exile. Nowhere else in the world was the experience of physical and spiritual oppression more real and concrete than in that ruined, desolate land that had become the province of strangers. Adherents of the religions that claimed to have inherited the faith of Israel attempted to convert the traces of Jewish history and faith that remained in the land into memorials of their own; churches or mosques were erected on every site that was holy to Israel.

Gradually, then, a dual remoteness developed: there was the physical distance between the people and the land, and the chasm between the land's actual state and its image in the Torah and in the visions of the prophets. The concept of the promised land thus took on a new, far more intensive meaning: the land that it once had been, and would be someday again. In the present, however, it was no more than a faint shadow of its exalted past and its marvellous future. Only one who remembered it and knew it would know its true image, which would symbolize for him both the present exile and the redemption to come.

Clearly, the contrast between reality and destiny bears within it a powerful tension, pregnant with conflicting impulses, and it is this that forms the background of rabbinic thought about the land of Israel, and of the halakhic enterprise. The dilemma confronted them in all urgency when the phenomenon of exile tangibly penetrated the very core of the land of Israel with the destruction of the Temple and the city of Jerusalem. How was the people of Israel to maintain itself as a people; how was it to continue to worship God and be sanctified by the holiness of the commandments, without the Temple and without Jerusalem? There are commandments, not only those involving

attaining a noteworthy degree of independence. The Babylonian sages, on the basis of their assessment of the respective political, demographic and spiritual conditions prevailing there and in the land of Israel at the time, demanded leadership authority superior to that of their Palestinian contemporaries, and even deemed it preferable for the Jews to remain in Babylonia than return to their own land. However, on no account did they demand for themselves the status they would have enjoyed in the land of Israel when the people were still living within its borders, and the Temple was still standing. This principle was not challenged until the rise of certain movements among the Jewish people after the Emancipation.

What was the source of this outlook? The bases are to be found in the words of the rabbis as they have come down to us, and hence the primary importance of their words on the subject of our study.[1] Whereas in the Bible the relationship between people and land was molded by the process of settlement, for the sages it was shaped by the continually growing diaspora, as the land became a more and more distant memory and hope, its actual, physical presence progressively swallowed up by what it symbolized. The sages drew on the whole biblical treasury of ideas regarding the land of Israel, but gave them a new dimension, stemming from the difference in perspective.

2

We shall not concern ourselves with details of the halakhah relating to the Land of Israel,[2] but we must note the principal trend characterizing the halakhic enterprise in this respect.[2] When the land of Israel was still the political, religious and ritual center of unquestioned authority, the sages sought to establish clearly both the religious dependence of the Jews of the diaspora upon Jerusalem and the Temple and their economic obligation toward settlement in the land. They thus emphasized acceptance of the rulings of the Palestinian sages, the festival pilgrimages to Jerusalem, the obligatory contributions to the Temple and to the poor of the land of Israel, and, in time of need, both military and political aid.[3] In the periods of decline, particularly after the destruction of the Temple, the halakhah reflected efforts to prevent the abandonment of lands and their transfer to foreign ownership, to encourage the redemption of lands that had been abandoned, to prevent emigration to the diaspora because of the prevalent economic conditions, and to strengthen the economic resilience of the Jewish population in Palestine.[4]

During this period the tendency to idealize the significance of living in the land of Israel gathered force; while at the same time decisive steps were taken in the precess of creating "vessels of exile." The work of Rabban Yohanan ben Zakkai at Yavne has already been noted in this connection.

Whether he saw in it provision for the short term, or whether he understood that the Jewish people would have to pass many generations without a Temple and without Jerusalem, he began to fashion halakhic patterns that would make possible a Jewish communality united by the holiness of the commandments while it internalized the absence of the Temple and made it a concrete dimension of its everyday life.

Meanwhile, the struggle over leadership between the Palestinian and the Babylonian sages had begun, and developed into a prolonged and bitter conflict. Stress on different elements led to a dispute over the correct practical interpretation of the commandment to settle the land of Israel in a period of exile. Does the precedence ascribed to settling the land apply even with the Temple destroyed? Does the authority of the Palestinian sages remain superior to that of their diaspora colleagues even when the population of the land has been reduced to a fraction of its former size? In the long run the exile, in which the Jews had become more firmly established than in their own land, won out. The Babylonian sages gained the upper hand, and their Talmud and its authority superseded that of the Palestinians.[5]

This victory did not imply a break with the land of Israel however, but rather a change in the perspective from which the Jews' relationship to it was determined. When the land of Israel was no longer the base for the leadership, the exilic communities had to bind themselves to it on their own initiative, for without such ties there was no source of legitimation for the halakhic authority of the diaspora sages nor for a way of living permanently in the diaspora that did not constitute assimilation. Responsibility for the continued Jewish presence, even of only symbolic dimensions, in the land of Israel and especially in Jerusalem, also eventually passed to the exilic communities, as the very existence of the Jewish population of Palestine came to depend upon *aliyah* and economic support from abroad. The Jewish population in the land thus came to be a kind of representation of the exilic communities expressing their recognition of the commandment to which they were obligated in this respect. It was also incumbent upon them to preserve the presence of the land of Israel in the living memory of the people. It was necessary to imbue their daily lives with this memory, to set the symbols of mourning for the destruction, and to find ways of expressing their expectation and hope of returning to their land. Moreover, they had also to make a distinction between those commandments that are incumbent upon the people wherever they might be and those that apply only in the land of Israel, and to give concrete expression to the fact that certain of the commandments cannot be fulfilled in the diaspora so that their felt and conscious absence colors the whole experience of exile.[6] The fulfilment of these tasks demanded halkhic implements, and even though these did not develop in a single generation, their formulation began, as we have said, with the work of the Tannaim in the period immediately following the destruction of the Temple.

3

When we turn our attention to the philosophical element accompanying the halakhic enterprise—that is to say, to the aggadah—we are confronted with an amazing fact. It appears impossible to point to any ideological innovation in the words of the sages concerning the land of Israel. All those motifs that we found in the Bible are reiterated by the sages: the land of Israel is a land of milk and honey;[7] it is the choicest land;[8] it stands midway between the lands and higher than the rest;[9] it is watered by rain and furnished with God's providential care;[10] it is sanctified by the presence of God within it and by the holiness of the commandments;[11] it was predestined for the people of Israel from the time of the creation of the world;[12] there is an ethical-religious condition attached to its inheritance, and it will not tolerate sin.[13] Even so, a new undertone can be detected in what the Sages have to say. Their style is different, and the careful reader will find that this change in style is accompanied by a change in content as well. The change in style is noticeable first of all in the fact that we are now dealing with an interpretation of the Bible—that is to say, a cataloguing and drawing of inferences from what is to be learned of the land of Israel from the testimony of Scripture, both directly and indirectly; and the interpretation has something of the nature of a translation. Things expressed in the Bible, and especially in the Prophets, in exalted, poetic language, are restated by the sages in factual, moderate terms, applicable to things as they really are. It is precisely in this, however, that the paradox stands revealed. The moderate, interpretive language of the sages, the prosaic terms that bring the poetry of the Bible down to earth, express an idealization far greater even than that of the prophets. For example, their descriptions of the bounteous produce of the land, its dimensions, its quantity, its quality and its variety, exceed any imaginable reality. If the Torah says that the land of Israel is "flowing with milk and honey," the sages report that this is no more rhetorical image: the words are to be taken literally.[14] If the Bible contains expressions figuratively describing the land as having a personality and a will of its own, in the Midrash these verses are no longer metaphorical. The land of Israel acts in accordance with the qualities of its own soul. It responds to the deeds of its inhabitants with anger or with joy. From this last quality the sages derived their understanding of the predestination of the land for the people of Israel: The land was especially marked for this people at creation not only because it is the most beautiful and bounteous of lands, but because of its unique spiritual quality. When the Sages speak of it as the loftiest of lands, they are not referring to physical altitude. A special sanctity pervades the land, and it is thus clear that simply living there is in itself of the highest significance. Settling in the land outweighs all the other commandments in the Torah.[15] Whoever lives there is assured of a place in the world to come, while he who leaves for good "is like a man who has no God."[16]

The new shade of meaning that we find in the words of the sages, then, lies in their perception that what the prophets said of the land of Israel was no mere rhetoric or poetic imagery. Things really are as the simple meaning of the text would have them—or even more so. No less amazing, however, is a second innovation of the sages. The descriptions of the physical plenty and spiritual sanctity of the land do not apply, as would appear from the language of the prophets, to the distant future, but to the present, to the concrete, tangible land of Israel, the very land upon which we stand, whose scenery we see and whose air we breathe. This is truly an astonishing paradox. While the land of Israel lies in ruins, and its sons abandon it because of the dire straits in which they find themselves and go off to seek sustenance and wealth in the diaspora, the sages, instead of interpreting Scripture by looking at the land, describe the land by reading Scripture. They see the land not as it is but as the Bible describes it, and a literal reading becomes their *midrash!*

After an initial astonishment, it becomes clear that the sages did, in fact, intend to provoke just this reaction—that this is a deliberate pedagogical device. Nor is it difficult to identify their educational goal. Their aim was to influence those who were inclined to leave the land of Israel to change their minds and remain despite the prevailing poverty and difficult conditions; or, at least to get those who had made up their minds to go, or had already left, to do so regretfully, and to take with them to the diaspora an ideal image that would link them to their land by the triple bond of love, longing and obligation. It was thus precisely because of the widening gap between the biblical image of the promised land and its actual circumstances that the sages felt the need to reaffirm that image and imprint it upon the national consciousness. Their aim was to remind the people of what they were liable to forget, to affirm what might be undermined.

The interpretive form is essential in this respect. Its purpose is to establish the material under study precisely in the reader's consciousness, to indicate, to explain in detail and to affirm, in order to prevent the content from fading away like some pretty poetic image. The beginning student reads and then says to himself, this is what I have read, this is what it means; this is what the prophets said of the land of Israel. And should one say: but the land of Israel as we know it from our own experience is not like this? It is here that we are brought face to face with the meaning of the pedagogical tactic employed by the sages. When they declare with such innocent and unambiguous simplicity: the land of Israel is truly just as the Bible says it is, do they not fear that their students will contradict them? No—and precisely because the bitter facts are well known to them and present in what they have to say. It is to these very facts that they are responding! There can be no question that they saw around them exactly what everyone else did. And even so . . . What, then does this "even so," this naive paradox which is really not at all naive, imply? In fact, the sages mean exactly what they say. The land of Israel does not appear as Scripture would have it. But at a second glance, directed and educated, it *does* appear so. It actually contains, here and now, all that has been ascribed to it, as it were, in these poetic outpourings. One must know how to extract from the depths of personal and historical memory those experiences and facts by which the true nature of the land is revealed. Transcending the spreading shadow of a difficult historical hour, the words of the Torah and the Prophets come to teach us how to see the land of Israel correctly, as it was and was meant to be—as it still is and still is meant to be.

When the sages aver, therefore, that the land is, in fact, precisely as the prophets described it, their purpose is to reaffirm and establish in the national consciousness a level of meaning already fixed in their own and their students' minds as a result of their prior learning and experience, because just this level of meaning was in danger of disintegrating. From the distance of ages, it appears as though at the hour of departure the sages were fixing in the memory of the people the image of the land that they were to take with them. This was not to be an image of the ruin because of which they were forced to leave, but rather that conception which had been shaped in their hearts well before, so that even as they left the land would remain a place where they desired and longed to be, their home. From distant, foreign parts they would remember the land as it had been and as it truly would be again. Thus would it be in their memory and hopes; thus would it be present in their thoughts, and thus would be its fixed truth, that no other truth could displace. And let there be no mistake: the land as it is, the physical land, with none of the miraculous reshaping that might come about in the age of the Messiah, would, to them, be the epitome of perfection.

It would thus appear that this idealization of the land of Israel according to the literal meaning of the Bible, accompanying and elucidating the halakhic solutions, provides a philosophical answer to the dilemma posed at the beginning of the chapter: How was the land of Israel to be retained as the single, unique homeland of the Jews, without which Israel could not exist as a people, without denying the legitimacy of the diaspora—since only there could the people continue to exist as a people? By putting forward a view of the land of Israel, despite its forlornness and ruin, as the symbol of a full Jewish life. A land that symbolizes the full and perfect life of the people, a land unique and irreplaceable in every respect, can never be changed for another. At the same time a land that symbolizes the ideal can be present and felt, by its emphasized absence, even in the diaspora. The real ideal, present/ utopian land of Israel remains the homeland. The people of Israel survive as a people among the peoples of the world, and it remains a chosen people. Even though not in its own land, it retains a vital and tangible relationship to it.

The pedagogical transformation implicit in the words of the sages concerning the land of Israel was only the first step in a long process. While the prophets idealize the words of the Torah, and the sages those of the prophets, the medieval scholars idealize the words of the sages. This process of idealization upon idealization eventually reached such heights that it might have broken the people's bond with the actual land. This discord, too, was eventually sensed, and then no less paradoxical an effort was needed to shatter the exaggeratedly idealized image that had been built up in order to rediscover the real, physical land with its stone and its dust, while at the same time not undermining its sanctity. We have barely begun to describe this process, and there is yet a long way to go.

2

From the Furthermost West

In the preceding chapter we noted a historical process that was completed during the Middle Ages, particularly after the Arab conquest. The land of Israel ceased to function as an active center. Its Jewish population was sparse and impoverished, and depended upon support from the exilic communities. The people's relationship to the land was from this time on an aspect of Jewish activity in exile. Our task now will be to examine the philosophical concepts which "institutionalized" the exiled Jews' emotional and practical relationship to their desolate land. To understand these concepts however, we must first examine three major factors in greater detail.

The first of these is the geographical spread of the Jewish diaspora, in contrast to what it was in Mishnaic and Talmudic times. In the Middle Ages, not only had the abandonment of the land of Israel and the transfer of property out of Jewish ownership reached their furthest extreme, the extent of the dispersion was also greatly enlarged. We now find large Jewish communities in lands distant from one another and far removed from the land of Israel. This had a far-reaching impact upon the degree to which the people remained unified and upon the shaping of its leadership, and it also had its effect upon how the Jews related to the land of Israel and their image of it. The communities were remote from one another and each formed its own leadership, while the land of Israel not only had ceased to provide a unifying leadership but was also effectively screened from sight by its physical distance. Travel in those days was such that this great distance—especially from the western communities of Italy, Germany, France, and England on the one hand and North Africa and Egypt on the other—meant that the Jews were effectively cut off from any possibility of direct contact with the land, and even from a continuous flow of factual information from it. Only imagination and sentiment could bridge the distance, and these shaped the people's image of the land, based upon the traditional sources and the immediate impact of their exilic environment, for only from these could imagination and sentiment, in effect, draw sustenance. There were, indeed, occasional travellers who brought up-to-date information, but their descriptions of what they had seen, filtered through the perspective of the dangers and hardships endured in reaching the holy land, generally nourished the

43

imagination more than they provided concrete information. The distant land of Israel was thus transformed into a legend.

The second major factor is comprised of the unique "religious" conditions within which the medieval diaspora was formed. The exilic communities during the Second Temple period had existed in a pagan environment. In the Middle Ages, however, the Jews lived among Christians and Moslems—under the rule of two religions which had, in a sense, grown out of the Jewish tradition, and which boasted of having inherited the mission of Judaism. This had a decisive effect on the nature of the exile, and on the people's relationship to the land of Israel. Precisely because Christianity and Islam recognized their ties to Judaism and had pretensions of supplanting it, life in exile was more difficult under their rule than it had been in ancient times. Formerly, in pagan lands, Judaism had generally been considered a legitimate national or "ancestral" faith. Under Christianity and Islam it was not, indeed, considered heretical, but it was also not viewed as a true religion. Its time had passed, and it should by now have disappeared into one of the two daughter religions. It was suffered, in that its adherents were permitted to live in Christian and Moslem countries, but in an inferior and despised status. They were surrounded by constant hatred, for the religions that presumed to displace Judaism could not accept the presence of Jews within their dominions, even as inferiors, with equanimity. The mother-religion's refusal to recognize her "offspring" was a continuous source of irritation, which bore no relation to the size and strength of the dispersed people. The exile thus became a focus of never-ending scorn and humiliation for the Jews. Their unique cultural activity was severely limited, and even though there were lands—and periods—in which they enjoyed relative peace and economic prosperity, their basic legal status remained the same, and fairly frequent outbursts of violence and blood-letting recalled this to anyone who tried to forget.

It is safe to say that the non-Jewish environment gave added validity to the way in which the tradition demanded that the Jews relate to their dispersion, for while it enabled them to establish themselves economically it consistently denied them any feeling of being at home. The Jews remained foreigners who existed on sufferance. Moreover, the Christian and Moslem environment affirmed the Jews' understanding of the religious significance of the exile as a divine punishment for sin. In both of respects, then, the Jews' relationship to their exilic environment was in accord with that of the latter towards them. Of course, this accord was contained within the framework of the religious dispute. The Jews did not accept the Christian and Moslem claims of having displaced Judaism, and they interpreted neither the sin that had brought about the exile nor the punishment for it as did the rival faiths. They viewed their dispersion as no more than a temporary state and, in contrast to Christianity, which believes in a messiah who has already come, they awaited their restoration to their own land by a redeemer yet to come.

It is at this point that the connection between the increased hardships of exile and the formulation of the Jews' relationship to the land of Israel is to be found. First of all, with the feeling of being in exile so intense, the Jews could not forget their land. During periods of relative peace and prosperity, of course, the land was relegated to the realm of ritual memory alone and aroused no feeling of obligation. Such periods, however, never lasted very long. Jewish settlement in a country generally provoked jealousy and religious fanaticism. The venting of this hatred reawakened their feeling of foreignness in all its force, and the land of Israel, symbolizing the present exile and the redemption to come, once more became central to the Jewish experience. Again, the fact that Jews lived under the rule of religions which had pretentions of supplanting their own faith was also significant for their relationship to the land of Israel. The Christians, too, viewed Israel as the "holy land", and Islam also considered it sacred; in other words, these faiths also sought to take over Judaism's relationship to the land of Israel, even though, in contrast to Judaism, the religious sanctity that they ascribed to it was not coterminous with any national bond. Their relationship to the land, mediated by Jewish tradition and bitterly disputed by the Jews, had the effect of endowing the historical/religious connection between Israel and its home with objective reality; and confirming the unique image of the land as one that bore no comparison with any other. It was viewed as a symbol whose significance transcended geography. The military conflict between Christianity and Islam over mastery of the land, the notable efforts of both these faiths to mold it in their own image by building churches or mosques, multiplying the number of holy places and encouraging pilgrimages— emphasized the objective, "universal" validity of the relationship between the Jewish people and Israel. At the same time, they also impelled great individuals among the Jews to act to prove their faithfulness to the land, and thus to demonstrate against the Christian and Moslem pretensions as successors. Indeed, whenever the Christian and Moslem armies fought over control of the holy land, Jews, too, went there to settle and fulfil their duty to Zion. In this, even as individuals, they were expressing the collective national consciousness. They saw themselves as representatives of the people, and the people, too, saw them as such.

Dispersion and geographical distance may have hidden the land of Israel behind a screen of legend, but the cultural and religious circumstances described above—together with their repercussions in the social and economic realms—recalled its image, shrouded in the distant glow, to the center of Diaspora life. The land of Israel, despite its remoteness, remained an important focus of Jewish national life. It stood at the center of the geographical and cultural map of the world that the Jew created for himself and by which he interpreted his fate. We are referring, of course, to its symbolic image, not to its physical presence.

Keeping this in mind will facilitate our understanding of the third factor in our analysis: the unique character of the theoretical works produced in the Middle Ages. Medieval literature was strongly influenced by the scientific and philosophical heritage of ancient Greece, and this is easily visible in the religious thought of the time. Philosophy had come to serve as a component of or organizing element in religious thinking, so that the latter now offered a comprehensive view of reality as man knows it from his own experience and thinking, and from those religious sources that bear witness to a particular, supreme type of human experience—prophecy. The great thinkers of this period set out to present a comprehensive, ordered and detailed account of all that is known to man about reality, to explain these phenomena by way of causal connections, and so to discover their ultimate purpose in order to draw conclusions from it regarding the duty and destiny of man and arrive at an understanding of what constitutes true merit on his part. Everything of importance had to be interpreted within this framework. Israel's status as a chosen people must be explained in the context of an examination of humanity, its status, its role and its history; while the land of Israel must be considered in relation to the structure of the world and the relationship between the material and the spiritual universe. In other words, the people of Israel, its land and the relationship between them must be located within a complete conceptual framework; and since philosophical and theological systems prefer the spiritual reality to the physical, the intellectual concepts of "knesset Israel" (the community of Israel) and "Zion" often seem, in theoretical works, more real than the actual people dispersed in its exile, and the land so remote that it could not be reached.

We are thus confronted with three factors, geographical/political, religious/cultural and philosophical/theological, all of which tend toward imaginative, emotional and intellectual abstraction. Small wonder, then, that in the Middle Ages conceptions of the land of Israel reached an extreme degree of idealization, or that it was viewed in the Kabbalah as a mystical symbol almost divorced from its physical being.

Since we are concerned with comprehensive doctrines which are the products of individual thinkers, a change in method is necessary. We shall no longer be dealing with the thought of a complete literary era but rather with the teachings of outstanding thinkers. We shall present the approaches that were most typical of the Medieval Ages: those of Judah Halevi, Moses Maimonides and Joseph Gikatilla. Maimonides represents the Aristotelian stream in medieval Jewish thought and Gikatilla the neo-platonic approach in its kabbalistic version, while Judah Halevi differed from and at the same time combined these two schools of thought with an original approach whose impact reached even beyond the realm of medieval thought, down to our own day.

3

Judah Halevi: A Land both Spiritual and Physical

Judah Halevi's conception of the uniqueness and special attributes of the land and people of Israel and the relationship between them are based on the teachings of the sages. He did, indeed, formulate them more systematically and in so doing infused them with new meaning, but only because he felt a need to reaffirm the traditional view in the context of a different culture and a different historical situation and to reestablish it at the intellectual and emotional center of the people. This is evident from the order of the discussion. The analysis of the special attributes of the land in the second book of *The Kuzari* opens with a summary of the scriptural and rabbinic teachings concerning its holiness.[1]

According to the sages, the dust from which the first man was created was gathered in the land of Israel. When he was expelled from the Garden of Eden, Adam went to the land of Israel and there attained prophecy. The battle between Cain and Abel, according to the Midrash, was solely over the inheritance of the land. What follows in the historical account no longer requires midrash: The Torah states explicitly that Abraham achieved prophecy only by virtue of the supremacy of the land of Israel, and only there did he find intimacy with God. Isaac and Ishmael, too, fought over the inheritance of the land, which was destined for Isaac because he, not Ishmael, was worthy of the "divine degree"—i.e., prophecy. The same is true of the quarrel between Jacob and Esau. The blessing, whose burden was the inheritance of the land, went to him who, by dint of his personal qualities, was destined to attain to prophecy. Nor did the people of Israel achieve true knowledge of God until they had left Egypt and set out for their own land. The question, then, is how was it possible for the people and some of its notables to be granted prophecy even outside of the land.[2] Halevi's response, in the words of the "sage", is that these were exceptional circumstances, resulting only for the sake of the land. Those who prophesied abroad were granted the gift of prophecy for them to use to rouse the people to return home. Their concern was for the land and one might say, therefore, that its presence affected them even in exile. At any rate, we note that

47

Halevi's primary theme is prophecy, which has to do with God's proximity and His direct concern for the people and its individual members. Whosoever dwells in the land of Israel is in the presence of God, and enjoys His direct and intimate care.

Following his exposition of the ancient history of the people, Halevi discusses law and legend having to do with settlement of the land.[3] It would seem that he intended to continue in line with these traditions, and for the same reasons which motivated the sages. He wished to revive in the consciousness of the people that venerable truth that had sunk from sight and been forgotten or relegated to the periphery of their concern. It must be stressed, however, that he worked in the context of his own time, using intellectual tools drawn from contemporary culture, and we therefore find that his ideas not only parallel those of the sages but also introduce far-reaching differences of interpretation.

Indeed, the literature of Jewish thought in the two generations that preceded Halevi's poetic and philosophical creativity did not assign much importance to rabbinical ideas about the land of Israel. Moreover, they devoted no in-depth theological discussion to the whole network of concepts relating to Israel's unique status as a chosen people (including the historical significance of the election of this particular people, and the Jew's relationship to the holy land and the holy tongue). Other topics with which Moslem theology was much concerned—such as the renewal of the world, the existence and attributes of God, individual and collective providence, miracles and prophecy—obscured those that related to the history of the people of Israel. Not that faith in the election of Israel and its unique destiny had ceased; on the contrary, it remained an inseparable element of conventional religious thought. Rather, this belief had become routine and thus marginal from the point of view of the intellectual and existential challenge it might have posed. Such marginality, in addition, clearly implies a dulling of these thinkers' immediate feelings about these matters.

It seems that the scholars and spiritual leaders of the people had become well integrated into the culture of the diaspora, and their yearning for their own homeland and feelings of unease with exilic existence were progressively fading. At the same time, they felt it more important to establish their thinking on the same level of theological speculation maintained by the gentile scholars around them. They saw in the generalized religious problems that concerned the Moslem and Christian philosophers a challenge to their own thinking. A particularly instructive example of this is to be found in the thought of Solomon Ibn Gabirol. Ibn Gabirol's poetry testifies to his deep involvement in the tradition and his faithfulness to the principal motifs articulated by the liturgy. His religious poems express his belief in the election of the people of Israel, the holiness of the land and that of the Hebrew tongue. However, his philosophical treatise, *Mekor Haim,* deals entirely with general theological matters, and the reader would find in it no direct evidence of its being the work of a Jewish philosopher.[4] It would seem, therefore, that those topics which emphasize the problematic opposition between Judaism and other religions and the peculiar uniqueness of the Jewish people did not particularly concern Ibn Gabirol, and that it was more important for him to show his strength in those matters that were of common interest to the religious thinkers of his time. This certainly testifies to a fair degree of integration into and acceptance of the circumstances of diaspora existence. It would appear that the Jewish philosophers of those generations were not disturbed, at least from an intellectual point of view, by the defective nature of life in exile.

Judah Halevi's book, *The Kuzari,* testifies to a radical change of direction. His perception of reality reflects a sudden transformation, which again made central the question of the uniqueness of the people of Israel, its Torah, its land and its language. *The Kuzari* expresses a deliberate effort to explore the full significance of this transformation, and to bring about a matching change in the religious consciousness of the people, and particularly of its leaders.

Halevi was writing at the time of the Crusades.[5] These wars constituted, among other things, the means for achieving a decision—through the creation of historical facts that could not fail to impress observers—in the long, drawn-out historical struggle between the great religions to dominate the world. Whichever faith could succeed in conquering the holy land would have concrete proof that it was the faith that God wished to reign supreme— this was the apparent theological significance of the recurrent wars between the European crusaders and the Arab armies. What was the role of the Jewish people in this struggle? It was crushed between the warring armies, apparently without any ability to take an active part in the "debate," in which the claims of either side were established by means of political and military power. On one matter the belligerent religions were agreed: the faith of Israel was no longer a true religion. The truth that it had brought into the world was now in the possession of its heirs. Only one question now remained to be resolved: which of them was its rightful successor? It was difficult not to be convinced by the weighty factual claims brought to bear by the rival faiths against Judaism. How could this oppressed and persecuted people, exiled from its own soil and dispersed among many lands, humiliated by all and without the ability to forcefully defend its honor, continue to claim that it was the chosen people and that its faith was the true faith? How could it go on clinging to its Torah, against so many aggressive contenders insisting that its time had passed?

These are the very questions around which Halevi focussed his treatise.[6] *The Kuzari* gives express and vigorous attention to the historical circumstances that we have described, and it brings the questions arising from the experience of persecution and suffering into sharp relief. No wonder, then, that Halevi rediscovered the importance of those historical motifs relevant to belief in the uniqueness and singular qualities of the Jewish people. Nor is it surprising that he wished to shed new light upon the role of the land of Israel in the life of the Jewish people. That which had seemed to the previous generation conventional truth had become a problem relating to the very roots of the people's existence, and at the same time it suddenly revealed within itself new and vital layers of spiritual and emotional meaning. In his book, Halevi sought to present the Jews' claim to precedence as bearers of the true religion and as that people to whom the holy land—which its warring "heirs" longed to possess—truly belonged. He was moved to rouse the people of Israel from the slumber of exile, and make it recognize once more the significance of its peculiar fate and the obligations that stem therefrom. In this comprehensive sense, Halevi's doctrine must be seen as an attempt at recapitulation.

2

The point of view informing Halevi's attempt to revive the basic elements of rabbinic thought concerning the special quality of the people of Israel, its Torah, its tongue and its land, stands revealed in the principal assumptions underlying his intellectual method. More precisely, it is expressed in those assumptions upon which he based his argument against philosophy on the one hand, and Christianity and Islam on the other, for the sake of reaffirming the traditional Jewish world view and way of life. We shall, therefore, describe these assumptions, if only very briefly, as they form the basis for any understanding of Halevi's interpretation of the relationship between the people of Israel and its land.[7]

The Kuzari opens with the story of the king of the Khazars. An angel had appeared to him in a dream and said: "Your intentions are pleasing, but your deeds are not."[8] The king was very pious in his observance of the Khazar faith, and he strove to worship his gods with increased devotion. However, the angel reappeared several times with the same message, and he came to understand that he must search for that religion that showed the way to the true service of God. The story appears at first glance to be very simple, almost childish, but, like the "myths" used in the tradition of the Platonic dialogue, it was designed to achieve a particular aim. We must ask, therefore, what Halevi wished to accomplish by setting his within a narrative framework.

First and foremost, Halevi wanted to remove the religious debate from the domain of the Aristotelian philosophers. He could have used an intellectual argument to prove the truth of the Jewish faith because logically it is not difficult to demonstrate the superiority of Judaism over both Christianity and Islam. Many Jewish scholars had done just that. But Halevi did not wish to do as they had, for he saw the philosophical argument as posing as great a danger to Judaism as it did to Christianity and Islam. He therefore selects a judge who is not a philosopher, but rather a man of common sense and a pure heart, before whom to present his claims. The Khazar king is thus an objective judge of Judaism, Christianity and Islam. He is a straightforward person of sound intellect, and he has no initial predisposition toward any one of the three religions. However, this in itself would not have been sufficient; for one who is to judge between religions should have some kind of positive preparation for the task. Otherwise, in Halevi's opinion, he would have no understanding of matters of faith. The philosophers considered the desire to know the truth to be an integral characteristic of man; to them, curiosity alone would suffice to motivate this kind of investigation.[9] Halevi, however, felt that curiosity alone cannot lead to religious truth; some kind of direct, religious experience was necessary. The dream of the Khazar king is just such an experience. Only after he has had the dream is he impelled to inquire into the identity of the true religion. Moreover, dreams were commonly held by the ancients to be one of the levels of prophecy. It is this religious experience, then, that provides the basis for the theological discussion that follows.

The first thing we learn from this introduction is, thus, that inquiry into the truth of religion, and any attempt to gain an understanding of it, must be based upon direct religious experience. The second is to be derived from the repeated recurrence of the same dream, which demonstrates that religious experience needs no external verification. All experience authenticates itself, and this is true of religious experience, too. This, too, as we shall see, is an anti-philosophical assumption.

The philosophers would accept the truth of a prophetic statement only if it agreed with the logical conclusion of the intellect.[10] Halevi does not accept this view. In his opinion, prophecy requires no external verification. Like all direct experience, it authenticates itself. My certainty that the table before me is really there stems from the fact that every time I look at it I see it just as I did before. The same is true of prophecy. Its message or vision is the kind of experience of which we can be certain. Once it has been repeated several times we can be sure of it.

The third truth demonstrated by the dream is expressed in the words of the angel: "Your intentions are pleasing, but your deeds are not"[11] which indicates that the various religions do not differ in their "intent." The intent of Christians, like that of Moslems and even of pagans, may be good and desireable. The real difference between them lies in the realm of deeds—that is, in their rituals. There is true worship and there is false worship. It is the commandments that make the faith of Israel unique, and these, the very commandments that demand practical action, embody within themselves religious experience. In other words, a person is not considered religious because he accepts intellectually certain tenets of faith, but because he has attained the experience of standing before God through his performance of certain commandments.[12]

The Khazar king's dream thus very concisely sets forth three interrelated truths which constitute the essential kernel of Halevi's doctrine: that prophecy is a form of direct religious experience; that it authenticates itself, and that its purpose is to determine a way of life—that is, a set of deeds by which man may arrive at the experience of standing before God. Let us now take another step forward in our exposition: in fact, what Halevi has to say about the need to base oneself upon direct experience was not directed against the philosophical outlook in general, but only when applied to theology. Halevi was thus able to base himself, up to a point, on a philosophical argument, and he exploited this expertly in his debate with Aristotelianism, whose philosophical method is also based upon experience.[13]

Those who encounter Aristotelianism from the perspective of modern philosophy usually describe it as a scholastic system based not upon experience but upon complex speculation, in contrast with modern philosophy, which is experiential. This view, however, is mistaken. It is not the distinction between speculative philosophy and systems based upon experience that separates Aristotle from the modern philosophers, but rather that between experimental philosophy and empiricism—that is to say, Aristotle and his followers were not involved in experimentation; they did not subject reality to practical test. However, they did base their systems on man's direct, unmediated experience; the basic Aristotelian statement in the realm of epistemology is that man can know with his intellect only what he learns from his senses, or through his senses. In other words, without experience we can know absolutely nothing. Thus, on every occasion in which experience contradicts a conclusion at which we have arrived by way of analogy, the knowledge gained through experience is to be preferred, and we must review our reasoning process to discover where we went wrong. Direct experience thus precedes all conceptualization.

Halevi bases his claim that the prophetic word must outweigh all the reasoned conclusions of the theologians upon this Aristotelian principle—for prophecy is based upon direct experience. Clearly, however, in so doing he gave Aristotle's words an entirely new meaning which contradicted their original intent, and this transformation is of great importance for understanding Halevi's whole conception of the world.

Aristotelian philosophy recognizes only one form of experience: sensory perception. It knows of no kind of experience beyond that which can be apprehended through the five senses. Thus, the things we know by way of direct experience concern the physical world alone. Halevi claims, however, that experience can also be metaphysical. Aristotelian philosophy did not recognize such experience because it was not shared by Aristotelian thinkers—after all, they were not prophets. However, anyone with a tradition of prophecy must recognize or accept the admissibility of this form of experience.[14] This statement has many implications. If we assume that there is such a thing as metaphysical experience, we must also postulate the existence of a metaphysical realm, which can be reached by special organs of spiritual perception, and we must also postulate the existence of such organs. The prophet, unlike the philosopher, is a person who has been blessed with an array of "inner senses" that are capable of placing him in the immediate presence of a system of entities that are neither physical nor intellectual; what we call revelation. It is an area of experience paralleling that of the normal senses but taking place on a higher level beyond that of ordinary human experience.

Halevi's desire to affirm prophetic revelation by transcending the framework of the Aristotelian theory of knowledge creates a similar "mutation" almost everywhere he touches upon Aristotle's philosophy: he accepts every doctrine up to a point, but always goes on to superimpose another "level." In the realm of epistemology he postulates a system of inner senses beyond ordinary experience;[15] beyond the accepted hierarchy of the forms of being—inanimate objects, plants, animals and humans—above which Aristotle postulates the existence of differentiated intellects (that is, pure intellects, which are not bound to and do not work through a physical body), Halevi places the prophet, who is on a level of being above that of man; and beyond the differentiated intellects he posits a level on which angels really exist; these are not the same as the differentiated intellects, but rather beings whose presence may be experienced through the inner senses. In other words, Halevi adds to the accepted hierarchy a level of experience and reality which transcend those known to ordinary man. It is easy to see how he could later base upon this the concept of the election of Israel that had come down to him in the ancient texts and invest it with new meaning.

Halevi argues that the people of Israel differs in essence, and not merely in quality, from other peoples, and he bases his argument on the emendation he had made in the classical hierarchy of existence. Just as the difference between man and animal is one of essence and not merely of kind—so that man is not simply a more perfect animal but a qualitatively different kind of creature—so the Jewish man is not simply a more perfect human but rather a qualitatively different kind of being. What is it that distinguishes man from beast? Surely it is his capacity for thought, for man has a mind, while the animal does not. And what is it that distinguishes the Jew from other men? It must be that peculiar quality of his intellect that transcends the mind of ordinary man—that is, the attribute of prophecy. The capacity for prophecy exists only in the people of Israel,[16] for they alone possess, actually or potentially, that array of inner senses that enables the prophet to stand in the unmediated presence of God.

This is the key to Halevi's famous "chauvinism," and before we judge him wanting because of it we must distinguish between what he actually meant to say and what we are apt to read into his words because of certain unpleasant modern associations.

First of all, we must give Halevi a good deal of credit for the fact that in his elevation of the Jews he bore no trace of hatred for the gentile world. He could not have been unacquainted with the kind of perspective that would have given rise to such feelings, for he lived in an age of cruel persecution, and hatred toward the peoples who treated the Jews so harshly would not have been devoid of justification. Yet there is no hatred in him, nor does he scorn or belittle the gentiles among whom he dwelt. Neither does he claim that the Jew is perforce superior to any other man where his ordinary human qualities are concerned (the Khazar king, for example is a man of superlative human qualities).

Each of the levels of being that exists in our world, while distinguished from that preceding it by its unique essence, contains within it all the qualities that characterize those below. Man is also an animal, and he has vegetable functions as well. His intellect sets him above the animals, but this does not mean that he is also superior to them when it comes to those qualities that are common to both. Experience, in fact, demonstrates quite the opposite: for the most part, the beast displays more perfect animal qualities than does man. The same is true of the Jew in relation to other human beings. Alongside that attribute that makes him essentially unique, he has all of the qualities of man and, insofar as he is human, he is not necessarily better than anyone else.[17] There is no guarantee that the Jew will be more perfect than others where morality or the capacity for intellection, which are human qualities, are concerned. It is the divine quality—prophecy—that makes Judaism unique. Moreover, this should not be understood to imply that human perfection on the part of the Jew is superfluous. The Jew, in order to fulfill that which makes him unique, must strive for perfection in all that he shares with the rest of the human race. Thus human perfection, ethical and intellectual, is indeed required of the Jew, except that for him such perfection is not the ultimate goal but rather a station on the way. Moreover, the Jews were not given this unique quality to enable them to oppress all other peoples, or to gain special rights in the apportionment of the world's land. On the contrary—it was bestowed upon them for the sake of the fulfilment of their mission to all mankind. The Jewish people in relation to the rest of humanity may be likened to the heart of a man, which, by virtue of its special quality, serves the rest of the body, giving life to all its limbs. Halevi sees all of reality as a single organism, so that his seemingly "chauvinistic", particularistic conception fits into a universalistic approach whose ultimate goal is the perfection and exaltation of all mankind. Within this broad framework, Halevi also interprets the course of Jewish history within that of the world at large, and predicts a state of harmony at the end of days when all humanity will cleave to the true God through the mediation of the chosen people. This, however, is an extended and complex matter which our framework does not permit us to examine in detail.

The unique quality of the people of Israel, as Halevi explains it, has its parallel in the existential nature of the land. As there is a people that is essentially different from all others, so there is a land that is essentially different from and superior to all the rest. In this matter, too, Halevi exploited elements that already existed in medieval scientific thought for his own purposes. Just as he had extended the classical ontological hierarchy to include the level of the prophet, he added to classical geography the concept of the uniqueness of the land of Israel. The idea that some region of the world is superior to all the rest because of its geographical position is not at all unusual. The Greeks claimed that the unique development of their own culture stemmed, among other things, from the fact that Greece was the finest of all the lands, standing in the center of the inhabited world and blessed with a temperate climate. The land of Greece was moderate in all its features, and this had a beneficial effect upon its inhabitants. It was thus precisely there that that great flowering of culture, whose crowning achievement was the development of science and philosophy, took place. The Arabs later adopted this theory for their own, claiming that theirs was the most important culture because it had developed in that region that had the most moderate climate. Halevi thus did no more than stretch forth his hand to grasp that object which all claimed for their own. It is the land of Israel that, in his view, is the choicest land, standing at the center of human habitation, in the very heart of the world.[18] This, as we have said, is a common claim, but Halevi's theory does not stop here; this centrality, to him, is no more than an external manifestation of the land's inner essence. Here, too, Halevi imposes a "second level" upon the accepted scientific view of his time. The primary reason for the distinction of the land of Israel does not lie in its moderate climate or its geographical centrality. These advantages are, after all, relative, and not of the essence. The land's truly significant attribute is that it, and none other, is the locus of prophecy. Only there does the "divine essence" prevail among men (true, there were rare and exceptional instances of prophecy occurring elsewhere, but even these took place for the sake of the land or by virtue of it). There must, therefore, be something special about the physical essence of the land that qualifies it for prophecy.

As we have said, Halevi stated that there are personages that cannot be grasped by the ordinary senses; they are also neither intellectual concepts nor ideas; these are the angels. The same level of existence also includes the "glory" of the Lord. This is an object that shows itself to the inner eye of the prophet by the will of God. All of the visions seen by the prophets are scenes actually depicted within the "glory", and it is by means of these that the prophet attains the experience of intimacy with the divine reality. This level of existence containing the angels and the glory is, of course, far above our own world; however, it influences what takes place in our lower dimension. One who knows how to act in a manner appropriate to this transcendent level of existence can bring about responses that will affect our own reality—this is the secret of the miracles in which the prophets were involved.[19]

We know about this world from the experience of the prophets who saw it in their visions, and from their descriptions Halevi is able to map out a heavenly "geography" paralleling that of our physical world. The land of Israel lies at the center of the world, Jerusalem in the center of the land of Israel, and the Temple in the center of Jerusalem, for the creation of the world began at the site of the Temple and spread out from there in concentric circles. But why should creation have begun precisely here, and nowhere else? The reason is simple: here lies the opening through which the upper world, that of the glory and the angels, is linked with the lower. Here stands the "gateway of heaven", and here, therefore, is the eternal nexus between the two worlds. The divine plenty flows down through this gateway, and it is thus here that prophecy occurs. Here our prayers rise to the upper world, and it is thus better and more efficacious to pray in the land of Israel than anywhere else. As there are different lands below, so has creation spread forth in the same way above, or, more precisely: our world was formed according to the model of supernal existence, so that there is a celestial land of Israel paralleling that below, a celestial Jerusalem and a celestial Temple; and the link between the worlds lies at their center, the site of the celestial and earthly Temples.[20]

The uniqueness of the land of Israel is thus "geo-theological" and not merely climatic. This is the land which faces the entrance to the spiritual world, that sphere of existence that lies beyond the physical world known to us through our senses. This is the key to the land's unique status with regard to prophecy and prayer, and also with regard to the commandments. Whoever performs commandments in the land of Israel, especially those limited to one land itself, acts in accordance with the rules of behavior appropriate to the celestial world. These are the rules governing the true service of God, which can be learned through prophecy and by means of which one may also merit prophecy.

We have thus learned that Israel is superior to other lands because of its location at the connecting point between the celestial and lower worlds. Clearly, however, this is no matter of mere geography; it also involves the various levels of reality. Halevi had studied the ontological hierarchy that was accepted among scholars of his day: inanimate, vegetable, animal, creature of speech, etc. Each such level is different in essence from that preceding it, but all are interconnected and influence one another. That is, each lower level strives toward that which lies above it, and each supervises that which lies below. There must, therefore, be some kind of continuity between the different levels. Indeed, this conception of ontology posits the existence of intermediate creatures between the inanimate and the vegetable, the vegetable and the animal, the animal and man. There should also be, therefore, some kind of intermediate form between man and the world of the angels and the glory. This, of course, is the prophet—or the people of Israel as a whole, whose members alone are graced with prophecy, and which is distinguished in essence from all other peoples by its prophetic capability. The same must also be said of the land, which is uniquely distinguished by its capacity for prophecy. It, too, enjoys a special ontological category. Physically it resembles other lands, just as the prophet's human attributes are like those of other men, but it also differs from every other land in its proximity to the supernal, spiritual level of existence. This, of course, explains the existence of those special commandments that may only be fulfilled within its borders and by means of which men may merit prophecy.

The land of Israel is thus distinguished by its location and its level of being, lastly, however, it is also unique in terms of time. Since it stands at the center of the world both physically as the focus of its spatial extension, and in terms of the superior qualities of its residents it is also the place from which the measurement of the cyclical units of time begins: the days, the weeks, the months, the years and the seven- and fifty-year cycles (*shmittah* and *yovel*). True, this would seem to be no more than a matter of human convention. After all, men could begin the measurement of time at any agreed place. To Halevi, however, it seems a marvel that all of cultured peoples should have agreed upon just these chronological units. Is this not clear evidence of the truth of the biblical account according to which all mankind shares a single, common tradition, whose origin lies in the time before the peoples were separated from one another? Moreover, how could such a convention have come into being if men had not had a common language? But how could they have arrived at a common language without a prior divine revelation? The origin of both speech and the measurement of time is thus to be found in divine revelation; things were meant to be so from their very beginning. Clearly, then, there is no question here of coincidence or arbitrariness. The order of time was fixed in this way for a reason essential to creation itself.

The same assumption upon which Halevi explains the spatial centrality of the land of Israel also explains its centrality in terms of the ordering of time: it was here that creation of the world began. The beginning of creation thus marked the onset of time, and the rhythm of time is that of creation, for having begun with creation, time was spaced according to its stages. Since creation began in the land of Israel, time began there as well: in its continual recapitulation of the cycle of days, weeks and so on, it ever and again repeats the rhythm of the creation that spread from there. This cannot be merely a convention of measurement then, for it is by the will of God and at his express command that the rhythm of time accords with that of creation. This phenomenon is expressed primarily in the Sabbath, which begins in the land of Israel each week at precisely the same time that God rested during the first week of creation. This is sanctified time, chronology that accords with creation. The same is true, however, of all the other festivals and holy days, and of the seven- and fifty- year cycles. Only in the land of Israel does the continual repetition of time conform to the rhythm of creation. It is from this that we may infer the sanctity of its time.[21]

The utter uniqueness of the land of Israel, geographically and on the levels of being and time, gave Halevi's conceptions of both space and time an absolute cast. The worlds above and below are fixed absolutely, as is the rhythm of time. The land of Israel defines the correct directions in which one must orient himself, spatially and in time; in fact, it objectively defines these directions. The Jew, at least, is thus always and everywhere oriented toward the land, and his life conforms to it even when he is in exile. His calendar is that of the land of Israel, and he physically directs himself toward it from where he stands. When he serves his God, he stands facing the land and follows its order of time. In other words, just as prophecy can occur only in or for the sake of the land of Israel, so, according to Halevi, true service of God can be only in the land or toward it. The people's yearning for its land thus can never die, for only there can the Jew truly and completely be what he was meant to be.

Halevi came up against a great many difficulties and contradictions, and, indeed, the Khazar king did not spare the sage perplexing questions. He first asks about the current state of the land of Israel. As far as he knows, the land is not marked by any special virtues. Nor has anyone heard that its current inhabitants excell in wisdom or righteousness. On the contrary, the land is desolate, and its inhabitants ignorant boors.[22] The sage responds that this is of course true, and, in fact, it only proves his point. After all, the people of Israel in exile also cannot be said to be outstanding in virtue. It is persecuted and tormented, and it is not characterized by any prophetic capability. The state of the people thus parallels that of the land: if the Jews are still the chosen people despite their exile, theirs is still the chosen land despite its desolation. This strange fact is explained by way of a radical paradox. Halevi might have argued, as did many Jewish apologists, that the Jews' special merits were visible even in exile, and used this as evidence of God's special care for His people. As one who witnessed all the glory of Jewish life in medieval Spain, Halevi in particular could easily have made such a claim. Interestingly enough, however, he does not—on the contrary, he saw in the seeming magnificence of Spanish Jewry a manifestation not of strength but of weakness, for it indicated their tendency to let themselves slip into an illusory complacency.

Instead, Halevi attempts to demonstrate the uniqueness of the people of Israel by its very sufferings. Jewish history is distinguished not necessarily by success or virtue, but rather by divine providence. The people's uniqueness is shown by the supernatural quality of its historical fate. This is expressed both in the tremendous successes that it reaped in its own land and in the extreme suffering it has undergone in exile. Great peoples such as the Babylonians, the Egyptians, the Greeks, the Romans and the Arabs flourished naturally enough: their rise and fall can both be explained by political, geographical and economic conditions. There is no natural explanation, however, for the success enjoyed by the Jewish people in its land. The Exodus from Egypt was not a natural phenomenon; nor was the greatness of the Kingdom of Israel in the time of David and Solomon, surrounded as it was by enemies several times larger and more numerous than itself. Neither, however, is the extreme suffering of the people in its exile a natural state of affairs. This is no ordinary suffering, for it is out of all proportion to the size and strength of the people, and it cannot be compared to that of any other nation. Can we not see in this people's extraordinary suffering, just as we did in its former brilliant successes, evidence of the fact that it is governed not by nature, but rather by divine plan? Does not the depth of its suffering testify to the fact that this torment can be no mere punishment for sin, but rather is informed by a higher intention? The very power and intensity of its pain testify to the exalted status and virtue of the dispersed people.[23]

This explains the destruction of the people, and the ruin of the land parallels and is also a result of it. The land can flourish only when it is inhabited by the people meant for it. To illustrate this, Halevi uses a parable characteristic of his way of thinking: that of the vineyard.[24] If one were to plant a high-grade vine seedling in soil that is unfit for it, while rooting some other plant in soil that would suit the vine, the vine would not flourish, and the soil would not reveal its true capabilities. However, if one were to transfer the fine seedling to its proper soil, the qualities of both would immediately be recognized. So it is with the relationship between Israel and its land. Only when the Jews dwell in their own land do they reach their full splendor, and only then does the land display its true attributes. As long as Moslems and Christians dwell in the land of Israel, it remains barren. In desolation and ruin it awaits its sons and daughters, and it thus demonstrates that, as the chosen land, it is destined only for the chosen people. Recognition that actually going to live in the land of Israel is one of the primary commandments that the Jew is obliged to fulfil would seem to follow as a self-evident corollary of this understanding. Judah Halevi's own departure at the end of his life on his famous journey to the land of Israel stemmed from this recognition.

Halevi's decision to set out for the land of Israel was also influenced by the events of his day, particularly the Crusades. Apparently he was affected powerfully by the fact that Christians and Moslems were struggling with all their might to prove that they were the true heirs to the Holy Land. He did not, however, react to this with jealousy and hatred towards the other faiths; rather, he was positively impressed by the Christians' self-sacrifice for the sake of a Jewish value. Was the Jewish people to be found wanting in comparison with the gentiles in this respect? If even Christians were attempting to conquer the land, then the Jews must surely go to settle there, in any way open to them. This could not, of course, be accomplished by a military campaign, but rather by individuals who were willing to risk the journey to live in the land and fulfill the commandments that can only be carried out on its soil. Thus, when the king of the Khazars chides the sage, asking him why he does not go to that land whose virtues he has expounded, the sage replies, with great sincerity, "You shame me, Khazar king."[25] The king has shamed him, for this is truly a primary religious obligation. At the end of *The Kuzari,* Halevi returns to the same idea. He relates that the sage has decided to settle in the land of Israel, and so hints at the decision to which he came at the end of his life: the people of Israel must attempt to return to their land by their own efforts, so that their full spiritual glory may stand revealed, enabling them to fulfill their mission to all peoples.

4

Maimonides: An Ideal Home for a Holy People

Our study of Judah Halevi's views about the people of Israel and its land emphasized his effort to renew the relevance of the rabbinic sayings and bring them back into the mainstream of Jewish experience. When we compare his approach with that of Maimonides, who also sought to restore the relevance of the rabbinic texts, and try to identify the basic requirements of each of these thinkers, we are struck by the differences between them. Halevi and Maimonides, we find, followed opposing streams in biblical Jewish thought, streams which are in conflict, but which also complement and clarify one another.

We note the difference between Halevi and Maimonides, first, in the fact that Halevi discussed the people of Israel, its history and its land, in a theoretical work, within the framework of a theological dialogue, while Maimonides did not. In his principal philosophical essay, the *Guide for the Perplexed,* Maimonides does not relate directly to these topics, and if we wish to find out what he thought about them we must look to his halakhic works, the *Book of the Commandments* and the *Mishneh Torah.* This difference cannot be chance; it is reflected in the way they approached their subject and even in their use of the sources. Halevi's approach was philosophical rather than halakhic, and even when he did demand particular actions, he formulated them not as halakhic obligations but as expressions of religious loyalty. Thus, in his use of the sources, too, he was primarily interested in the aggadic stream, and even the halakhic material served primarily to help him develop the aggadic aspect. Maimonides, on the other hand, approached the subject as a halakhist, and he therefore made use primarily of the halakhic sections of the sources. His own views become apparent only upon examination of his emphases, his explanations, and the systematic relationship between these and the philosophical propositions that he posited and developed in his theoretical works.

A comparative study of the particular philosophical assumptions of these two thinkers reveals a relationship between their stylistic and methodological differences and the ideological ones that underly them. True, Halevi admired philosophy, particularly Aristotelian philosophy, and considered it an outstanding human achievement.[1] He even drew upon certain of the assumptions of Aristotelian philosophy, but these served him as no more than points of departure for reaching toward that which lies beyond human grasp. As we have seen, he viewed prophecy as an extra-intellectual, superhuman achievement resulting from an experience of intimacy with God, and what he had to say about the people and land of Israel is both sustained by this understanding and is an element in its description. Thus, to be a Jew in the land of Israel is in itself a first step toward prophetic experience.

Maimonides saw things quite differently. We shall not enter here into a detailed discussion of the relationship between philosophy and Torah in his doctrine,[2] but it must be understood that Maimonides saw prophecy as an intellectual plenitude, for which theoretical, philosophical perfection was a necessary precondition. True, he does not *identify* philosophy with prophecy, for the prophet has a particular kind of spiritual yearning and educational leadership role in which the philosopher has no part. Nevertheless, Maimonides views prophecy as human perfection, and even the greatest of the prophets, Moses, is no more than human, although he has indeed reached the very height of human perfection.[3] Thus, Israel's attribute of prophecy does not place it on a level of existence different from and above that of other peoples. The peoples' uniqueness lies in its having received a divine Torah at the hand of the prophets, and it retains its uniqueness only insofar as it obeys the Torah's commandments. This would seem to be the reason why Maimonides does not concern himself directly with the uniqueness of the land and people of Israel in his theoretical works: He deals directly with the uniqueness of the Torah, while he deals with that of the people and the land, which stems from the Torah, in the context of the latter—that is, in the context of *halakhah*.[4]

Thus far, we have distinguished between Halevi and Maimonides in terms of their respective approaches and their basic theoretical assumptions. These differences, however, have their source in the differing orientations in the ancient sources upon which each of them drew, and this is expressed, in relation to the subject of our concern, in their understanding of the concept of holiness. Halevi, as we have seen, saw holiness as a quality inherent in certain bodies or objects. They produce in the person who comes in contact with them if he is blessed with the necessary sensory perception, a particular kind of spiritual experience. Just as physical bodies produce a tangible response in those who have the appropriate senses, so things holy produce a spiritual, extra-sensory response in those who have the corresponding inner sense—that is, the capacity for prophecy, which Halevi defined as the experience of being in the direct, unmediated presence of holiness. Maimonides' understanding, however, is quite different. In his view, holiness is essentially pure spirituality,[5] and things therefore cannot be holy in themselves; they can only symbolize man's yearning to rise to a level of pure spirituality. That is to say, holiness is the significance that man, by his thoughts and actions, ascribes to these things in relation to himself.[6] It is thus not difficult to see that Halevi, with his basically aggadic approach and his experiential, extra-intellectual perspective, was developing (using the theoretical concepts of his time) the priestly approach found in the Bible—which focused upon experiencing the presence of God in the Temple and contact with the divine by means of ritual. Maimonides, on the other hand, with his basically halakhic approach and his ethical/intellectual perspective, developed (also using the theoretical concepts of his time) the prophetic stream in the Bible, at the core of which lay the belief that it is man's moral and religious behavior that forms the basis of that way of relating to the world which sanctifies both man and his physical surroundings. These two approaches are not entirely detached from one another, even in their further development by Halevi and Maimonides. Prophecy and moral/intellectual purity have their place in Halevi's thought, as does ritual holiness in that of Maimonides. Even so, juxtaposing their two approaches brings out the strong tension issuing from the conflict between them.

2

The idea that the holiness of things is no more than the symbolic significance that man attaches to them by his behavior is all-inclusive in Maimonides's doctrine and well rooted in his philosophical views. It applies to synagogues, Torah scrolls, and other ritual objects[7] as well as to the land of Israel, Jerusalem and the Temple. This is clearly articulated in some of his halakhic formulations. The land of Israel was sanctified by the Jewish people when it settled there. That is to say, it is the relationship bound up with national possession of the land based on the Torah that sanctified it to the people of Israel and none other. This is implied in the halakhic extrapolation that distinguishes between the former and latter acts by which the land was sanctified.[8] Joshua's conquest made it holy for a time, but when the people were exiled to Babylon this sanctity came to an end. It was renewed by those who returned from the first exile; however, since this time the people acquired the land not by military conquest, but by reappropriating their possession through settlement alone, it was sanctified, in those areas where the returnees actually made their dwelling, forever—that is, their legal ownership of it was established permanently, and with this legal determination, the sanctificatory relationship between people and land also became eternally binding. The assumption that holiness devolves from this sanctificatory relationship is brought out by a further halakhic principle:[9] any tract of land conquered by the people—that is to say, by decision of the authorized leadership of the people in accordance with the laws of the Torah (as opposed to conquest by individuals or otherwise than in accordance with the law)—is considered sanctified, even if it is beyond the borders of the land of Canaan.

The land of Israel is thus quite simply the land of the people of Israel, the land that is their national possession, and since it belongs to the people of Israel, it is sanctified. And what is the practical implication of this holiness? It is the people's obligation to fulfill those commandments that are binding upon it when it dwells in its land as a national group.[10] The same ideas emerge from what Maimonides had to say about the duty to settle in the land of Israel. It would seem no coincidence, then, that Maimonides cites the rabbinic sayings concerning this obligation in that section of his work devoted to "the laws of the sovereign."[11] The context is rich in meaning, for Maimonides interprets this obligation as stemming from the existence of Jewish sovereignty in the land of Israel. Let there be no mistake about this. The duty to fulfil this commandment derives not from any intrinsic holiness of the land, but from the over-all halakhic way of life which depends upon the existence of an independent Jewish society, and this is only possible, according to the halakhah, in the land of Israel. The Jew must live among his sovereign people in order to fulfill the commandments—this is Maimonides's basic assumption, and the sanctity of the land is founded upon it.

Up to this point, the halakhic formulation of these matters accords with Maimonides's Aristotelian philosophical-political ideas, so that there is a simple agreement between his halakhic and his philosophical/intellectual approach. However, anyone attempting to understand in this fashion all that Maimonides had to say about the relationship between the people of Israel and its land will rapidly become confused. Several of his halakhic determinations do not fit in with this system, at least not according to any simplistic interpretation of it. First of all, Maimonides distinguished keenly between the original and the later holiness of the land, and stated that its later holiness is eternal: it remains even when the Temple is not in existence and the people does not dwell in its land. Secondly, he differentiated between conquests made beyond the borders of the land of Canaan after all of the latter territory had itself been taken, and such conquests before all the land of Canaan was in Israelite hands. Only in the first instance would the further territory be considered part of the halakhic "land of Israel"; in the latter case, it would not.[12] And this refers precisely to the sacred significance of national possession of the land, for it is not the political sovereignty of the people of Israel over any territory it might conquer that Maimonides limited, but the applicability of those commandments that can only be fulfilled in the land of Israel. It would seem, therefore, that the land of Canaan is better fit for sanctification than, and is prior in holiness to, any other land. The greatest difficulty, however, lies in Maimonides's explicit statement[13] that the holiness of Jerusalem, or, more precisely, that of the site of the altar on Mt. Moriah, precedes Joshua's conquest of the land and the settlement of Jerusalem by the people of Israel, and is eternal. Is this not the same as saying that there is an intrinsic holiness to the site of the altar? And is this intrinsic holiness not then imparted to Jerusalem and to the entire land of Israel?

These questions remain unanswered, but before we attempt to answer them we must reiterate that Maimonides is not speaking here as a philosopher or a theologian. He expresses these views as a man of the law who is not free to decide otherwise than in accordance with the legal sources. All of the distinctions cited above, both those that conform simply to Maimonides' philosophical propositions and those that do not, are drawn from the ancient texts. Having understood this, we are once more confronted with the difficulty that students of Maimonides' thought encounter with regard to almost every subject of which he wrote: How did Maimonides relate to halakhic principles that appear opposed to his philosophical propositions? Did he accept them for the sake of appearances, because political considerations demanded that he set the authority of the halakhah beyond question, or did he find some more profound way of making these statements accord with the propositions he had accepted from Aristotelian philosophy?

This question of interpretation has divided students of Maimonides' ideas from the greatest of his earliest followers to the most famous contemporary scholars of his works.[14] Since our own discussion is not designed to provide a comprehensive understanding of Maimonides' thought, it shall suffice for us to note the crux of the controversy. The primary view, with which others have taken issue, is that of those who hold that Maimonides heeded the Torah out of absolute conviction, not only for the sake of appearance, and that his halakhic decisions reflect his true opinions. That is to say, he accepted the theoretical assumptions which underlay the halakhic principles he expounded and sought to understand them in accordance with his overall philosophical outlook. On the one hand he gave the Torah a philosophical interpretation, but on the other, he demanded that philosophy recognize the conclusions stemming from the fact of the Revelation at Sinai and the historical events that established the people of Israel as the recipient of the divine Torah. This history—from the days of the patriarchs, down through the people's slavery in Egypt, its exodus to freedom, its wanderings in the desert, the giving of the Torah, the conquest of the land of Israel, the building and later the destruction of the Temple, the exile and the redemption that is to come, and the commandments that were given to Israel—is made up of unquestionable facts.[15] The philosopher must take them into consideration just as he does the facts of nature—that is to say, he must draw the conclusions that follow from the fact that divine providence is everywhere apparent in the history of the people of Israel, just as he draws those that follow from natural events. And he must find a way of understanding what follows from his historical knowledge, on the one hand, and his knowledge of nature, on the other, so that they accord with one another, for the wisdom and the will of God are revealed in both.

This last statement is extremely important to an understanding of Maimonides' halakhic philosophy. Nature, he contends, generally has no concern for individual persons. The laws of nature are "concerned" only with the maintenance of the various species, and from this perspective the

individuals that are born and die are no more than representatives and repro-
ducers of the species to which they belong. Since we view nature as a divine
creation, we may interpret the laws that maintain the different species as an
expression of God's "general providence." According to Aristotelian philosophy, so Maimonides maintains, this general providence attaches to the
human race as well; individual persons do not live forever. The Torah, however, teaches us that men enjoy a special providence insofar as they live in
accordance with their destiny, that is, in accordance with the Torah.[18] The
Torah, then, is the revelation of God's providence over men, which applies
to particular individuals, as it does to the particular community, that people
which lives in conformity with the commandments of the Torah. We must
note that it is from the eternal value of particular individuals and particular
communities with all of their small details—that is, with all of the particular
actions that went to make up the personality of the individual or the culture
of the people—that the significance of history derives. Only that perspective
from which the deeds that make up the lives of men and of peoples are
important makes the past worth remembering, because it testifies to the
significance of the lives of men.

Maimonides' understanding of providence makes history eternally
significant. It provides a context of significance for the lives of individuals
and of peoples. If we bear this in mind, we shall also understand the importance of history to the halakhic determination of the sanctificatory relationship between the people and its land. There is, indeed, no contradiction
between the philosophical assumption that the holiness of the land of Israel
is not inheret but stems from the people's sanctificatory relationship to it,
and the halakhic proposition that the sanctification of the land by those
returning to Zion after the Babylonian exile made it holy to the people of
Israel forever. Maimonides did no more than supplement the philosophical
premise with an educational and historical factor, which was missing from
Aristotelian philosophy but emphatically present in the Torah. The distinction between original and later holiness is essentially historical, stemming
from the relative power of the act that sanctifies: the legal effect of conquest
is not the same as that of settlement on the basis of prior possession. Unlike
the fact of conquest, the latter creates a historical continuity, maintaining the
legal bond between people and land.

The importance of the educational-historical factor is particularly striking,
however, in Maimonides' observations concerning the eternal holiness of the
site of the altar on Mt. Moriah: "The site of the altar was defined very
specifically and was never to be changed. For it is said: 'This is the altar of
burnt-offering for Israel' (1 Chron. 22:1). It was on the site of the Temple that
the patriarch Isaac was bound. For it is said: 'And get you into the land of
Moriah' (Gen. 22:2); and in the Book of Chronicles it is said: 'Then Solomon
began to build the house of the Lord at Jerusalem in Mount Moriah, where
the Lord appeared to David his father; for which provision had been made in
the Place of David, in the threshing-floor of Ornan the Jebusite' (II Chron.

3:1). Now there is a well known tradition that the place where David and Solomon built the altar in the threshing floor of Araunah was the same place where Abraham built the altar upon which he bound Isaac. This, too, was the place where Noah built an altar when he came out of the Ark. It was also the place of the altar upon which Cain and Abel offered sacrifices. There it was that Adam offered a sacrifice after he was created. Indeed, Adam was created from that very ground; as the sages have taught: Adam was created from the place where he made atonement."[19] (translation quoted from Isadore Twersky, ed., *A Maimonides Reader*, p. 142, source of translation not given there).[19a]

Careful examination will show that Maimonides' explanation for the unique sanctity of the site of the altar does not go beyond the limits of his philosophical method. He attributes no intrinsic holiness to the place, but rather describes a history of sanctificatory acts which have marked it for the service of God and atonement for sin. It is history, then, that has given this place peculiar significance. It symbolizes on the one hand the fundamental relationship between God and His people, which has undertaken to sanctify His name in the world, and on the other the status of this people's role in the history of the nations, from the very beginning of the human race. That is why this place is uniquely and eternally holy.

This explanation for the sanctity of the site of the altar on Mt. Moriah fits in with that of two events, each of which, in Maimonides' view, was also unique in history and fundamental to an eternal order: the creation of the world, upon which the natural order is founded, and the Revelation at Sinai, which established the ideal order of human life. The binding of Isaac symbolizes perfect, unhesitating obedience to the divine command, the perfect devotion of him who believes in the Torah.[20] This makes the place holy, for man's total obedience to the divine command takes place within history, and in accordance with the conditions to which he is subject in space and time. In this respect, indeed, the site of the Temple symbolizes the land of Israel as a whole, for it is there that the Jewish people was obligated to live its full national life in every respect, in accordance with the Torah. Maimonides, then, sets the holiness of the altar, of the city within which it stood, and of the land, in a historical context.

3

What Maimonides had to say about the duty of the Jew to dwell in the land of Israel must also be interpreted on this basis. Political considerations demand that living in the land be obligatory when a sovereign Jewish kingdom stands upon its soil, for it is in relation to the Jewish community as a whole that the obligations of the individual are determined. Moreover, only when there exists an independent Jewish community in the land is one bound to fulfill the commandments that depend upon the land, so that considerations of policy accompany those of a political nature. Maimonides, therefore, does not consider it obligatory for every individual living in the exile after the destruction of the Temple to settle in the land. On the other hand, only in the land of Israel can the Jewish kingdom laid down by the Torah ever exist. The halakhah is quite clear in this respect: the *Beit Din HaGadol,* the High Court, upon which the Torah kingdom depends, depends in turn upon the existence of the Temple, and this can stand only in the land of Israel, and only on Mt. Moriah. A Jewish kingdom outside the land of Israel, even if, politically speaking, it were entirely sovereign, could never fulfill these halakhic criteria. From the point of view of the Torah it would still be exile.

Moreover, Maimonides appears to feel that a way of life based upon the Torah, even partially so, can be maintained in exile only if it is upheld by the existence of a Jewish community, even of only symbolic dimensions, in the land of Israel. Maimonides thus considers the Jewish people as a whole obligated to maintain such a community, for this small representation is vital to their ability to interpret and fulfill the divine command; that is to say, even when it is in exile, the land of Israel constitutes the basis for the people's active obedience to the commandments of the Torah. This principle is as explicit in Maimonides' doctrine as it is in Halevi's, even though the reasoning by which each of them arrives at it derives from opposing points of view. Halevi devotes a lengthy passage to establishing the proposition that the land of Israel is the geographical center from which true calculations of the order of time—weeks, months, and years—are to be made.[21] The reason why this was so important to him was because it made the land of Israel central to the life of the Jewish people even in exile. Even in the diaspora the units of time marking the Jewish calendar, its Sabbaths, holy days, and festivals, were still established in accordance with the land. Indeed, Halevi, following his understanding that holiness is an intrinsic quality, insisted that the centrality of Jerusalem was no matter of convention but stemmed from its geographical and theological superiority. The Sabbaths and festivals conform particularly and uniquely to the land of Israel—that is, only there, in that time, are there true Sabbaths and true holidays. Maimonides could not be further from such an explanation, but his halakhic conclusion is nevertheless the same:

> With regard to the commandment of the Most High concerning the calculation of months and years, which is the same as the commandment to sanctify the new month . . . this can only be fulfilled by the High Court, and only in the land of Israel. For this reason, we no longer carry out the practice of witnessing the New Moon, because the Temple is no more . . . Know, then, that the calculations by which we know when to celebrate the New Moons and Festivals may be done only in the land of Israel; but when there is no other resort, and there are no sages in the land of Israel, then the court nearest that land may decide which are to be leap years and determine New Moons even from beyond its borders . . . Herein lies one of the great elements of our faith, which cannot be known or sensed but through profound and careful study. When we, today, make calculations

outside of the land of Israel, following the order of leap years to which we hold, and say that a particular day is a New Moon or a holiday—it is on no account on the basis of our own calculations that we make that day a holiday. Rather, it is because a court in the land of Israel has already determined that this day is a holiday or New Moon, and it is because they have said that this day is a New Moon or a holiday that it is celebrated as such, whether they acted on the basis of mathematical calculations or on the basis of testimony   We make our calculations today only in order to know the day fixed by people living in the land of Israel, for it is by this very order that we make our calculations and determinations today—and not by testimony; and it is upon their determination that we rely—and not upon our own calculations. Our calculations do no more than reveal that day to us. Understand this well. And I shall add a further clarification: Were we to suppose, for example, that there should be no more Jews in the land of Israel—and God could never allow such a thing, for he has promised us that the remnant of the people shall never be entirely uprooted and eradicated—were we to suppose that there was no court there, nor any court abroad that was in close proximity to the land of Israel— then all of our calculations would on no account be of any use, for we may make calculations abroad, set leap years and determine the beginning of the new month only on the terms that I have described, as I have explained: "For the Torah shall go forth from Zion, and the word of God from Jerusalem.[22]

A careful examination of these very clear words will show us, again, that Maimonides ascribed no intrinsic superiority to the land of Israel with respect to determining the units of time. He is speaking, rather, of a halakhic convention, for according to the Torah it is the Palestinian sages who have the authority to determine the calendar. Obedience to the commandment of the Torah is thus the sanctificatory act in this case. However, according to the Torah the calendar may be fixed only in the land of Israel, so that if it is not done at the instruction of a court in that land, the act can no longer be considered to fulfill the commandment. Moreover, this statement makes sense only in light of the historical attestation to the principle of divine providence. Indeed, as we saw above, it is on this principle that Maimonides bases his confidence that the last remnant of the Jewish community in the land of Israel shall never disappear, so that the bond with the land that constitutes the basis for the people's ability to carry out the commandments binding upon them in exile will never be severed. Maimonides' opposition to Halevi's outlook on the theoretical level thus did not prevent his coming to the same practical conclusion. From a historical point of view, the land of Israel shall always be the center of gravity for the Jewish way of life, in accordance with the Torah.

4

The practical conclusion is one and the same, and the agreement of two such great men, so widely divergent in their views, is of immeasurable significance for the world of the medieval Jewish diaspora. It expresses a national consensus that is now greatly revitalized. The land of Israel is the holy land. Only there, from the point of view of the Torah, is a complete Jewish life possible, and only by its relation to the land can the people of Israel maintain its unique quality, the quality of Torah, even in its dispersion. Moreover, both of these doctrines are marked by their idealization of the land of Israel on the basis of the relevant rabbinic sayings, whether this stemmed from an understanding that the land's holiness was intrinsic or from the converse view that it derived from the people's sanctificatory relationship toward the land.

However, we must not minimize the importance of the ideological differences between these two thinkers. It may not affect their halakhic conclusions, but it does affect their meaning, and the experiential content of the commandments is determined by the meaning attributed to them no less than by the act itself; the deed fulfils the commandment only if it is performed with the proper intention, and intention is awareness of the meaning of the act. Moreover, the differences in their understanding of these meanings is expressed in their specifications of the obligatory deeds as well, for these determine where the emphasis is to lie in formulating a comprehensive Jewish way of life both in the diaspora and in the land of Israel. From this point of view, we are faced here with two quite different models of concepts of life based upon the Torah, the one stressing the ritual aspect of Judaism in order to draw out the full experience of the presence of God on the part of both the individual and the people, and the other emphasizing the ethical/political and spiritual/intellectual aspects of the life of the individual and of the community. The land of Israel that served as a foundation for Halevi's model differs from that described by Maimonides, and the images these two thinkers drew for themselves of that ideal way of life in accordance with the Torah that would exist in the land at some future time were indeed greatly different. Halevi visualized a people whose lives centered on the ritual symbol of the Temple service, while Maimonides foresaw it living by an ideal political order that would lead it to cleave intellectually to the true metaphysical concept of the world and to the fulfilment of the ethical good.

These two visions of the ideal way of life that was to be lived in the land of Israel, with all the tension between them, together influenced the religious thought of the Middle Ages. Both together shaped the living relationship of the people to its land, enabling them to continue to view it as its home even as it remained in exile.

5

A Symbolic Entity—The Land of Israel in the Kabbalah

Maimonides, who expressed his views on the land of Israel in legal terms in his halakhic works, had his effect upon the halakhic debate surrounding this subject, but the people's intellectual conception and visual image of the land, and their emotional relationship toward it, took shape primarily under the influence of Halevi's reworking of the rabbinic sayings. However, the concept, emotional attitude and image described in *The Kuzari* and in Halevi's poems about the land of Israel underwent a reinterpretation in the literature of the Kabbalah, which added a dimension of its own. From the beginning of the thirteenth century until the expulsion from Spain, the Kabbalah constituted the ideological basis of the thinking of those scholars who led the Jewish communities. It was the Kabbalah that came to their aid in their struggle against a thin crust of intellectuals who considered themselves followers of Maimonides and who were working toward a consistent rationalistic world view that appeared extremely dangerous to the halakhic scholars, in view of the circumstances obtaining in Christian Spain.[1] This trend gained further impetus after the expulsion in 1492. The elements of Aristotelian philosophy in Jewish thought were reduced to insignificance, while mysticism burst through the bounds of the scholarly domain and began to spread among the people as well.[2] In the long transition period between the Midddle Ages and the modern era, it was the Kabbalah, more than any other stream in Jewish thought, that shaped the people's mental conception and image of the land of Israel. The most striking expression of its impact is to be found in the messianic movements, and especially in the tremendous messianic outburst sparked by the appearance of Shabbetai Zevi.[3]

The background to the growing influence of the Kabbalah upon the people was the perceived worsening of conditions in the diaspora, both internal and external. Internally, the people were experiencing a spiritual deterioration that was expressed in the alienation of the intellectual elite from the community and its ways and in the conversion of many to Christianity. From without, there was the curtailment of rights, blood libels, persecution and expulsions. The powerful yearning for redemption from this ignominious state was frustrated by the helplessness of the Jewish leadership. The possibility of any change being effected by political means, by working within history, was nil. Only an event that transcended the natural course of history, a spiritual occurrence originating in a higher sphere of reality, could possibly bring about an immediate transformation in the people's situation. The Kabbalah expressed and responded to this popular mood, providing a way for the individual to achieve spiritual redemption by transcending physical circumstances to take part in the spiritual life, or by providing the way in which the people might be redeemed through a messianic transformation transcending the laws of history. Redemption was conceived of as a transcendence of the sphere of physical existence, and the land of Israel, that beloved place toward which the people's desire for redemption was directed, thus also took on a transcendent significance; beyond its concrete, physical actuality, it became a spiritual entity, a symbol. In the Kabbalah, then, the idealization of the land of Israel reached its peak, so that one could now speak of a spiritual *"aliyah"* to a symbolic land, which involved not physical movement from one place to another, but rather an internal spiritual development through mystical cleaving to God at prayer.

This development placed the land of Israel, in symbolic form, at the center of exilic Jewish experience; as such, it was present in the life of the Jewish community. Prayer was more than yearning—through intense spiritual effort, the land could become an internal reality. Of course, this intimate experience also bore within it the possibility of arousing a movement for actual settlement.

The Kabbalah generally demanded strict observance of the commandments, not only with regard to one's spiritual intention but also in terms of physical action, and from a halakhic point of view there are commandments of potentially redemptive power that could be fulfilled only in the land. An important representative of this approach was Rabbi Moses ben Nachman, Nachmanides (1194–1270), who settled in the land of Israel toward the end of his life.[4] Nachmanides the halakhist stated that, legally speaking, the commandment to return to the land was binding even "in the present day"; and Nachmanides the commentator, in his interpretation of the Torah, exalted the land in terms similar to those used by Judah Halevi. But Nachmanides was a kabbalist as well, among the first of the Spanish school, and he hints at the mystical image of the land in his interpretive writings. He refrained, however, from developing this image, for it involved secret lore that he did not wish to reveal. The mysical image was thus left to be developed in the kabbalistic literature that appeared later, particularly in the *Zohar*, which presented itself as the work of Shimon bar Yohai, a Palestinian sage, written in the land of Israel and portraying in its narrative and descriptive passages the reality and scenery of the land. In fact, the *Zohar* was written in Spain by a Spanish kabbalist, Moses de Leon, and what it describes is the scenery of the Iberian peninsula.[5] But this, paradoxically, is the source of the *Zohar's* power. If one studies this book with perfect devotion, he could transport himself into the reality of the land of Israel as he might have imagined it while still in the very depths of exile. Perhaps precisely for this reason, the intense experience of intimacy with the land expressed in the *Zohar* appears to have carried no practical impulse to actually settle there. Redemption was here and now, the internal spiritual achievement of great individuals.[6]

Nachmanides on the one hand, and Moses de Leon on the other, represent two possible and opposing responses. Their theoretical and experiential background, however, was the same, and it is this that we must come to understand in the course of our discussion. From a methodical point of view, this places us in a difficult position. The symbolic, kabbalistic significance of "the land of Israel" cannot be understood without first coming to grips with the basic elements of the kabbalistic system; however, the context of our present discussion does not permit of a lengthy elaboration of these fundamental ideas. We have, therefore, chosen for our purposes a work which, although the land of Israel is not its central concern, can serve as a basis for describing the kabbalistic system and its symbols to the reader who may be unfamiliar with them: Rabbi Joseph Gikatilla's (1248– ?) *Sha'arei Orah* (Gates of Light). The symbolic character of the land of Israel is discussed in this work within the framework of its overall characterization of the system, so that through it we may examine the transformation that took place in the way the significance of the land was understood in the course of the emergence of a new way of looking at life and at the Torah.

2

The teachings of the Kabbalah interpret reality as a system of symbols. Differentiated objects are no more than an external expression of the unified, continuous, internal life of the divine. Insofar as it can be characterized by this understanding of reality as comprising the continuous unity of divine life, the Kabbalah is one of the many branches of neoplatonic thought. Its Jewish distinctiveness is disclosed initially by its view of the Torah and the other books of the Bible and of the commandments, the first two as keys to understanding the symbols presented by reality, and the last, when performed with the proper intent, as a spiritual means of influencing that reality, by unifying it and returning it to its source, and so redeeming it from separation, change, and death.[8]

The idea of emanation constitutes the broad basis for this interpretation of reality as a system of symbols. Emanation is the continuous, gradual pouring forth of differentiating internal elements from within the comprehensive, infinite unit of God. In other words, God is the one, infinite source of all that is. Our experience may, indeed, seem to show us a plethora of finite, changing objects, coming into being and disappearing, and we may sense conflicts and contradictions in the world around us and in our thoughts, but in fact all

originates from the source of infinite unity. It is only man's limited understanding that makes him see the unity of the source and the multiplicity of its
derivatives as contradictory. If one probes deeply into the way in which the
divine life reveals itself, however, he will come to comprehend the unified,
continuous process by which these limited contents pour forth from their
source. It is this process that is called emanation, and three striking symbols
are used to express it: the beaming of light, the flow of water, and speech. All
three evidence the marvellous phenomenon of multiplicity streaming out of a
unity that is yet maintained, of movement from within to without, without
the external being severed from the inner essence. The divine essence
breaks forth, revealing itself, contracting, and differentiating, level by level.
Each level, up to the formation of the tangible, physical reality of our world,
embodies a necessary stage in this process of revelation. Taken together,
these are the *sefirot,* the principles upon which the reality of our world
stands, from which all being flows and to which all returns. He who knows
these principles, and the complex system of relationships between them, can
overcome the conflicts created by multiplicity; he may conquer finitude,
alienation and suffering. He knows how to return each tiny part to its source,
and to draw down the plenitude of infinite life into the world. As we have
said, the Kabbalah sees the Torah as the key to understanding the symbols
present in reality. The Torah is the plan by which the world was created; it is
the web of names taken on by God in each new stage of the process of
emanation. He who understands the Torah in this way, and fulfils its commandments on the basis of his knowledge of its secrets, is the true kabbalist,
who shall bring about the redemption of Israel and of the world.

These things, which are characteristic of the kabbalistic literature in general, are fundamental to the *Sha'arei Orah.* The book expressly undertakes
to provide the beginning mystic with a systematic guide to understanding the
web of divine names that makes up the Torah and to give him an idea of the
relationship between these names and the objects and circumstances present
in reality. It describes the specific meaning and intention of each and every
name in the Torah, and how it unifies supernal, spiritual reality with that of
the physical world. This is necessarily an extremely complex system, and in
order to become familiar with it one must first acquaint oneself with the
overall structure of the divine emanations—that is, with the *sefirot* and their
principal appellations. Only thereafter can one begin to discover the endless
richness of names ensuing from the infinitude of possible configurations
created in the course of the formation and conduct of the world.[9]

The *Sha'arei Orah* follows the tradition that there are ten such *sefirot.*[10]
This is the ultimate reduction of the sequence of limited numbers by which
one may count to infinity, differentiate unity and unite it once more through
counting. Each *sefirah* has a name and also several further basic appellations
which express the "psychological" mechanism of the self-revelation of the
divine inner essence. The *sefirot* are: *ratzon*—i.e., will (also called *keter*—

crown); *hokhmah*—wisdom; *binah*—understanding; *hesed*—mercy and *din* justice (or *gevurah*—might), which are mediated by the *sefirah* of *daat*—that is, knowledge (or *tiferet*—glory); *netzah*—eternity, *hod*—majesty, and *yesod*—foundation (these latter three, in fact, repeat the previous pattern formed by the principles of mercy and justice and the *sefirah* mediating between them); and, lastly, *malkhut,* kingdom, by means of which the upper *sefirot* conduct the affairs of the earthly, material world; *malkhut* is thus the level that unites the heavenly and the earthly, the spiritual and the physical.[11]

This, then, is the overall structure of the divine emanations. However, as we have said, this multiplicity itself leads to still further differentiation. There is no end to the possible configurations resulting from the relationships of the *sefirot* with one another and with the reality issuing from them. Each fairly outstanding configuration has its own name or symbol. Thus is created a rich and ever-expanding vocabulary of symbolic names, enabling the mystic to understand the world around him and his own internal life, to interpret these in accordance with the Torah and to connect them once more with the unity of divine life.

3

A world view which sees the Torah as a guide to God's self-revelation in creation must assign a central role to the people of Israel. It is they, the chosen people, who were given the Torah, and through them all peoples are blessed with closeness to God. The Kabbalah interprets this traditional view by identifying the people of Israel with a certain level in the divine emanation.[12] Moreover, this people's secret nature has roots in all of the *sefirot,* and comes to the fore in one of them. Thus, the upper *sefirot* are identified with the Patriarchs (*hesed* corresponding to Abraham, *gevurah* to Isaac and *tiferet* to Jacob).[13] The matriarchs too, as well as Moses, David and Solomon, derive from various emanations. The spiritual counterpart of the people of Israel, however, is the tenth *sefirah, malkhut,* which conducts the physical world by means of the plenitude that comes down to it from the other *sefirot,* just as the people of Israel mediates between the peoples of the world and the supernal beings. We thus find that the *sefirah* of *malkhut* is also called *knesset Israel*—the community of Israel,[14] and it is closely related to the people of the same name. When the people of Israel lives in accordance with the Torah, the *sefirah* of *malkhut* unites with the upper *sefirot* (particularly *tiferet,* which it reaches by means of *yesod*) draws down the divine abundance over Israel and thereby over the whole world; when the people of Israel sins, however, the connection between *malkhut* and the upper *sefirot* is broken, and the flow of the divine plenty ceases.[15]

We shall return to this idea, which we mention here only in order to fill out the scheme charted above, further on; before going into it in detail, however, we must note the meaning that the relationship between the people and its land takes on in the context of this symbolic conception. As we can well imagine, the land, too, is viewed symbolically, and since it is connected with the people of Israel and called by the same name, it unites with them to assume the same symbolic form. The *sefirah* of *malkhut* is called *Eretz Israel,* the Land of Israel, as well,[16] and just as the roots of the symbolic essence of the people of Israel are to be found in the upper *sefirot,* so it is with the land. In the mystical nature of the land we thus encounter holiness within holiness; Jerusalem and the Temple face the upper worlds, Mount Zion symbolizes the *sefirah* of *yesod,* and by means of the Temple service the very highest of the *sefirot* are drawn down to reveal themselves through the Temple, Jerusalem, and the land of Israel.[17]

In order to understand these things in greater detail, we must further define the significance of the symbol in kabbalistic thought. Generally speaking, a symbol is a tangible object which alludes to a thought, image, or feeling that has no tangible presence—that is, it is an object which expresses something else that is related to it in some way. This holds true for the Kabbalah as well. However, the Kabbalah has a unique understanding of the relationship between the symbol and the meaning it expresses. Its practitioners were, indeed, most careful to caution us against the grave error of identifying the symbol with the entities to which it alludes. They were particularly concerned with the danger of anthropomorphism: the symbolic relationship must not be interpreted as revealing an identity between the two realms; we would be wrong to see in earthly phenomena the tangible presence of the supernal spiritual reality. The tangible object does no more than allude to something which, in the upper spheres, is not material but spiritual, so that it can only be comprehended by means of its symbols.[18] Even so, however, the symbols do represent the supernal reality, for they are the end result of its continuous downward flow and ever-contracting outward revelation—that is, supernal reality presents itself to us by means of objects that come down from it to represent it. In their deepest essence, the symbol and its meanings are one, and it is thus possible to use these objects to act upon the upper spheres of reality. If the people of Israel and its land are symbols in this sense, then we must see in them a limited revelation of the plenitude of the divine life itself.

Moreover, as reality becomes more and more differentiated, and as it is perceived through its endless multiplicity of aspects, the symbolic system becomes ever more detailed. The symbols, too, are endless in number, and in their very infinitude they point back toward the infinite unity. All of their allusions, taken together, comprise a single meaning. Again, if the people of Israel, the land, and the Torah are principal symbols for the process of emanation, then their inner essence must be the same. As the *Sha'arei Orah* puts it, "And God, blessed be His Name, took His portion of the land, which is Jerusalem, and He took Israel from among men, . . . and since God's portion of the land is Jerusalem, and His portion among the nations, Israel,

Jerusalem and Israel are called by His name . . ."; and it is from this that the eternity of the people of Israel and the holiness that never departs from the site of the Temple are derived. The land and people of Israel are thus not merely objects that are related to one another; they are different aspects of the same essence, and even in symbolic form they are identified as the single *sefirah* of *malkhut.*

4

In developing these symbols, the author of *Sha'arei Orah* works in, according to his own system, several of the principal motifs found in biblical and rabbinic thought on the relationship between Israel and its land. We have already seen how the idea that the people and land of Israel are "the portion of God" is interpreted: one might say that they are actually part and parcel of Him. People and land are different aspects of the unity of divine life as it exists at a certain level. The centrality of Israel among the peoples and of its land among the rest will be interpreted in the same way. The plenitude of divine life, the outpouring of being and direction, flows down to the "princes of the nations" (who have a part in the divine emanations) by means of *knesset Israel* in its supernal, symbolic sense; and in the same sense this plenitude flows out to all lands by way of the land of Israel. The land, geographically surrounded by other countries, bearing within it the people of Israel surrounded by seventy nations, symbolizes the supernal reality of the *sefirah* of *malkhut,* surrounded by entities that it must maintain and direct.[19] Similarly, the levels of holiness within the people: priests, levites and ordinary Jews, and those of the land, including, in ascending order, the land of Israel as a whole, Jerusalem, the Temple, and the various levels of sanctity within the Temple up to the Holy of Holies, symbolize the complex network of relationships between the *sefirah* of *malkhut* and the upper *sefirot* that work through it.[20] The latter include, from time to time, the *sefirah* of *yesod,* which is also called *Mt. Zion,*[21] *tiferet,* the primary vessel for the divine conduct of the world,[22] and sometimes even *binah,* which holds the secret of true repentance and redemption.[23] Here we find the key to the eternal holiness of the site of the Temple as well: since it was fixed as the locus of the divine service, its holiness never departs from it, even after its destruction, for its status in relation to the inner essence of the divine life can never change. In fact, even the destruction has a symbolic significance that is related to the working of the upper spheres.

Up to now, we have dealt with interpreting the symbolic nature of certain bodies as they stand in relation to one another: people and land, city and Temple. However, we must recall that in the kabbalistic view these bodies are not static; rather, they are stages in the divine emanation, which is an active process of continuous flow downward from the infinite source, and upward from the bottom of the metaphysical ladder. This continuous activity is the key to the unity of these bodies which are maintained and revealed by one another, and the symbols that allude to a seemingly static system of fixed bodies in fact provide the setting for those symbols that embody the continuity and unity that lie in activity, in *assiyah*. These include, first and foremost, the divine service of sacrifice and prayer, to which we must add the historical event which, in the mystical view, is fundamentally sacred, for it expresses the divine conduct of the world.

The secret nature of the divine service, carried out by means of sacrifice, prayer, and the fulfillment of the other commandments of the Torah, lies in the joining of the lower reality with its supernal source. It is by way of the commandments that Israel becomes a chosen people, and they are the vessel by which it is bound with its land. When, through their performance, it is joined with its source, it rises to a higher level of reality and, conversely, it exudes the divine plenty, through itself and through the land, to all the world. The primary symbol used in this connection is that of intercourse, the meeting of love between God, symbolized by the *sefirah* of *tiferet,* and the people of Israel, symbolized by *malkhut.*[24] The Temple, in this symbolic conception, is the bedchamber of *knesset Israel* and God. When Israel serves its God, they are joined together in intercourse, and this too takes place on levels within levels, the highest of which is reached in the Yom Kippur service when the High Priest enters the Holy of Holies, for then the elevation of the people reaches as far as *binah,* the *sefirah* of redemption.[25] However, when the people of Israel sins—heaven forbid—God and *knesset Israel* are parted. The people of Israel is exiled from its land; that is, it is removed from its position within this self-supporting framework wherein it had lived in holiness, in direct relation to the source; and the *Shekhinah,* God's indwelling, which still connects it with sanctity even in this terrible state, goes with it.

This is the true, inner significance of the exile. Its full extent may be learned from what the *Sha'arei Orah* has to say about the difference between prayer in the land of Israel and that offered up abroad. In addition to its other meanings, the *sefirah* of *malkhut* also symbolizes communal prayer. This follows naturally from the previous set of symbolic associations: *malkhut,* as we recall, is *knesset Israel,* and, indeed, when the Jewish people gather for prayer they unite to become *knesset Israel.* However, *knesset Israel* is also the reality of the land of Israel. May we not thence infer that when the Jews pray as a community they rise inwardly to the spiritual level of the land of Israel? The author of the *Sha'arei Orah,* as we shall see, does hint at such a possibility, leaving the exiled people some opening for hope even in the depths of its despair. At the outset, however, he makes quite the opposite inference, showing by this association just how great the superiority of prayer in the land of Israel really is; for there the worshippers already stand on a certain level of holiness, so that their prayer can rise, raise them up, and effectively draw the divine plenty down into the world. Outside the land of Israel, where the path of prayer is blocked by accusers, critics and various other obstacles, this is not the case. To be outside of the land of Israel is thus to be distant from the true *knesset Israel,* outside of the symbolic framework of holiness that brings these things together. Even from there, however, there is a way in which one may still make his prayer effective: he can direct it so as to pass through the land of Israel and Jerusalem, through the Temple. This cannot be achieved, of course, by merely facing in their direction at prayer; rather, one's primary task is to comprehend the inner meaning of prayer and direct his feelings and thoughts to pass "through" or to be mediated by the symbolic meaning of the land of Israel. This, it would seem, is what leaves the people room to hope that they may still hold fast to the reality of the land of Israel even from exile. It is self-evident, however, that in this regard worshipping abroad cannot be compared with prayer actually offered in the land of Israel.[26]

The historical event, as we have said, acquires its significance through the sacral deed. The story of the love affair between *knesset Israel* and God is contained in that of the people's exile and redemption. When the people is exiled, the *Shekhinah* goes with it. God is no longer present among the people, and has deserted His land, His city, and His Temple. The latter are all despoiled; the divine abundance ceases and the people can no longer sustain itself in its own land. It departs for the lands of the gentiles, for these are still reached by a little of the divine plenty that maintains the lower world, coming to them through the "princes" of the nations, who have some connection with the upper worlds and receive a little of this abundance through the "pipelines" that were broken with the destruction of the land. However, instead of the entire world being maintained by the merit of the people of Israel living in its land, the latter, straitened, scorned and humiliated, are now maintained by the mercies of the gentiles. All of the outward phenomena of the exile thus symbolize its inner meaning: distance from the supernal source. Redemption will come when the Jews repent, when they fulfil all of the commandments of the Torah with the proper intent, for this has the power to connect the people once more with its true "place," its station in the order of the supernal elements. In this sense, repentance holds the key to redemption.[27]

5

The contents of the *Sha'arei Orah,* despite their brevity, present a model that recurs over and over, with many variations, in the kabbalistic literature. Were we to undertake a more detailed discussion we would be obliged to distinguish among the various kabbalistic systems, which have interesting differences among them, both in terms of their overall understanding of the theory of emanation and its symbols and in terms of the intensity with which they feel the pain of exile and the hope for redemption. We should have to devote an especially long passage to those doctrines that influenced broad segments of the Jewish people at critical historical turns, such as the *Zohar,* on its various levels, and the Kabbalah of Safed, particularly the Lurianic Kabbalah.[28] In the present survey, however, we have sought to do no more than offer a typology of the mystic's relationship to the land of Israel, and for this purpose we must make do with using a single example to note those characteristics that are common to all of these systems.

We shall conclude by demarcating the differences between the *Sha'arei Orah*'s conception of the land of Israel and those of Judah Halevi on the one hand and Maimonides on the other. Halevi was closer to the mystical worldview in his understanding that the land of Israel, Jerusalem, and the Temple lie in physical proximity to the passage between the upper and lower worlds and that it is through the divine service of sacrifice and prayer that the people of Israel merits having God's presence in its midst and in its land. To him, however, the upper and lower realities lie alongside one another; they are still two separate forms of existence. The land of Israel does bridge between the two, and the Temple is built according to a plan that symbolizes the supernal reality. However, these symbols are not swallowed up by their meaning; rather, they help man raise himself to the level of their higher significance by means of his inner spiritual powers. At the same time, the concrete, physical land, since it stands on a special level of reality, has experiential importance in its own right. Maimonides, on the other hand, was distant even from this kind of perspective. To him, the land of Israel is physically no different from any other land. Its holiness is an expression of the people's sanctificatory relationship to it. If it has a symbolic, educational significance, this stems from the historical events by which this relationship was demonstrated in its most elevated form. In the kabbalistic conception, however, the symbol actually embodies its significance in itself, and so represents it, so that its separate existence is no more than illusory. Even if one is most careful not to identify the form of the symbol with what it symbolizes, their inner essence is conceived as identical, so that the symbolic deed has direct consequences on those levels of reality to which it relates, and man can influence the upper worlds by his actions below.

In the Kabbalah, then, the land of Israel was transformed into the embodiment of a supernal, spiritual reality. This meant, on the one hand, that if one was able to go to the land of Israel, he might actually enter this spiritual reality and become totally united with it; and, on the other hand, that even beyond its bounds, from the distant exile, there was a way of "intending" one's devotions in the direction of the land of Israel and "arriving" at it by means of a symbolic experience. This, as we have said, is the highest level of idealization to which the relationship of a people to its land can be raised. Clearly, this kind of idealization created a close, living, and intimate bond between the religious person and the land, for the land was present even in the exile if one directed one's intentions towards or through it in prayer.

However, this also involved a dilemma that must not be overlooked. While strengthening the Jew's desire to go to the land of Israel, since this symbolic deed might be of critical importance in bringing the redemption nearer, such a conception tended to provoke a simultaneous sense of recoil from the very same act, for just because of its symbolic significance it seemed, from a religious point of view, extravagantly presumptuous. Was one permitted to come so close to the preserve of holiness before he could be absolutely certain that he had been cleansed of the impurity of exile? Moreover, if the mystic often demonstrates an ambivalent attitude of strong attraction and simultaneous inner reserve as he approaches the decision to go and settle in the land,[29] a terrible disappointment may well await him there once he has made up his mind and departed for it. He will reach the ruined, oppressed and despoiled land of Israel, only to find life there inferior to the life he had led in exile, not only in physical terms, but also in the realm of the spirit. How, then, is he to explain this terrible paradox to himself?[30]

It is, thus, not surprising that the renewal of the people's concrete bond with its land was bound up with a radical change of values. The Zionists, even if they were religious and even as they drew upon kabbalistic thought, had to reinterpret the symbolic idealization of the land if they were to give it back its physicality, make that physicality important in itself, and use it to rebuild the earthly life of the people.

PART III

Regaining the Land of Destiny as a Homeland

1

Nachman of Bratslav: A Return to the Physical Land

In the period following the expulsion from Spain the literature of the Kabbalah, which was now the leading intellectual movement in Jewish life, was characterized by a growing messianic ferment. Its concern with the issue of exile and redemption, on both the personal-spiritual level and in the national sense, produced a tension between its perception of the people's acute suffering and its towering hopes. The dimensions of the significance of the exile become ever more profound, and with them those of the hoped-for redemption. The land of Israel, of course, holds a central place in this stream of thought. Its importance was demonstrated concretely when it became, in the latter part of the sixteenth century, not only a principal subject of mystical and messianic thought, but also a spiritual center, which drew the finest Jewish scholars of the time, both in halakhah and in metaphysics. It was there that they created original and tremendously profound new systems of thought whose influence spread throughout the diaspora. The sixteenth-century land of Israel witnessed the most consistent effort ever undertaken to make the Kabbalah a way of life for both the individual and the community.

The redemption was expected to grow out of the daily lives of the Jews in their land. It would seem that the mystics, by devoting their lives to study and to examining and fulfilling the commandments with the proper intent,[1] were seeking to take hold of the physical land of Israel and raise it up to its source. In so doing, they also set the stage for Shabbetai Zevi's audacious attempt to break through the sealed gateway leading to redemption.[2] Even after the wild hopes he created had been tragically dashed, however, the Kabbalah of Safed, and especially the Lurianic Kabbalah, still remained the spiritual foundation by which the people's faith and hope were preserved, and which kept alive the search for new theoretical and practical ways of bringing about the redemption. The influence of these kabbalistic systems persisted very powerfully right up until the first stirrings of the Jewish Enlightenment and the Zionist movement. Moreover, the onset of these movements cannot be said to have delimited the boundaries of the Kabbalah, for not only did it continue to influence the opponents of these movements, it even infiltrated their domain. The kabbalist image of the land had a multi-faceted effect, both direct and indirect, upon the image which hovered before the eyes of generations of dreamers of the return to Zion, non-religious as well as devout.

This huge body of mystical literature immeasurably enriched the Jewish people's understanding of the symbolic significance of the land of Israel, particularly with regard to their understanding of its desolation in time of exile and the spiritual path by which it might be redeemed. Several of these works even contain inklings of a way of thinking that gropes toward the cultural and political realities of the modern era. The writings of the Maharal of Prague[3] provide a particularly striking and interesting example of this tendency. The idea that there is a "natural" relationship between every people and its land and that each people has a natural right to lead an independent existence upon its own soil is already present here. Moreover, on the basis of this idea we may discover in the Maharal's thought a definition of exile not unlike that given by Zionism, describing the diaspora as "unnatural," an abnormal situation which cannot endure forever since it distorts the natural law of history.

The people of Israel thus must eventually return to its land, which is its natural place in the world, in order to restore its national independence and so fulfill its predestined task in the world.[4] Within the limited framework of the present discussion, however, we cannot go into the fascinating variety of ideas that arose during the period of transition between the Middle Ages and the modern era. Of all this rich collection, we have chosen one theoretical doctrine of special importance, that of Rav Nachman of Bratslav.[5]

The particular importance of Rav Nachman's concept of the land of Israel lies in the fact that it indicates with exceeding clarity the borderline distinguishing the patterns of experiential and intellectual response characteristic of the Middle Ages from those of modern times. The Bratslaver experienced the transformation in the nature of the exile that was taking place in his time with acute intensity. In his intellectual and emotional response, he illustrated on the one hand the problems involved with the Kabbalah's extreme idealization of the land, and, on the other, the direction that the change which would eventually lead to the formation of the Hibbat Zion movement was taking. The novelty of his approach may be summarized in one sentence, fraught with tension: Rav Nachman rediscovered the importance of relating to the physical reality of the land of Israel as the foundation for the continued existence of the Jewish people. He was not, however, to go as far as the conclusion reached by the adherents of Hibbat Zion, namely, that the land must actually be rebuilt on the people's own initiative.

2

The Bratslaver saw his pilgrimage to the land of Israel (though he remained there only briefly) as a response to the circumstances of Jewish life in exile in his time, and especially to the spread of Sabbateanism in its Frankist incarnation.[6] He was seeking to remedy the blemish that the Frankists had cast upon the essential nature of the people of Israel and to combat the danger that they represented. From our historical perspective, Sabbateanism and Frankism may both be described as early, extreme, and perverted expressions of a phenomenon that was to become the most prominent characteristic of the exilic community in the period of the Emancipation: the posing of assimilation as a Jewish ideal, or a path towards redemption. There was a qualitative difference between this and the kind of assimilation the Jewish people had known throughout the history of the dispersion. The defection or desertion of individuals, even a great many of them, is nothing new to Jewish history. But a Jewish movement that made an ideology of assimilation or conversion, that saw the redemption of Judaism in the destruction of its particularistic existence—this was indeed a novel occurrence. Such was the ideology of the assimilationist movement of the nineteenth century. In its view, the time had come for the Jewish people to give up its particularity. The gentile environment was no longer pagan, and was ready to accept the universal ideals central to Judaism. For this purpose, however, Judaism had to be set free of its antiquated ways and become identified with its pure ideal. It would thus be released from exile and find redemption, while penetrating and becoming a part of the culture and society of its enlightened surrounding.[7] As we have said, Sabbateanism and Frankism appear to be early, extreme and distorted manifestations of this kind of ideology. The destruction of Judaism from within, through the desecration of its commandments and conversion to other faiths—this was the path out of exile. Judaism was to be fulfilled by its own self-negation.[8]

The historical, sociocultural, and intellectual background to the psychological and spiritual perversion manifested in Sabbateanism and Frankism is extremely complex, and this is not the place to go into it in detail. Rav Nachman, however, apparently felt that this movement, perverted as it was, expressed a general, qualitative weakness in the character of the Jewish people, and that only a powerful struggle that came to grips with the very root of it could curb the danger and rectify the damage that had already been done. In the following lines, we shall attempt to derive the perception of the malady from the remedy that Rav Nachman proposed.

The reason that Sabbateanism and Frankism, which are manifestations of the *Sitra Achra,* (powers of evil) had such a seductive power was that the exile had become an inner, psychological reality, a state of distance from the primal source of Jewish life and from the unmediated reality of Jewish existence. It had deepened into an abstract, foreign, and hollow way of being. The foreign, gentile world was so solid and so influential that the inner nature of Judaism seemed a distorted shadow beside it. This feeling on the part of the people is demonstrated, in fact, by the contemporary attitude toward the land of Israel, and Rav Nachman's decision to go there attests to it. The land of Israel is that place where the Jews had once lived a full, real

Jewish life, and as such it represented at least the dream of that reality. In the exile whose presence ran so deep, however, it appeared at times that all had been forgotten. Was there really such a land? Was it a real, physical country? In other words, there comes a moment when the marvellous dream, despite its loftiness, or perhaps because of it, affects one less by its wonder than by the fact that it is a dream, a once-upon-a-time reality with nothing behind it. The dream no longer represents an extant reality but a misty existence such as one might behold just before waking from sleep into a foreign world, whose actuality is mighty, stable and imposing.

Of course this is not true of the land of Israel alone. What about *knesset Israel?* Does the people living in exile truly exist as a people, or is *knesset Israel* perhaps no more than a meaning represented by no living symbol? And what of the Torah—does the traditional way of life define an extant reality whose mark on the world is perceptible? Thus, precisely that overwhelming spirituality by which the Kabbalah had sought to preserve the presence of land, people, and Torah within the internal dimension of Jewish life was transformed, in this setting, from a solution into a mere illustration of the problem. The power of its extreme idealization faded before the burdensome actuality of the foreign environment. This, apparently, was the inner weakness that gave the crazed Frankist fantasy its seductive power, which Rav Nachman himself seems to have sensed quite strongly.[9] The Frankist vision is no more than an attempt at redemption in reverse; release from the vicious circle of abstract Jewish existence through self-destruction and alienation, in an environment whose actuality forces itself upon the Jew and oppresses him from every side.

Rav Nachman's doctrine of the land of Israel represents, at the very least, a daring psychological effort to confront this perception of reality. In this respect, it might be described as a quasi-Zionist response to a set of circumstances that sustained a movement of quasi-assimilationism. This description, however, should be viewed within the full context of the spiritual phenomena with which we have been dealing. While carrying on the kabbalistic tradition of thought, Rav Nachman awoke to the danger it entailed, that of an overspiritualization that might ultimately deprive the symbols of their actuality. His response, therefore, was to reaffirm that the symbols are important in themselves, for only by their means can the sphere of spiritual significance be reached. There can be no bypassing the actual people of Israel, by whom the meaning of *knesset Israel* is borne, of the Torah and the commandments, or of the concrete, physical land of Israel, a real land of rocks and dust, a land that can be touched, whose soil men tread. Let us recall once more that the element of the land of Israel in the triad formed by people, Torah, and land represents the dimension of concrete actuality. In their own land, the people's life in accordance with the Torah is full and complete, and their mark upon the world is clear and powerful. It is no wonder, then, that a comprehensive response to the abstraction of Jewish life in the diaspora should involve the land of Israel. Rav Nachman went there quite simply in order to touch the actual land. He had to behold in broad daylight the reality that lay beyond the dream in order to reintroduce a physical dimension into the shadowy life of the diaspora. In this respect, his pilgrimage was clearly a mystical act of a symbolic nature. The special significance of his symbolic act, however, lay in its revival of the people's consciousness that the land of Israel actually exists, and that the reality of Jewish life everywhere, even in the very depths of exile, is derived from it.

3

As we have said, Rav Nachman continued in the kabbalistic tradition, even though he was aware of its flaws. His works are replete with the motifs we noted in our discussion of the mystical image of the land of Israel, some of which he develops and even expands: The land is a symbol of supernal holiness; Providence reaches the world through the land of Israel, as does the divine plenty, when the world is as it should be. It is the foundation of holiness and of faith, and the commandments can be fulfilled perfectly only upon its soil. Sin caused it to come under the dominion of the *kelippot* (the forces of evil) which conceal its sanctity. This is the secret for Canaanite rule over the land of Israel prior to its conquest by Joshua, and for its current domination by the gentiles. Although its sanctity may be obscured, however, it abides forever. The people of Israel know its secret, and when, by the hidden power of the land, they have repented completely, the land will be released from the governance of the *kelippot* and they will be redeemed, and with them all the world.[10]

Ideologically speaking, there is nothing new in any of these formulations, except for some emphases in which a kind of Zionist perspective can be detected. These include Rav Nachman's accentuation of the idea that living in the land is a mode of repentance, for fulfilling the commandments that depend upon the land puts an end to its domination by the *kelippot* and reveals its holiness. Rav Nachman associates this idea with God's refusal to allow Moses to enter the land of Israel. Had Moses entered the land, he would have driven out the *kelippot* before the proper time—before Israel had repented completely.[11] If this teaching has a practical import, it is that re-demption, in Rav Nachman's opinion, must be preceded by a return to the land. At the same time, however, he stressed another, associated idea: while the defects of the exile can be remedied only by the power of the land, the people will not become worthy of the land until they have corrected these defects.[12] Rav Nachman expressly admitted his perplexity in this regard, and this was the core of the hesitation he evinced between his sense of obligation to go and live in the land and his opposing feeling that the mission he had to fulfill could be accomplished only in the diaspora.

The principal innovation in Rav Nachman's doctrine of the land of Israel then, is that action precedes speech. It must be understood, moreover, that to Rav Nachman it is not the word that explains the deed, but rather the deed that explains the word which, once the deed has been done, may also function as a kind of action or sequel to the deed. This statement is to be taken at face value. What was new with Rav Nachman was not the fervent yearning that bestirred him to go and see the holy land at least once in his life; others, impelled by the same yearning, had done this before him. Rather, it was the symbolic significance of the act and the words that accompanied it, whose purpose was to apply the relevance of the act to his continued activity as a spiritual leader in the diaspora. In light of his deed we are able to understand, first of all, Rav Nachman's repeated emphasis that the land of Israel of which he speaks is "quite simply this land, with these very buildings and homes, to whose shores Jews travel."[13] One cannot enter into the holiness of the land of Israel without coming into physical contact with the actual land. Just this understanding, however, involved a serious spiritual dilemma, which demonstrates the significance of the exilic experience described above: "Rav Nachman related that when he was in the land of Israel, the important people there who had come from these countries to make their homes in the land of Israel, as is widely known—these people told him that before they came they could not imagine that the land of Israel is of this world; they had felt that the land of Israel was an entirely different world, as would befit its great holiness as described in the sacred texts and in conformity to the degree of sanctity ascribed to it in our holy Torah . . . But when they got there, they saw that the land of Israel really is of this world, for it is just like any other country, and its soil looks just like that of our own countries . . . For there is no visible difference between the land of Israel and any other land, though this is not to say that it is the same as any other, and even so the land of Israel is very, very holy, and happy is he who is able to tread even four cubits upon its soil, etc. . . . And the land of Israel is truly different and utterly distinct from every other land in every respect . . . Yet, even so, in the material sense the eye of man can distinguish no difference between the land of Israel and any other land; only he who has achieved faith in its holiness can discern a slight difference . . ."[14]

In this passage Rav Nachman gives vent to his astonishment at the disappointing contrast between the kabbalistic image of the land of Israel and the reality. However, the careful reader will find that this contradiction is simultaneously affirmed—or, rather, that it is in the very course of his affirmation that Rav Nachman voices his surprise. Things could not be otherwise, for the land of Israel is a real country, symbolizing the physical, actual dimension in the life of the people. The holiness of the land must have its source precisely in its geographical reality, and in the physical sense there is no difference between one country and another. "The principal virtue of the land of Israel," says Rav Nachman elsewhere, "is to be discovered in the Torah's praise of it as a land flowing with milk and honey, and in the seven species of fruit for which it is renowned. The main intention of these passages is to show that it is there that the supernal pleasantness flows, the root of all the pleasantness and sweetness that inhere in all the tastes in the world; and this is the source of the pleasantness and sweetness of the fruits of the land of Israel. It is there, by means of these good fruits, that one may bind himself to the supernal pleasantness by sanctifying the act of eating them by fulfilling the commandments that depend upon the land, all of which have to do with various kinds of food . . ."[15]

Of course, anyone who imagines that simply being in the land, whose physical aspect is like that of any other, will provide him with an experience of exaltation and holiness risks a terrible disappointment, and this is the very essence of the danger inherent in the kabbalistic idealization. What if, contrary to one's idyllic expectations, there should be no difference between his inner experience of his physical presence in the land and the impression made upon him by its external appearance—if he should feel no sanctity in his experience of being in the land? And what if, because of its desolation and neglect, the pilgrim to the land of Israel should feel not elevation and holiness but rather distress and even spiritual descent? To this Rav Nachman responds, in the passage cited above, that in order to discern the land's holiness in its physical appearance, one must believe in its presence. Faith, in this context, is defined as the action of a powerful will to seek and to find. Admittedly, however, it is no easy challenge that one faces, and even the believer will find that that difficult spiritual goal which he seeks cannot be reached by any direct route. One's natural response to the desolate land cannot be one of holiness and exaltation. The believer who knows the secret truth must, therefore, outwit his own soul to call forth an obscure presence from its innermost depths.

The strange report of Rav Nachman's journey to the land must be understood in this context. His behavior was certainly most peculiar, and the reader will sense immediately that this was no simple idealistic pilgrimage; rather, there is a distraught spiritual deviousness about it, expressed in the unceasing tension between his firm decision to make the journey, despite all of the difficulties involved, and his constant, deliberate frustration of his own desires. Rav Nachman's behavior on his journey seems fraught with irony toward himself. He discloses none of his spiritual greatness; on the contrary, he appears to be on a course of descent, of self-degradation and concealment of his true spiritual stature. This is doubtless attributable in part to a complex combination of humiliating circumstances in which he unwittingly became entangled on his perilous, adventure-strewn journey to the land and back. At times, however, it appears that he brings these demeaning situations upon himself by his own behavior, and that his self-belittling actions are intentional.

Just so, and not otherwise, must he arrive in the land of Israel, and just so must he to appear during his sojourn there. Most of the time he acted as though he were fearful, unhappy, and oppressed. Could it not be that he sought thus to outwit his own soul, to circumvent his potential disappointment at his meeting with the land by anticipating it, and so succeed in achieving the fulfillment of his great expectations? May he not have hoped that the first spark of an inner exaltation would begin its rise out of the very depth of his external descent into the land's depressing physical reality? This, indeed, is how Rav Nachman saw things. In his own words: "In order to achieve greatness—that is, to attain to something so marvellous that it touches upon greatness, one must first fall to meanness. The land of Israel is the peak of greatness, and in order to reach it one must therefore plunge into the uttermost degradation. That is, those *zaddikim* who are on the highest level of greatness and wonder can reach the land of Israel only by degrading themselves utterly, so that no exaltation or grandeur are to be seen about them on their journey there, for they much conceal themselves . . . and undertake to suffer humiliation and scorn and so on. It is in just this way that they succeed in emerging victorious and passing through all of the obstacles and hindrances they encounter unharmed, and so they are able to reach the land of Israel, and in this way they arrive at a most exalted, marvellous and awesome achievement."[16] So did Rav Nachman on his journey appear to crush himself to the ground, so that he might reach the inner court by way of a gate so low that it could be entered only by getting down on all fours.

So much for Rav Nachman's way of dealing with the problem of the contrast between the kabbalisitic ideal of the land of Israel and the reality. Let us not forget, however, that this problem was all the more serious for him and had come to occupy the center of his attention because it was the material dimension of the land which he needed in order to counteract the circumstances of the exile in his day. In these circumstances the reality of the symbol, despite its physicality and forbidding appearance, was more important than its higher meaning. It was for just this reason that the difficulty was so intense, but precisely because of this Rav Nachman was ready from the outset to deal with it and to which end he undertook his pilgrimage. But what was he actually seeking to accomplish by his journey? What was the object of his coming? Here we must turn our attention to a fact no less startling than the irony toward himself that characterized his behavior on the journey. When, after all the hardships, humiliations, and perils he had endured Rav Nachman finally reached his journey's end and entered the land of Israel, he appears to have been quite uninterested in remaining there for any length of time. As soon as he had touched its soil, he was already thinking of going back, ready even to forgo a visit to Jerusalem. He thus gave himself practically no time to attain to the holiness of the land of Israel during his sojourn there, although he later testified of himself that by walking no more than four cubits upon its soil he had performed sacred feats of unimaginable spiritual grandeur. It would seem that simply by reaching the shores of the land and actually touching its soil he had done what he had to do. He did not even put his inner experience of the land into words while he was there.

The careful reader will find that only after his return to the diaspora did he make any explicit mention of the experience of exaltation and holiness that was to be had in the land of Israel; it is as though he sought to let his listeners share in an experience that had arisen from the depths of his previous silence. Moreover, after his return from the land of Israel he not only represented himself as having been there, he now bore the land within himself. His teaching, from here on, belonged to the land; all his ways were its ways, and he devoted himself wholly to sustaining the reality of the land with him in the exile.[17] By his pilgrimage, then, he dedicated himself to a sacred mission, whose fulfillment demanded that he bind himself to the land through actual, physical contact and bring this contact back with him to the exile. In the countries of exile his talk of the land of Israel, which he called the Torah of the land of Israel (and was not confined to matters relating directly to the land; henceforth, everything of which he spoke partook of the Torah of the land of Israel), was the sequel to the deed that had been done in silence—or one might say that the meaning of his talk was to be found in the deed that he had performed.

4

There is a qualitative difference between Rav Nachman's pilgrimage to the land of Israel and those of others who had preceded him, such as Judah Halevi and Nachmanides. A similar distinction, however, can be made between Rav Nachman's journey and that of the Hovevei Zion who came after him. Rav Nachman did not go to the land for the sake of dwelling there in an attempt to bring about the end of days through prayer and study; but he also was not trying to bring about the redemption of the people by settling the land and regenerating its desolate wastes. He went to gain a sense of the actual presence of the land, which was essential to him for its own sake, for it was a vital dimension of Jewish life that had fallen away from the people in exile. It is for this reason that he felt that the defective nature of the exile could be remedied only by means of the land—that is, by way of physical contact with its soil—even though the main tasks necessary for bringing about the redemption could still be accomplished only among the people in exile.

As we have said, Rav Nachman's ideas on this point are riven with confusion and ambiguity. On the one hand, he felt that the Jewish people's true place was in its own land, and he knew that making the journey there was ultimately a matter of will alone. He expressed himself on this subject openly and clearly, his words having the ring of a Zionist demand. The argument that travel to the land involved insurmountable difficulties and dangers, he claimed, was only an excuse. Jews took even greater risks just to earn a livelihood, and overcame them with the help of the Holy One. If they really wanted to go to their land, they would do so, and the Holy One would surely come to their aid in this as well.[18] Moreover, one had to be ready to face any kind of suffering for the sake of the land of Israel, for it is the essential basis upon which holiness, faith and the commandments are constituted; the Jew was duty-bound to go there even if he had to go on foot.[19]

He believed, in any case, that the really prodigious dangers involved in the journey were reserved for the great *zaddikim,* who had to do battle with the *kelippot* (shells of evil) on their way; for simple Jews, however, the passage presented no unusual difficulties.[20] It is no wonder, then, that Rav Nachman's hasidim felt that he had wished to encourage them actually to go and settle in the land of Israel.[21] On the other hand, he himself clearly went there with the intention of returning to the exile, for he understood his primary mission to be that of correcting the defective nature of Jewish life in exile through the influence of the land of Israel. True, the obstacle to going to live there was internal; its source lay in the realm of thought. The exile was like a screen, concealing or dimming the will. As long as this internal obstacle remained however, it was stronger than any external circumstance. The primary task, therefore, was to remove it, and this could be accomplished only in the exile.[22]

Here once again we are brought face to face with Rav Nachman's unique understanding of the exile. The Jew's inner life had lost its solidity because of the concealing screen, the dominion of the *kelippot,* and this unhappy state could be overcome only by the influence of the land of Israel—but the land could exert its influence only when the flaws of the exile are rectified. The careful student will find, at any rate, that no less than he emphasized the commandment to go and settle in the land of Israel, Rav Nachman stressed the idea that the reality of the land could be drawn into the exile, and that the redemption of the land could be speeded in this way.[23] In other words, Rav Nachman felt that before the exiled people could return to its land, he had to bring the land of Israel to the exile.

We can now understand more clearly the connection between the Frankist defect and pilgrimage to the land of Israel. The Frankists were likened to the Canaanites; like the latter, they symbolized the *kelippot* that had extended their rule over the land of Israel. This time, however, it was that aspect of the land of Israel that existed in the exile that was involved. Rav Nachman journeyed to the land of Israel and returned to the exile to rectify this defect by drawing the influence of the real, physical land of Israel back with him. But what was the nature of this activity? How did Rav Nachman understand the land of Israel as actually being present in the exile? Our reply to these questions must be couched in the kabbalistic terms of *kavvanah,* intention, and *devekut,* devotion: the Jew's spiritual tie with the unique, particular nature of Jewish life, which was of the essence of the land of Israel, was to be strengthened. However, there is a qualitative difference in the content of these ideas. The "intention" and "devotion" were to be directed toward the real, literal land of Israel, a land of dust, stones and earth.

In this connection, we must note a symbolic linguistic extrapolation which recurs several times in Rav Nachman's teachings concerning the land of Israel: *adamah,* earth, is related to *dimui,* image. The land of Israel, which is earth, holy earth, is the power of the imagination. But what does this power have to do with the metaphysical and kabbalistic understanding of the soul? Quite simply, the imagination is the organ of prophecy; by its means, the prophet attains to the actual, direct presence of the supernal reality.[24] Here, then, we encounter the perfect interpenetration of the symbolic and physical dimensions of the land of Israel. The real land of Israel is that aspect of the supernal reality to which we can attain by means of the images it leaves in our own minds, so that it is only by means of the direct, physical presence of the land that we can arrive at true devotion to the supernal reality. The obvious meaning of the symbol constitutes its deeper meaning as well.

The physical land is the concrete dimension of holiness that dwells in the lower world. If we have understood this symbolic linguistic extrapolation correctly, then, it would imply that devotion to the land of Israel must consist, first and foremost, in having a true image of the land as it really is. It must be present in the mind's eye of the pious and devoted while they are still in exile; they must yearn for this land by impressing its true image upon their imaginations. Moreover, the worshipper must intend actually to lay hold of the land, as though he were stretching forth an imaginary hand to grasp it with all of his might: "Even though we have been appealing for so many years to return to the land of Israel and are still far away from it, none of our prayers or cries, even of the very lowliest among us, has ever been in vain. For with every cry and every prayer some small part of the land is conquered, and one day all of these points that we have subdued by our prayers shall come together as one whole, and then we shall quickly return to our land.

"Even the cry of a very defective person, who does not have the power to conquer even a small part of the land of Israel by his prayer, is of great consequence, for it functions as would a protest in the realm of the laws of property, according to which the occupier's possession of a tract of land is never sufficient to prove his rightful ownership for as long as anyone continues to protest it. Thus, even though we have been divested of the Land of Israel, which is our land and our inheritance, and we do not have the power to wrest it from our enemies, because of our defective deeds, we continue ever to pray and to cry out that it is our land and our inheritance, and thus we lodge our protest against the *Sitra Achra,* so that all shall know that its possession by the forces of evil proves nothing, for we have inherited the Land of Israel from our fathers, and ultimately, with the help of God, we shall wrest it from our enemies."[25] It is most instructive to compare this description of how one is to direct his intention at prayer toward the land of Israel with that given by Joseph Gikatilla. Rav Nachman is not content with directing prayer "through" the land of Israel so that it can reach the supernal *sefirot* directly. He wishes, by means of prayer, to lay hold of the land itself. One's "intention" functions as an act of conquest and repossession, and the symbolic act, in this context, is not metaphorical; it is real. The land of Israel is actually reconquered for the Jews by means of prayer offered up with the correct intention, that is, with yearning actually to be in the land of Israel, bodily and spiritually.

At the same time we must not gloss over the fact that it is a symbolic act, which will lead to redemption only in some future time, that is involved. Just as Rav Nachman's pilgrimage was of a symbolic nature, so, too, does the people's hold on the land from exile have a symbolic character for him. He sees the symbolic act as having a concrete effect, but it functions on the internal level. He solved the dilemma arising from the conflict between the people's ideal expectations of life in the land and the real circumstances to be encountered there, too, from the perspective of the exile, by means of a symbolic gesture, and it must be admitted that this kind of solution from afar is a relatively easy way out. From this perspective, ultimately, even the simple reality of the land is an idea, and on this conceptual level it is not all that difficult to discover a dialectical unity between the land's destruction and its holiness.

The transformation wrought by the Hibbat Zion movement involved an additional and no less revolutionary step away from the idealization of the physical land and toward the demand that the people possess the land itself, not symbolically but physically. This step could not be taken until there was a change in their definition of what was actually to be sought in the land of Israel. No longer was this confined to its holiness or even to the simple experience of its reality; the new movement wanted it to fulfill all of the roles played by a national home. Hibbat Zion arose when the people of Israel began to feel that it needed a land of its own like any other people—that is to say, a physical foundation upon which it could establish itself on the demographic, economic, social, and political levels. The fulfillment of this need demanded more than symbolic pilgrimages or a spiritual hold on the image of the land of Israel, and the intensity of the dilemma to which the contradiction between the Jew's expectations of the land and its actual state was thus increased sevenfold. Rav Nachman did not have to confront the problematics of this situation, but one might say that he came very close to its threshold.

2

The People Redeems itself—The Land of Israel in the Ideology of the Religious Hibbat Zion Movement

Hibbat Zion, from its inception, was a religious-traditionalist movement. Its founders knew, of course, that they were introducing something new into the traditional world, both in their evaluation of the historical situation of the Jewish people and in the practical ways in which they proposed to solve its problems. It appeared to them, however, that the tradition permitted of such an innovation, and that their plan might even be an expression of greater loyalty to the commandments. Their dream of a return to Zion was itself, in their view, that same ancient vision that had inspired the people of Israel since patriarchal times. Indeed, there certainly was nothing new in their relating to the land of Israel as the homeland of the Jewish people, or in their yearning to be redeemed there. Even secular Zionism, which had cut its ties with religion and with Jewish tradition, saw its relationship to the land of Israel as expressing the continuity of the historical consciousness that had held the people together for generations; and the choice of the name "Zion" bore witness to the fact that for them the land of Israel was not merely a territory but rather an ancient symbol that embodied the entire national culture.

The Hibbat Zion movement, in its early stages, took the same view. The land of Israel was the land that had been destined for the patriarchs, where the tribes that went out of Egypt had settled, where the prophets had uttered their messages and the sages had taught; and it was the land of which generations of Jews captive in the exile had dreamed. Moreover, even their reawakened desire to settle once more in their ancestral land did not, initially, seem all that revolutionary. There had been, as we know, numerous precedents for such a course of action. In fact, shortly before the Hibbat Zion made its initial appearance, there had been movements for settling in the land of Israel among the adherents of the two great conflicting Jewish factions in Eastern Europe, the hasidim and the followers of the Vilna Gaon.[1] Hibbat Zion, as it were, took its inspiration directly from these two sources and brought them together in itself.

Even so, the significance and the image of the land of Israel for the members of Hibbat Zion were quite different than they had been for the thinkers surveyed in the preceding chapters, including Rav Nachman of Bratslav and the other great hasidic leaders, and the Vilna Gaon and his followers. As we have said, it seemed to the founders of the new movement that Jewish tradition not only permitted this change, but even, if one understood its values in their authentic, original sense, required it. In fact, however, a large proportion of that segment of the community that had maintained its loyalty to Jewish faith and tradition clearly remained unresponsive to the Hibbat Zion initiative, and later turned against it with increasing ferocity. As an alternative traditionalist image of the land of Israel developed, the innovative quality of the image presented by the new movement became more and more obvious and accentuated, so that ultimately even religious Zionist thinkers came to view it as revolutionary, at least in comparison to the image put forward by the latter-day tradition.

What was new and different about Hibbat Zion becomes clearer in the context of an evaluation of its historical circumtances. Hibbat Zion arose in response to those trends that characterized the Jewish people as it entered modernity: the weakening of the religious communal framework, the growing economic pauperization of the masses of the Jewish people, their confrontation with the seductive power of the rich secular culture, the spread of secular learning, the Reform movement, and increasing tendencies toward heresy and assimilation. It was also responding to the new opportunities that had developed in the modern era for a national solution to the Jewish problem. The ideals of the Emancipation and the growth of the European nationalist movements gave rise to hopes that the enlightened peoples of the world would recognize the Jewish people's right to return to its own land and there live its own national life. Hibbat Zion thus sought to overcome the dangers inherent in the circumstances of modernity by exploiting to the full the opportunities it offered, and this meant that it internalized, if only in part, the modes of thought prevalent in the surrounding culture.

This trend did not yet constitute a break with traditional thought. On the contrary, the new ideas were to a large extent intended to forestall the danger of such a break occurring. Even so, the Hibbat Zion drive to settle in the land of Israel was not the same as that undertaken by the hasidim or by the followers of the Vilna Gaon. The new movement set out to possess and settle the land of their fathers, and this change in goal constituted, in and of itself, a new view of the land. For long generations the Jews had viewed their land through the prism of its holiness, to the point that even its function as a national homeland had been raised to the realm of the sacred by the influence of a supra-historical messianic vision. Hibbat Zion placed the emphasis once more upon the character of the land as a national home, and it restored the ancient, biblical image of the land of Israel by using ideological tools provided by modern, secular culture. It was this fact, which was not overlooked by the ideological leaders of the Orthodox movement that was then taking shape in opposition to the spreading influence of secular culture, that led to the controversy that accompanied Hibbat Zion in its early days. It also made the change in the image of the land of Israel and the way in which it was understood progressively firmer and better defined. Hibbat Zion's developing ideology had to dig deeply into traditional thought in order to bring a buried layer of meaning to the surface. It had to unearth the original meaning of the rabbinic texts from the thought of the medieval scholars, and the original significance of Scripture from the rabbinic texts. Even this, however, was not sufficient. The ancient concepts had to be interpreted in the context of a historico-cultural situation that had its own ideas of the image and meaning that a homeland should have in the life of a people.

2

The new ideology unfolded gradually, and we must differentiate among its several stages. The forerunners of Hibbat Zion (the most important of whom was Rabbi Zvi Hirsch Kalischer) developed their ideas in response to the Western Enlightenment; later on, its founders were affected by the growing ferment taking place in Eastern Europe; and the movement was organized against a background of antisemitic outbursts, which brought to its ranks, and to those of political Zionism, a group of non-religious intellectuals who had come very close to assimilating.[2] In this chapter, we shall limit our discussion to the image of the land that appears in the ideology of Hibbat Zion's religious stream. We must, however, bear in mind that the transformation it represented was formulated and reached its sharpest definition in relation to the development of the secular versions of Hibbat Zion and of Zionism, so that it was affected by the dual tension produced by the opposition of Orthodox ideology to Zionism, and that of secular Zionism to religion.

Hibbat Zion's forerunners acted in response to the changes in Jewish life in Germany and France toward the end of the first half of the nineteenth century. These included an enlightenment movement that had quickly led in the direction of assimilationism or Reform; the opportunity that now existed for achieving equal rights, at the cost of forfeiting the insularity of the Jewish community and undermining its distinctiveness; and the rise of the European nationalist movements, which could be seen as models for emulation, so that their successes were a source of encouragement and hope. The progress of European culture endangered the Jewish way of life, but it might at the same time provide a remedy for the very blow it had dealt. If the people of Israel were once more to settle in its land, it would resume its own national character and thereby buttress its religion. This was the great hope.

It was in this spirit that Rabbi Alkalai, in his time, had called upon the Jew to demonstrate patriotic loyalty to his own land.[3] Like the other peoples around them, the Jews, too, had to organize to regain their national independence in their own land, and there seemed a chance that the peoples of Europe, newly awakening to their own nationhood, would understand this desire and aid in its realization. Of course, Alkalai did not mean by this that the people of Israel was to set itself up as a secular nation; on the contrary, the national framework would enable it to develop its religious dimension to the full. Earthly nationalism would be no more than the foundation upon which redemption in the messianic sense would arise. A similar understanding is also characteristic of Kalischer's ideas.[4] Kalischer saw the dangers inherent in the movements of enlightenment, assimilationism, and Reform and sought a positive solution to them. Unlike most of the leaders of Orthodoxy in his time, the yearning of Jewish intellectuals to express themselves in a full spectrum of creative endeavor was not anathema to him. If the satisfaction of this desire in the diaspora meant assimilation, then it was incumbent upon them to return to that land where it would be possible to lead a full Jewish life. Thus, the most fitting response that Orthodoxy could make to the Reform movement would be a return to Zion—a return to the source. Like Alkalai, they buttressed their thesis with numerous citations from traditional texts. However, Orthodoxy's innovative elements were expressed in three proposals for practical action. First, the Jews had to go to the land of Israel, to settle there and work the land, and not just to learn Torah and pray at the holy sites, as had been the practice of the Jewish community in the holy land until then. Secondly, a pan-Jewish organizational framework had to be created to mobilize the people's economic resources to settle the land. Finally, the Temple service in Jerusalem must be restored immediately, "in our own time," insofar as the halakhah permitted this.

The novelty of the first two of these proposals is clear. They are founded upon a nationalistic principle—that of action by means of the people's collective, organized power to establish its comprehensive national framework. However, it is the third proposal, that which on the face of it appears contrary to the liberal spirit of progress characteristic of modern times, and expressive, rather of an Orthodox—one might even say reactionary—approach, that embodies a daring attempt to break through the walls of Orthodoxy by employing its own concepts. The proposal transferred to the "here and now" that which Orthodoxy had sought to relegate to the suprahistorical, messianic future. Using extremely conservative language which, for opposite reasons, alienated both secularist liberals and the adherents of Orthodoxy, Rav Kalischer in fact expressed in his demand for the restoration of the Temple service that idea that was most characteristic of the spirit of the Emancipation: to be redeemed, the people of Israel had to take the initiative. No longer was it to await miracles; it must act on its own. Kalischer's proposals for settling the ancestral land and erecting an organizational and financial apparatus would both be acting on this same principle. But it is

רזשעז

this third idea that most daringly and consistently fulfills it, for the restoration of the Temple service "in our own time," if only within the limited framework of the halakhically possible, meant taking an independent initiative on the religious-messianic level. The supra-historical utopia, and even the ritual religious center around which it revolved, could now be entered from within history!

We must immediately limit the above remarks to their precise context. Kalischer had no intention of changing the symbolic image of the land of Israel that had been formulated by medieval philosophy. His conception was kabbalistic, and as the philosophical/rationalistic aspect of his thought serves only to lead into its mystical core, so the elements of national independence, settlement, and economic and political development in his plan for redemption do no more than lead into its principal, miraculous aspect. Like Alkalai, he, too, believed that the miraculous redemption had to be preceded by a reawakening "from below." The ground had to be prepared for the messianic event. In other words, as a clearly Orthodox thinker, Kalischer expressed even the innovative in what he had to say along Orthodox lines. He cited numerous authorities to prove that the greatest sages in every generation had thought as he did, and that the ideas that appeared so daring represented no more than the fulfillment of long-standing halakhic obligations. The novelty of his ideas lay only in his recognition that conditions now permitted of practical action. One might even say that the very development of these conditions must be interpreted as a concealed message from on high: the Holy One expected His people to do its part. Even so, a new dimension had been added to the image of the land, even if it was intended only as a temporary outer covering. The beginning of the redemption would come about by way of the rehabilitation of the land of Israel as a national homeland in the political sense.

3

Truth be told, the impulse for action released by Rav Kalischer's initiative was not particularly impressive, and its achievements on the practical level were negligible. Its ideological and propagandistic aspects appear to have been stronger and also more important than its organizational operations and the settlement activity it generated. In other words, simply stating that something must be done exhausted practically all of its active impetus. It is difficult to avoid the impression that this was not only a result of limitations in the realm of personal ability, but also an expression of the general situation of the Jews in Western Europe. Hibbat Zion, in the ideological form in which it made its appearance in the beginning of the second half of the nineteenth century, did not express the suffering that was directly affecting the people's daily lives, and it proposed no immediate solutions to their pressing social and economic problems. Rather, it expressed concern over

Lincoln Christian College

the assimilation that the practical solutions offered by the Enlightenment and the liberal religious movements involved. This may well be the context in which we must understand the great importance, which appears rather strange to us today, that Kalischer assigned to the speedy restoration of the Temple service. The effect of this symbolic ritual act—or, more precisely, of the fact that he dared contemplate such a thing and to press for it publicly— was to provide relief for a distress that was primarily spiritual in nature. Matters were different, however, in Eastern Europe. Here, the Hibbat Zion idea arose in response to the material distress of the Jewish masses and to their growing disappointment with the solutions offered by the Enlighten- ment movement.[5] This is not to say that the spiritual aspect—the yearning for a full Jewish life and fears of the secularizing influence of the Enlighten- ment—was of no consequence. However, because of the physical plight of the people, this was accompanied by a sense of practical urgency. Thus, the Eastern European movement was less interested in the demonstrative, sym- bolic proposal to restore the Temple service in Jerusalem. In fact, for the sake of placating the religious leadership, which was increasingly suspicious of excessive messianic pretensions, its adherents found it desirable to play down the religious audacity inherent in the Hibbat Zion idea while emphasiz- ing the practical needs.

It is characteristic of Hibbat Zion in Eastern Europe that it sought to base its halakhic legitimacy upon the immediate needs of the Jewish masses. The halakhah, its adherents claimed, could not be silent in the face of such needs; and if, moreover, it could be shown that solving the people's im- mediate material distress by having them settle in the land of Israel would also prevent their conversion, a risk inherent in the practical solutions possi- ble in the diaspora, there could be no better halakhic legitimation of Hibbat Zion's ideal. This did not, of course, imply that it had given up its messianic expectations, but these could be excluded from the immediate considera- tions that demanded action. In other words, there were vital, practical needs pressing for settlement of the land. If there were to be messianic results, that would be all to the good, but even if not, the ideals of Hibbat Zion would still be fully justified.[6]

In other words, the idea of Hibbat Zion in Eastern Europe was based on the growing recognition that the Jewish people had to change the way it earned its livelihood; that it had to become "productive." The old pipelines through which that livelihood had flowed had been stopped up, and it was now necessary to return to productive labor, to agriculture and to working with its hands; thus would it put an end to its distress. However, the only possibility for carrying out such a plan on a large scale, while at the same time preventing assimilation among the gentiles, existed in the land of the fathers.[7] The Eastern European approach thus represents dual differences in emphasis: the independent value of working the land as a national need in its own right; and the urgency with which it related to the act of settlement.

These differences were expressed both in real accomplishments—a beginning, however trifling its dimensions, was made in settling the land—and in the way the image of the land of Israel as a homeland, in physical, concrete terms, was formulated. The literature of the Eastern European Hibbat Zion movement bears out this statement. In contrast to Kalischer's writings, it was increasingly concerned with the problematics of the relationship between the image of the "holy land" and that of the "ancestral inheritance" in the concrete, physical sense. It felt a need to prove that these two images were not contradictory, that the "ancestral inheritance" that could serve as a foundation for the physical life of a people like any other did not obviate but rather complemented the image of the holy land which bore within it the tombs of the patriarchs and precious relics of bygone days. Moreover, there was no contradiction between the quest for a solution to the material plight of the people and its yearning for redemption in the religious sense. On the contrary, both could be pursued at once, and along the same lines.

The fact that this statement needed proof at all testifies to an internal difficulty. Viewing the land of Israel as a solution to material distress profoundly disturbed an image that had been formulated over generations, and involved an emotional and ideological transformation. The problem was reflected in a two-pronged skepticism which Hibbat Zion had to devote considerable energy to combatting: could this ruined, desolate, Godforsaken land, whose existing Jewish community was unable to sustain itself and was in constant need of support from the diaspora, really offer a solution to the physical plight of the exiled people? And was it permissible even to think of the holy land in utilitarian terms? The movement had, therefore, to reshape the image of the land to make the people see it as a place in which to live, in the simple sense; a place where an individual could earn a livelihood and where the people could live with social and political dignity, even as the ancient holiness still pervaded it.

"He likens redemption to livelihood and livelihood to redemption," wrote Rabbi Yonah Dov Blumberg in his *Pamphlet on the Commandment to Settle in the Land of Israel,* "and the latter is even greater than redemption, as is shown in the place cited. It is thus explicitly shown that these two extremes, which comprise the substance and the form of the people, are inseparably bound up with one another; and this is the pleasure of the Holy One, Blessed be He. But settlement of the people of Israel in its own land acts in fulfilment of both these aspects: livelihood—the substance of its life as a people; and holiness—its spiritual life, which is its inner form . . . How greatly our sages of blessed memory praised the land of Israel in relation to livelihood alone! Thus, since, as we have said, the ultimate value and mission of the people of Israel is to hold fast to both these ends—that is, to be both 'a people' and 'holy', many of their number have laid hold of this exalted idea, and it is as though the one had found its mate. It is for the sake and commemoration of this idea, exalted in its holiness, the yearning of the soul, that these who delight in Zion strive; they are of the third type that we mentioned, those who walk the middle way, choosing the golden mean between fire and water. It is for this worthy (with respect to substance) and holy (with respect to form) ideal that they stand, for this is the shape of the true divine plan, which shall stand for ever and never cease, as we have explained. Therefore, the finest of these delighters in Zion have raised this standard, and God's banner over them is love, and they stand beneath this flag, which stands as an eternal standard among our people, and on it is inscribed, in golden letters and appropriately, 'Banner of the holy people', substance and form, the spiritual and the material . . ."[8]

This passage is vigorously polemical. It is, of course, opposed to viewing the land of Israel as a source of material sustenance alone, but it is no less opposed to seeing it only as a holy land, and its argument appears to be directed primarily against the latter view, which was characteristic of the religious camp. It opposes the religious objection with its claim that the material life of the people has value in and of itself, that the national mission of the Jews is to unify the material life with the spiritual and that the need of the hour is to perfect the material dimension, which is symbolized by return to the land precisely in the physical sense.

4

In the interest of clarity, we might say that Hibbat Zion sought to replace the legendary status of the biblical description that the land of Israel had assumed in the exile with its original literal sense. It must be recalled, however, that the "legend" that had been formulated over so many generations expressed the "literal" experience of the land that was to be had in exile. It was not the ideological screen alone that concealed the biblical land of Israel, for this screen represented the land's actual, geographical remoteness and the people's experience of life in exile in foreign parts. A theoretical, conceptual transformation in its image was therefore not enough. It was necessary to make the people conscious of the land as it really was, and as it might become. For this purpose, aids for teaching the facts and demonstrating them visually were required.

In discussing the image of the land of Israel in the Hibbat Zion literature we must therefore devote particular attention to two literary areas which went beyond theoretical exposition: *belles-lettres;* and that characterized by a descriptive, scientific approach. Lyric poetry and fiction gave form to the romantic image of the ancestral land. They revived in the people's collective "memory" a past in which it had sat beneath its own vine and fig tree; and the future for which it hoped was depicted in the image of this idealized past. We might mention, as an example, the stories of Abraham Mapu, and especially his book *Ahavat Zion,* whose influence upon the Hibbat Zion awakening was considerable.[9] The descriptive and scientific literature, whose pages contained drawings and pictures of the scenery, brought the land as it was, its character and its possibilities, closer to the people's consciousness.[10] It was in this way, then, that the new image of the land of Israel, pervaded both by romantic yearnings and by realistic facts, took shape.

The ideological literature that accompanied these experiential and scientific descriptions set out to gain acceptance for the new image and to stir the people into drawing practical conclusions. It included, first of all, anthologies of source material, drawn in particular from aggadic and halakhic rabbinic texts dealing with the vitality of the bond between the people of Israel and its land,[11] the presence of the land, as a memory, in the daily life of the exile,[12] and the commandment to go to the land of Israel, to dwell upon its soil and make its desolate wastes bear fruit once more.[13] Seemingly, there was nothing novel about such anthologies of ancient texts; their like had always been current, at least in scholarly circles. Even so, these collections and their methodical arrangement were of a nature hitherto unknown, for they were intended to create a clearly defined layer of consciousness, firm and demanding of action, associated with the land of Israel. The collection juxtaposed the sources to one another and allowed their collective import to work its effect, raising what had been merely known, or known only in the company of many and various other matters of Torah, to a level of direct significance and primacy that demanded response. One might say that as the stories, poems, and factual descriptions "recalled" the presence of the concrete, actual land of Israel to the people's consciousness, so these anthologies of sources reminded them of that relationship to the real land of Israel which, according to the Torah, imposed obligations upon them and revealed anew that they were truly required to respond to these obligations.

However, this mode of self-persuasion, as we have said, also played a polemic role vis-a-vis the Orthodox opposition, which became especially powerful when the Zionist movement began drawing its support from a primarily non-religious Jewish public. What Orthodoxy did now, in fact, was to consolidate the exilic image of the land of Israel. It, too, unwittingly contributed an element of its own to the old image, but this element was dogmatic in character, constricting and sealing out the new. Orthodoxy certainly could not disregard the religious bond between Zion and the people of Israel. Precisely because the land was so close to its heart, it set out to battle on its behalf against both the religious and the secular branches of Hibbat Zion at once, over the image of Zion and the preservation of its sanctity. Orthodoxy's land of Israel was, emphatically, the land of the past, but this same dogmatic emphasis also distinguished its view from that of the past. The latter, one might say, had no need of the land of Israel in the material sense, as a national homeland. However, what had slipped inadvertently into the traditional image that the land of Israel had had in the Exile had now, in the Orthodox image, become intentional, for it arose in response to the nationalistic conception and was meant in rebuttal of this new understanding. The true land of Israel was that of the messianic future, which could not come about by means of any historical initiative. It was this image of the land of Israel as the holy land and nothing more that Hibbat Zion and the religious Zionist movement thus set out to combat. They had to prove that their romantic depictions of the historical past, and their realistic depictions of the historical present, were not in conflict with the sources. Since it involved them in controversy with thinkers who saw themselves as representing the authentic tradition, this effort to reconstruct the ancient portrait of the land took on a revolutionary aspect, at least from the perspective of the contemporary religious consciousness of a large segment of the people.

"This movement of revival," writes Rabbi Itzhak Nissenboim, one of the leaders of religious Zionism in Poland, "involves, in many respects, a fundamental 'revolution.' It draws out by the roots the world view implanted in our people by its long life in exile, and revives the ancient world view that it had when it dwelt independently in its own land, which is the view expressed in the Torah. This revolutionary revival is most clearly striking where the land of Israel is concerned, and we cannot yet predict all of the massive consequences that this may have for the order of our lives and the inner values upon which they are based." There follows a brief historical survey of the process that had led up to the formation of the exilic image of the land: "The people completely forgot its physical land as it had been, sustaining those that tilled it, and grew accustomed to seeing it as a spiritual land existing on the earth below . . ." The author concludes with the following words: "No, a total revolution had to come about in this relationship to the land of the fathers, recreating it almost anew, as the prophet Isaiah foresaw when he declared, 'For, behold, I create Jerusalem a rejoicing, and her people a joy' (Isaiah 65:18). Jerusalem shall no more be a city of weeping and of tombs; and its people, dwelling therein, shall no more be a people shrouded in mourning and lament, waiting for death . . . For they shall rejoice in their life and delight in their land. This new creation is being realized in our days by the movement of national revival which has made the land of Israel its uppermost priority. It is creating new values there, erecting settlements, garden cities and schools, and transforming the people into farmers, vinegrowers, agricultural laborers, speakers of Hebrew and men of towering physical strength, and in so doing it is restoring the original character of the land, to one 'flowing with milk and honey.' This is the value assigned it by the Torah."[14]

It is typical of the ideology of Hibbat Zion that it sought to locate this revolution within the traditional continuity. It may have been radical in relation to the concepts current among the contemporary religious community; in light of the entire historical continuum, however, it was a revival. Nonetheless, careful examination of the stylistic structure of this ideology and the interwoven concepts upon which it was based, including the idea of "revolution", will show that this revival of the past was conceptualized in terms of a different present, a new, nationalist-secularist present, which religious and Zionist thought sought to encompass. It represented, indeed, the closing of an ideological circle at the point of its ancient beginning, but at the very same time it opened up a new ideological path.

3

Why the Land of Israel?

Among religious Zionists, the question most central to the controversy over the significance of the land of Israel was: is it God's command that we return to the land of Israel, to settle there on our own independent national initiative, or are we trespassing a divine prohibition in doing so? For the secular Zionists, on the other hand, the validity of such independent initiative was not open to question; it was axiomatic. No longer would they await emancipation in the form of a grant by others of freedom and equality; they demanded "auto-emancipation." It may be said, too, that as this rebellious motif of independent initiative grew in intensity it strengthened the secular approach, which demanded that man exploit all of his abilities in his search for happiness. It was this apparently secularist tendency that made even religious Zionism suspect in the view of the ultra orthodox. A movement that defined itself as secular thus had no need to argue over the acceptability of independent initiative, and the land of Israel's potential to fit the role of a homeland in the modern, nationalistic sense appeared to it to be self-evident. Even secular Zionism, however, became embroiled in a debate which, though framed in pragmatic terms, was essentially concerned with the image and meaning of the land. Why, it asked itself, must it necessarily choose the land of Israel?

This question could not, of course, have arisen with the first stirrings of the Zionist idea. The continuity of the relationship between the people of Israel and its land should be clear from our discussion in the preceding chapters. It was thus natural that the first glimmerings of the idea of a national revival for the people in its land should point to the land of Israel, and this was true of secular Zionism as well. True, it was religious thought and the traditional way of life that had sustained the people's relationship to the land of Israel, but this was part and parcel of the national history, and breaking with religion, even rebelling against it, did not annul the deeply-rooted ties that bound the nationalist movement to that history. This is an important matter which requires clarification and emphasis, and without which our understanding of the discussion that follows would be hampered.

Every national movement aspiring to affirm its people's consciousness of unity in a political framework attaches itself to a particular land, the homeland. The fact that its people dwells in that land and makes up the majority of its population is its primary justification. The national movement sets out to do no more than realize a historical fact: This people, dwelling in this land, is deserving of political independence therein. To be sure, the fate of the people of Israel has been at variance with that of other national groups; it dwells in exile, amidst foreign peoples. However, this difference is not absolute, and it does not noticeably distinguish the point of departure of Israel's national awakening from that of other peoples. On the contrary, having arisen in response to the reorganization of the nations of Europe and developed concurrently with other nationalist movements, Zionism did no more than demand for the people of Israel that which every such movement asked for its people. It called, first, for affirmation of the fact that the people of Israel was a nation. As such, it was deserving of political independence. Where? In its own land, of course—that is to say, in that land that it had always seen as its own, and which, one might add, the peoples amongst whom it had been dispersed also recognized as such. This ideological relationship is essential to any national movement, and it was necessary to Zionism in just the same way. Just as it would not occur to anyone that the French people should demand national independence in any land but that called France, so it should not occur to anyone for the people of Israel to seek its national independence in any land but that called Israel. If there were no land that bore this name, Zionism would be an impossibility. Nor should this matter of appellation be taken lightly. As a new movement gets underway, its name performs a crucial function. It must symbolize the national consciousness, which lies at the very foundation of the movement. Had it not taken the name of "Zionism", even a territorialist Jewish national movement could not have emerged.

This, then, makes sense of our previous statement that breaking with religion, and even rebelling against it, could not annul the essential relationship between the Jewish nationalist movement and the people's past. On the contrary, it was precisely its abandonment of religion, which meant loosing the principal bond that had held the people together through the years of exile, that strengthened its need to hold fast to the national history. It had, therefore, to reinterpret its link with the past in a way that was relevant to the present but that also, above all, preserved that link. What matter, then, that for generations the people of Israel had seen its land as the holy land? It now wanted that land as its national home. This land and no other, for only this land could the Jew think of as his own, and only in relation to it could he conceive of his people as a nation. The ideologies that we shall survey are no more than later attempts to rationalize what had appeared so natural and simple as to need no argument when the Zionist idea first took shape. Moreover, this may well explain the peculiar vagueness that characterizes most of these ideological debates, for the contenders refuse to admit their permissibility in the first place. A people's link with its land should be considered a given, an incontrovertible fact. Any need of explanation, or proof, was tantamount to conceding that the link was suspect. Thus, an attempt at rationalizing must appear to contradict itself. If the relationship is not a fact, there is nothing to explain!

This brings us to the crux of the matter. The Englishman, the Frenchman, or the Italian need not explain why their nationalisms binds them to their particular lands. This tie is a fact which needs no explanation. Now we would, indeed, miss the truth if, on the basis of a crude distinction between Israel and the other nations, we were to deny the reality of the Jewish people's relationship with its land. That relationship too, is a fact. From the perspective of modern nationalism, however, this did not appear well enough established, for their bond lacked that demographic, economic, and political character that brings with it a clear political right. There was no doubt that the people of Israel had been sustained by its consciousness of its relationship to the land of Israel, nor that the nations among whom it dwelt, who had also at various times ruled the land, recognized this relationship. However, throughout the period of the exile the land of Israel had not served as the people's home in those respects relevant to the definition of secular nationalism.

At this stage, the problem did not involve legal rights to the land. Long before this became an issue the question being asked was whether the Jews' modern national need, because of which Zionism was demanding a national homeland, directed them exclusively toward the land of Israel. No other peoples asks such a question; they dwell in their lands, nothing more need be said. Nor would the people of Israel have raised the question, if the return to its land had been a simple matter. But when serious obstacles began to appear, making the possibility of mass settlement there appear doubtful, and at the same time other, tempting "unoccupied" territories were being proposed, coming to grips with the problem of the gap between the image that had bound the people to the land of Israel in the past—the holy land—and that of a future independent, secular, national homeland—seemed unavoidable.

The image binding the people to its past was vital, but not in terms of its religious content, which was no longer relevant. One might well, therefore, inquire whether the land of the past, with all that it had meant, must necessarily also be the land of the future, which would signify something quite new. As it was phrased, the question was one of practicality. Any unoccupied territory could offer the Jews what the land of Israel, simply as a piece of land, had to offer them. If it was territory that Zionism wanted—why did it have to be the land of Israel? The fundamental significance of this "practical" enquiry, however, is easily discernible. Can a national movement separate its future from its past? Will it not wreck its very foundation if it seeks to realize itself by breaking with its history? Thus, the two images of the land of Israel to which Zionism, as a modern nationalist movement had given rise, appeared antithetical rather than complementary. The image of the people's home, associated with the unity of the national past, stood opposed to the territorial image associated with political independence, representing the perspective of the future. We must emphasize that although it was expressed in a struggle between two opposing factions, the "Zionists for Zion" on the one hand and the "territorialists" on the other, the conflict involved the very core of secular Zionism, setting its essential relationship [as a nationalist movement] to its religious past against its equally essential relationship, in its secular dimension, to the modern concept of a homeland. It was this that fueled the flaming passions that characterized the controversy for as long as it remained a live issue. The territorialists accepted the severance of these two images for the sake of saving the people, while the "Zionists for Zion" fought for the unity of past and future and the interpenetration of the old and new images, sensing that the only possibility for the continued survival of the people of Israel, not only in the limited present but into the historical future, lay in upholding this unity.

2

Most of the essays that sought to justify remaining loyal to the land of Israel for "rational" reasons make disappointing reading today. The pathos in them seems to silence all considerations of common sense. They do, indeed, present an array of evidence purporting to prove that with respect to its geography, climate, economic and political conditions and so on, the land of Israel was more perfectly suited to fulfilling the aspirations of Jewish nationalism than any other country in the world.[1] But these homilies have a peculiar ring to them, and it is difficult to understand how the authors themselves were convinced, even as they wrote them. Can one really demonstrate unequivocally that any one land is particularly "suited" to the requirements or characteristics of a people? One gets the impression, moreover, that these were no more than rationalizations, coming after the fact, for some other consideration which had to be defended against rational argument because it was essentially irrational. This other consideration was, indeed, revealed in these pathetic discourses. The "Zionists for Zion" spoke, first, with zealous ferocity in the name of a mighty passion, against any other proposal. They spoke of their love for the land of Israel, making it tantamount to betrayal to seek out any other land. It had been no "practical" consideration that had led them in the direction of Zion to begin with, and the "Zionists for Zion" thus felt that to draw upon such considerations now was already to take the first step toward betraying their passion. One had to be devoted to the land for its own sake; this was the nature of true love. How could one explain love "rationally"? There was only one explanation possible: love is identified with national existence; if some other motive were to be taken to underlie the national enterprise, the basis for the nation's existence would disintegrate, leaving nothing but a miserable agglomeration of materialistic interests.

A particularly instructive expression of this feeling is to be found in Ahad Ha'Am's essay, "The Weepers,"[2] which was written in response to the outcome of a debate that took place at the sixth Zionist Congress. Ahad Ha'Am deliberately refrained from arguing against the rationalist arguments of the territorialists. With demonstrative composure (in itself almost pathetic), he spoke of the exclusive bond between the people of Israel and Zion as an established fact whose validity could never be upset by any resolution: "We look unto Zion, and only unto Zion, not as a matter of free choice, but out of natural necessity. For we believe with perfect faith that only there, by force of the historic passion that binds the people to its land, shall our spirit be strengthened and purified, and all of our inner powers be stirred into life. Only thus shall we be able to overcome the tremendous obstacles that stand in the way of a national undertaking of this nature, one which sets out to affect a fundamental transformation in the way of life and the psychology of a people uprooted thousands of years ago from its soil, and accustomed for generations to humbling itself before strangers and enslaving its spirit to them . . . The truth of this statement cannot be demonstrated mathematically, but it is our faith, and though it is borne out by the history of our people and the character of its spirit, its principal foundation lies in our inner consciousness, and it is this faith that we call 'Zionism' . . ."[3]

It is thus faith, in the sense of passion, with which we are concerned, an inner consciousness that identifies with the essence of that movement which is called Zionism. We shall return to this essay of Ahad Ha'Am's and to the nature of the passion that imbues it. Our concern at present it to highlight the "strategy" that reveals his basic attitude. From the perspective of the "Zionists for Zion," there was no need to enter into arguments over practical considerations. Such considerations were irrelevant from the start, because the matter under discussion was different in kind. The only way to win this argument was by not arguing—that is, to rest one's case, with utter composure, upon the indisputable fact. The fact itself would prove decisive.

In one sense, if it were polemics that concerned us, Ahad Ha'Am's approach would exhaust all that there was to be said on the subject. However, it is worth a more penetrating look. Passion is indeed a matter of fact, but it is set in an external and internal context, and it has its particular significance. Ahad Ha'Am speaks in this essay of a "historic passion," of the "historical basis" of Zionism and of the vital part this must play in the realization. What did he intend by this? What is the nature of the passion which imbues his essay? Where does it come from? How great is its intensity, and what is its significance? If we wish to answer these questions, we must return to the first stirrings of the movement. Ahad Ha'Am himself refers in the same essay to earlier stages in the controversy over alternative solutions to the national problem, other than the land of Israel. It seemed to him that the attitude of those who remained loyal to Zion had been firmer then, more dignified and more soundly based upon fact. In other words, we may see in Ahad Ha'Am's essay a reflexive affimation of a response which he considered, at the outset, to have been instinctive and natural, and so healthier and better established than that which obtained later. This, incidentally, is typical of Ahad Ha'Am's approach. He bases his nationalism upon a biological "will to live", to which the natural reaction is as to a fact.[4] A healthy person does not ask why he should continue to exist. His will to live is, to him, a given. When he does raise such a question, then, it shows him to be dangerously ill. The same is true of the existence of a people, and of its relationship to its land. The very fact that a homeland other than that in which it came into being as a people should even enter its mind attests to a degeneration of the healthy national organism. Ahad Ha'Am, of course, could not but contend with this disease, which was increasingly infecting the people's life in exile. It, too, had factual validity. The people, at all events, would not recover unless it could be shown an example of perfect health, and that example was to be found in the early stages of the movement.[5]

Let us return, then to a response voiced in one of these earlier stages, in which we can identify a primal, instinctive awakening:

A voice has been heard abroad, proclaiming that the borders of the West are open to us; but it is not this that our souls desire. Not from the West shall our eternal salvation come, nor shall our glory be raised up from across the sea. We are strangers here, and we shall be strangers there as well. We must choose another path, a path that has led us twice to a peaceful existence and to our inheritance, and surely this third time, too, will not deceive our hopes. This way leads to Zion! to Zion! to Zion! To the land of our fathers, the land of Israel . . . Too long have we wandered in strange lands, ever subjected to insult and abuse. Too long have we been trampled by human tyrants and inclined our ears to their judgements; are we human beings, as they are, or mere leeches sucking the juices of the earth? Enough, Enough! The end of our bitter exile shall come, and, after thousands of years of wandering, we shall find peace for our weary souls in the land of our fathers. There we shall dwell, in the dignity of quiet tranquility, upon our own soil, sustained by the work of our hands, and we shall know no evil; there we shall no longer be strangers; there we shall labor with vigor, and little by little Israel shall rise to its feet. It will regain its strength after its awful defeat, and once more become a great and free people, as in former times; only there shall we look upon other peoples as equals. Those writers speak falsely who declare that we, the members of this people, have no more to do with the land of our fathers, that it is strange and foreign to us—for this land is very, very close to our hearts, so that together with the exiles of Babylon we proclaim, 'If I forget thee, O Jerusalem, let my right hand forget its cunning.' We shall spill our blood; we shall sacrifice our very marrow for the sake of the land of our fathers. Many of our number are willing to work its soil by the sweat of their brows; and we shall set our minds to learning its character, so that we may be able to bring forth the fruit of blessing from it, and see it blooming with all the spendor of its beauty . . . Pay no heed to those false prophets who advise you to seek rest for your weary soul once more in foreign lands. They are pagan healers, and all their counsels are as nothing. You have only one way, and only by taking it will you find eternal salvation, and your honor shine forth once more. That way is to Zion! to Zion! to Zion! To the land of our fathers, the land of Israel! . . .[6]

The fact is obvious. The passage consists of a succession of passionate declarative statements, which set out to do no more than recall, arouse, and affirm the people's relationship to the land; one might say that most of its "explanations" for the exclusivity and irreplaceability of the land of Israel are tautological. It can be only the land of Israel because it is Zion, because it is the land of our fathers, because it is—the land of Israel. What little can be added to this passionate tautology is that in other lands we will remain strangers among peoples that do not want us; that in other lands we will be dependent upon the opinions of others, and, on the positive side, that in the land of Israel we will be at home, living upon soil that is our own. This last statement, indeed, contains the essence of the idea which recurs repeatedly in many impassioned variations. The land of Israel is understood from the outset to be ours. This also explains why the fact that it is the land of our fathers, Zion, the land of Israel is given such emphasis. It bears the name of the people, symbolizes its identity and thus belongs to it—not politically, economically or legally, but in a more primal, basic sense. It belongs to the people in the same way the people belongs to itself, mediated by the name that embodies the people's consciousness of itself.

If one cared to go into practical considerations, one could demonstrate that even in the land of Israel one might still be dependent upon the will and the opinions of strangers, and that if a truly unoccupied territory were to be found and a Jewish majority were to be created there, it would become a Jewish possession and provide a base for Jewish independence. But such considerations never even arise in this context because of the overwhelming force of this sense of belonging which is prior to political or economic possession, arising as it does out of the people's consciousness of its own national identity. The above passage is a powerful affirmation of this consciousness. At this early stage of the movement's awakening, the consciousness of identification rejects any other proposal for relieving the people's distress as posing a threat to its very essence.

Let there be no mistake. The young people voicing this impassioned call turn to the land of Israel in the name of the national past. It is Zion, the land of the patriarchs, the land to whose memory our fathers have sworn their loyalty since the time of the Babylonian exile. But this relationship to the past is thoroughly contemporary. Its source lies in the primary motivating force of the modern nationalist movement. Affirming their relationship to the past in and of itself affirms the validity of their national consciousness in the present. It justifies the national pride of a people which desires once more to become a people like other peoples, dwelling in its homeland and relating to it as any other people does to its land. From such a perspective no thought of any land other than the land of Israel could be entertained. But the image arising out of the heritage of the past was itself interpreted in the spirit of the modern national movement, bound to its land by the sweat that irrigated its furrows and the blood spilt in the war for its liberation.

Let us complete this picture with a no less passionate and instinctive passage expressive of a psychological response typical of the Zionists of western Europe:

We must yearn for and covet this land, our homeland, sevenfold, for if we do not conquer it—or at least consider conquering it—we shall never succeed in having others see us as a people equal to themselves, of the same human worth as they . . . The Jew whose home is the whole world, yet has no home in all the world, is never accorded that true honor, which none withhold from the foreigner, the gentile; he lacks an internationally recognized ordering of his relations with the peoples among whom he dwells, and he is reviled and hated because of his religion and origins . . . If we wish to gain the rights of native-born citizens among other peoples, we must acquire a homeland, a land truly ours, an ancestral inheritance that will be our possession forever. What people, what state, what country would desire to give someone the rights of a citizen, emancipation, legality, and equality, without knowing who he is and whence he comes? . . . Endeavor, first of all, to find yourself a country, a homeland in which every one of your people will enjoy unquestioned and unlimited civil rights by virtue of his religion and birth, and no enlightened country will then disqualify or limit your civil rights . . . The Jewish people must have a home, a land and state of its own. When? As quickly as possible. How? This demands careful and detailed study. Where? There is no question about this. In all of the globe, there is only one, special place where we can seek to build our homeland and our state: the ancient land of our fathers, our legal possession, which was taken from us by force, and from which we were exiled and dispersed over all the world. Any other place would be no more than a new land of exile. If we wish to regain our honor, in our own eyes and in those of others, we must strive with all our might to regain possession of our ancient homeland, to build up and establish the Hebrew state once more. There is no other remedy. Without this, others shall never consider us a people of equal worth, and we shall never succeed in casting off the accusation that we are mere landless flotsam and jetsam . . . In order to establish and justify this right of ours to ourselves and to others, we must take up the thread of our people's history once more, in the place where it was broken off, or, more precisely, where destiny broke it off by force. Yea, the holy land, truly and in reality, can once more be our own. For "the earth is the Lords and the fullness thereof." Of old He divided up the earth among all of the peoples under heaven, and bestowed upon each and every people its fixed, eternal place. "Italy for the Italians, and the land of Israel for the Jews." This is "the land which the Lord swore unto your fathers to give them, as the days of the heavens above the earth." But this land is ours not only by the law of God but also by the law of man, because the land which we took from the Amorites by our sword belongs to us by the right of conquest. This is the land in which our forefathers and mothers dwelt, acted and moved, where our prophets and visionaries lived and taught, and from where our sanctuaries spread the work of God and His teaching among all the peoples;

this is the land where the idea of the one God, the light unto the gentiles, made its first appearance, and where the Bible—the Book of Books for all peoples—was written, and the only place where it can properly be understood and lived by, in accordance with all of its details and nuances. We must set our sights only upon this land, if we wish to erect a secure and independent national home which all shall acknowledge and none shall deny . . .[7]

In some ways, this passage, by Dr. Yitzhak Rielf, is similar in outlook to the pamphlet cited earlier. However, Dr. Rielf, whose words reflect the prevailing disappointment of his contemporaries with the outcome of the prolonged struggle for emancipation that had taken place in Germany, was extremely sensitive to the problem of the legal status of the Jews in the lands of their exile. A homeland for the Jewish people would bring self-esteem to all of its members, and this would be the basis of their legal status. To be considered equals among equals, the Jews needed an address that defined their identity. Once they had such an address, they would no longer be thought of as "flotsam and jetsam", but as individual human beings. It was precisely for this reason that Dr. Rielf sought the land of Israel, for it was an honorable, legal status that he wanted, and this could be had, for the Jew, only in his own land. There were two reasons for this, and both are accentuated in the passage cited above: first, the Jewish people could claim a valid, legal right to this land alone, both by the word of God, as it appeared in Scripture (which the Christians respected as well!) and by the laws of man; and, secondly, it was in this land that the testimony to the universal contribution made by the Jewish people to world culture was preserved. The first of these assured the Jews recognized legal status; the second gave the legal claims added weight. The people of Israel were not simply full citizens of the society of the peoples of the world; they were among its more distinguished members.

Be this as it may, the problem that Zionism set out to solve, according to Dr. Rielf, was that of the status of the Jews, and its recognition by those around him. The land of Israel alone symbolized and distinguished Jewish nationalism. Again, the reliance in this passage on support from the religious heritage that sustains the national relationship of the people of Israel to its land is instructive. Dr. Rielf's enthusiastic phrases do, indeed, testify to his deep faith in the promise that had been made to the patriarchs, and, particularly, in the election of the people of Israel. His emphasis, however, is not on the religious content of these elements in itself, but on the implications they hold for the national status, precisely from the point of view of secular nationalism—that is, the exalted religious content of Judaism provides him with a significant claim to be used in the debate over the national legal status of Israel among the peoples.

Let us now return to the restrained, measured writing of Ahad Ha'Am. What did he mean by emphasizing the "historical foundation" that existed in the land of Israel alone? What did he mean when he said that only in the land of Israel would the "moral strength" be found to realize the national revival? He certainly was not speaking of anything connected with the physical character of the land. He was referring, rather, to a profusion of national memories: historical events, stories, customs, ways of life, symbols, matters of philosophy, prayer, and poetry that were all bound up with the land of Israel. To think of any other land would be to deny all of these—and it was they that comprised the very essence of the national character in its inner, spiritual aspect. The land of Israel symbolized the uniqueness of the people's consciousness of itself and of the experiential elements it shared. One could, of course, dwell outside of the land without rejecting these elements. But to aspire to go to any other land, to devote oneself to any other land as a national home—was to sever oneself from the source that sustained the national way of being, precisely in a situation that demanded complete dedication to the national goal. Would this not be completely absurd? It is thus, then, that we must interpret Ahad Ha'Am's concepts of "historical foundation," "historic ideal," and "moral strength." Nationalism drew its strength from the will to live that sustains the people's elementary sense of right, which is the motivating force behind the national movement. A movement that refused to recognize its historic identity, however, is working against its own will to live. Its attempt at revival is more a way of committing suicide and must necessarily fail. If Zionism devoted itself to the land of Israel, however, it would affirm the continuity of the people's historic consciousness, and draw from this affirmation the vitality it needed to realize its undertaking.

If we compare Ahad Ha'Am's ideas with those of the "Bnei HaNe'urim" cited above, or with Dr. Rilf's, we will discover a number of differences in emphasis. The "Bnei HaNe'urim" were more sensitive to the foreignness that the people felt outside of the land of Israel; Dr. Rilf to the problem of their legal status. Ahad Ha'Am, by contrast, placed a greater accent upon the people's inner evaluation of itself in relation to its history. However, all three share an essential common core. Reflecting on the primary, instinctive response of the national movement as it first stirred into life, Ahad Ha'Am highlighted the critical value of the dimension of historical self-consciousness to an exiled people that sought to make a dramatic turn on its historical path. The strength to make this turn, to break with the past, would be derived from reaffirming, though in a different way, its consciousness of this historical continuity. The land of Israel alone could, symbolically, embody both continuity and change.

3

Up to now, we have discussed reactions which were never developed methodically. Ahad Ha'Am's ideas were, indeed, grounded in his overall apprehension of the nature of nationality in general and that of the people of Israel in particular. However, he deliberately—one might almost say methodically—refrained from giving these ideas methodical development. He was well aware that the force of his argument lay in his self-assured invocation of a solid fact. In the heat of the controversy that surrounded the Uganda proposal, however, such a position could not be maintained for long, especially in debate among thinkers for whom, unlike Ahad Ha'Am, the idea of the land of Israel solely as a spiritual center would not suffice. For one whose plan called for Zionism to create a spiritual center for a people that would continue, for the most part, to dwell in exile, it was obviously impossible even to consider any "territory" other than the land of Israel. How could a "territory" that did not symbolize the historic experience of the people serve as its "spiritual center"? This was not true, however, for those who held that the task of Zionism was to provide a homeland for the entire people.

Those who saw Zionism primarily as a way of relieving the demographic, economic, social, and political distress of the Jews, who looked to Zionism for a comprehensive solution to their difficulties—that is to say, those who really aspired to gain a national territory where the people of Israel would be established within an all-embracing national framework like any other people—could not do without the rationalistic arguments of the territorialists. This was not only because the same rationalistic argument was fundamental to their own nationalist-Zionist ideology, but also because the pathos of their devotion to the land of Israel was challenged by another concern: their sense of responsibility for the people of Israel, which was in urgent need of refuge.[8] Was their love for the land of Israel greater than their love for the people? And what if it turned out that the land of Israel was beyond their grasp—was the people to be forsaken and any other proposal rejected out of hand? Under the pressure of these questions, which set the urgent needs of the present against the demands made by history, there was no avoiding a thoroughgoing, detailed examination of the considerations involved and the determination of standards by which these considerations could be evaluated and weighed one against the other.

We shall begin with the writings of Moshe Leib Lilienblum, which develop, in particular, the motif to which Dr. Rielf had assigned priority. His ideas are founded upon two basic assumptions: the first concerns his definition of the essence of the Jewish problem, the second his definition of the nature of nationalism and of the relationship obtaining between a people and its land. Lilienblum saw the Jewish problem basically as one of status. The people of Israel was a hated, persecuted minority because it was foreign to all the lands in which it dwelt and could not muster enough strength to stand up for its rights. This foreignness and weakness were manifested in its lack of status. Because the Jewish people did not have the status of a nation among all the rest, its members—as individuals—were inevitably bereft of civil rights. As long as this situation persisted, there would be no respite from hatred, and persecution would continue. The Jew would be seen as a competitor, and every effort would be made to get rid of him. A radical solution to this problem, then, must consist in creating conditions that would make the national status of the Jewish people like that of any other people, thereby ensuring the civic status of its individual members.

What, then, were the conditions necessary for the establishment of national status? The answer to this question derived from the experience and ideology of the European national movements. National status was based upon a population that comprised a majority of those dwelling upon a particular tract of land, from which it drew its livelihood. It derived from the power wielded by an ethnic majority in a sovereign political framework. This, then, was what the Jewish people required. It had to become a majority in a particular tract of land from which it would draw its livelihood. It must establish its power within a political framework. Lilienblum absorbed this understanding, by his own testimony, from modern European nationalist ideology. What most concerns us and is of great importance, however, is that he saw in the concept of modern nationalism itself the historic victory of an idea whose origin lay in the cultural heritage of ancient Israel—that is, in the Bible. The culture of ancient Israel was outstandingly nationalistic. It was founded upon the principle that each and every people was to live in its own homeland and develop its own distinctive culture. Medieval Europe, inspired by Christianity, had sought to establish an opposing, cosmopolitan order but failed in the attempt, and the national movements of the modern era were reaffirming the nationalist cultural ideal of the Bible. This was an impressive historical victory, and Lilienblum took pride in it. Paradoxically, however, the victory of this Jewish outlook had damaged the status of the Jewish people in the lands of its exile. The fact that the Jewish people lacked the conditions necessary for establishing its national status was now more obvious than ever. In an era of nationalism, the people of Israel became weaker, and its image, in national terms, was distorted.

These ideas had direct implications for the question of the people's relationship to the land of Israel. Let us note, first, an obvious consequence of the previous analysis: the modern secular, nationalist idea was perfectly acceptable from an internal Jewish perspective. By going back to Scripture, we return to the national secular foundation. This proposition was greatly cherished by secular Zionism, for it affirmed the historical continuity that emerged from the rebellion against the nature of Jewish life in exile. But did it necessarily mean that only the land of Israel could serve as the national homeland of the Jewish people? Did returning to the biblical conception, in its modern-day interpretation, also demand a return to the land of the Bible? Lilienblum's reply was affirmative, and his reasoning derived primarily from the first of his guiding assumptions. The problem of the Jewish people was basically one of national status, and the solution to it had thus to affirm their status as it unfolded. A territory certainly was required, but the search for one could not be conducted without regard for this problem of status. The people of Israel could demand as its national territory only that tract of land which it—and the surrounding peoples—could verify as its own. That is to say, Lilienblum saw the question of a people's national right to its land as being of critical importance not only from a pragmatic perspective. It was crucial, first, in terms of the way the people saw itself. If Zionism was to be a legitimate nationalist movement in its own eyes and to others, it must look to that land to which it had a legitimate claim. Every national movement acts this way. It seeks to institutionalize an existing situation, and this is the source of its legitimacy. If the people of Israel want to be like any other, it must take the same path.

There is, of course, no necessary logical connection between the claim that national self-definition for the people of Israel would constitute a return to the biblical stratum of its culture and the argument that its national status could be established only by a return to that land to which the people of Israel had a legitimate national claim—that is, to the land of the Bible. In spiritual terms, however, these parallel arguments complemented and rein-forced one another. The people of Israel was returning to itself by returning to its own land so as to be a people like any other. In any event, the proposi-tion that the modern definition of the nationalist ideal was a victory for an original Jewish approach gave especial prominence to the fact that secular nationalist thought, while introducing a transformation in the people's rela-tionship to the land of Israel, was also maintaining historical continuity. In order to unite the traditional image with the modern concept, it returned that image to its source and reinterpreted it in the spirit of the new concept.

4

A far more detailed and methodical ideology—perhaps the most meticu-lous of the approaches surveyed in this chapter—is to be found in the writ-ings of the socialist-Zionist thinker, Ber Borochov.[10] His need to develop so rigorously defined an approach arose from the fact that his point of depar-ture, firmly rooted in the Marxist world-view, drew him in the direction that had led others to adopt the territorialist alternative, and so did not permit him to remain oblivious to the challenge they presented. At the outset, indeed, it seems puzzling that an ideologue with a materialist outlook, who felt that the national culture was simply a "superstructure" whose form was determined by its material foundations, should attach importance to those "sentiments" that bound the Jews to the land of Israel, the symbol of the past, rather than determining his goal on the basis of direct considerations of socio-economic and political utility. The careful reader will, in fact, find that he had great regard for such utilitarian considerations, so that he did not reject the territorialist idea out of hand, at least in principle; and although he decided in favor of the land of Israel, he mustered these very considerations to his aid in his argument against those put forward by the territorialists. He was forced, therefore, to examine all aspects of the territorialist controversy seriously and in depth, and we shall see that his realistic approach sheds the light of clear rationality on his emotional motives as well.

As already noted, Borochov was a Marxist. His approach, however, was not rigidly dogmatic. He was a realist, and well aware of the uniqueness of the situation of the Jewish people. His decision to take up the Zionist cause had its source in the clarity of his understanding of this uniqueness. According to the Marxist world view, every national or social movement has its roots in the unavoidable historical process, in economic relations. Zionism was no exception to this rule. The class struggle, which was fought out first of all between the landed aristocracy and the bourgeoisie and later between the latter and the proletariat, had swept away the economic base upon which the Jewish people had rested throughout the Middle Ages. Until now, the people had maintained itself by acting as an intermediary between the classes in gentile society, and so had fulfilled a necessary social function. This function, however, had disappeared. The staff of life that had supported the Jewish masses was broken. Alternative trades into which they might have entered were already taken up by members of other classes and were thus closed to the Jews, and their attempts to squeeze themselves in set them up as dangerous competitors. The Jews were thus crushed between the warring classes, hated and persecuted by both, and there was nowhere for them to escape. True, once the revolution had reached its successful conclusion and a new, classless social order had been established, the Jewish problem, too, would vanish. But could the people hold out until then? Borochov's reply, based upon an in-depth analysis of the contemporary situation, was extremely pessimistic. In the wake of the growing class struggle, the situation of the Jews was rapidly deteriorating. The discrimination, persecution and violence to which they were subject would only grow more intense in the near future, and he could not see how the Jews could survive them. Their only hope of safety lay in leaving the homes they had made in the midst of other peoples, organizing themselves as a nation in their own right, and passing through the social revolution at the same time as and together with the others. Zionism was thus to fulfill the vital function of rescuing the whole people, and its realization was a matter of the utmost urgency. Time had run out for the people of Israel. It stood on the brink of a holocaust.[11]

Here, however, is where the difficulty comes in. Other national and social movements reach their goals by means of the impetus of the historical process that had brought them into being. In other words, the masses were impelled to action by their distress, and it was this that dictated the activity that would lead to the creation of a new order. If they have proper leadership, it organizes and directs the spontaneous movement created by the masses and by means of it succeeds to power. The situation of an exiled people is entirely different in this respect. The solution to its problem lies in creating something that has no existing foundations in the present. The plight of the Jewish masses does not, therefore, inevitably direct them toward the solution they require. Here, a positive, planned enterprise, neither initiated by the masses nor achieved by the impetus of their desperation alone, is needed. It is not enough to create a new political order. A new way of life has to be formulated, and this has to be undertaken at the outset. The sense of what Borochov was saying was simple. Realizing the Zionist goal meant creating a Jewish majority in a place where one did not yet exist. It meant building up the economic and demographic foundations required by such a populace and working far-reaching transformations in the people's lifestyle and in its vocational training. This was a tremendous undertaking, and it would not come about spontaneously. Its realization required a pioneering elite that would voluntarily take upon itself the task of laying the groundwork for such a project. Only after this had been accomplished would it be possible for the masses to be motivated by the impetus of their plight.

Zionism was unique, therefore, in that it demanded a planned enterprise, and the motivating force it required was thus different from that which impelled an ordinary mass movement. The urgency of the people's distress would not be sufficient. Zionism needed the propulsive power of a goal, a vision. Where was this motivation to come from? Here, too, Borochov rested upon a negative factor for support. The pressure of antisemitism affected all strata of the Jewish people equally. The poorer elements would do no more than react to their worsening poverty and to the violence to which they were subject; they were clearly incapable of positive action. They sought only immediate refuge. However, there was a thin stratum of Jewish intelligensia that had succeeded in penetrating the barrier of hatred to achieve professional advancement and employment that ensured its material sustenance. This group, affected primarily by social and psychological pressure, responded differently. They felt unwanted. Their non-Jewish peers rejected them socially and slighted their dignity. The distress they suffered was spiritual and psychological, and this conditioned them to participate in some voluntary, visionary activity that would resecure their self-respect and restore their dignity in the estimation of others. Borochov, however, was aware that this negative motivation would not suffice to propel them to positive action. The thrust of their distress was not enough; love, too, was needed. In other words, a realistic analysis showed that the Zionism demanded by material factors could not be realized in the absence of a spiritual, idealistic motivating force. Without love for the people, its culture and its values, the Zionist enterprise would never come to life.

This was the background to Borochov's preference for the land of Israel. The land symbolized the positive force required by Zionism: love of the people, its past, its culture and its values. On a theoretical level, Borochov would certainly have accepted the materialist view that the love of a people for its land is the byproduct of material circumstances. Once such psychological and cultural traits had come into being, however, their importance in their own right was not to be disregarded. They were not, indeed, strong enough to overcome material processes, and this was the reason why the people's love for the land of Israel had not led it to return in the past. Even now, love alone would not draw the Jewish masses back to the land. They would flow to any place where conditions promised to ease their material plight. Precisely this, however, determined the issue in favor of the land of Israel. The negative factor of distress would not move the Jewish masses to go to some empty territory, there to erect a foundation for their own independent national life. On the contrary, it would lead them to places where others had already created the foundations for their own national lives. The result would again be exile, and this new exile would quickly develop the well-known characteristics of the old. In this situation the positive factor motivating the pioneering elite was of critical importance. Its force alone could move this vanguard to establish that base upon which the only really plausible solution to the plight of the Jewish people could rise. Borochov thus saw the love of the people for its land as a crucial factor in the realization of Zionism.

As we mentioned previously, this consideration alone was not sufficient to strike down all the arguments of the territorialists. What if it should finally turn out that the land of Israel was not attainable? Borochov warned against reaching such a conclusion too hastily. The land of Israel was so precious to him that he would agree to give it up only if he had absolutely no alternative. The situation, therefore, had to be studied carefully to see whether the perceived obstacles were really as grave as they seemed. Moreover, the problems raised by the territorialist proposals themselves were not to be dismissed lightly.

Realization of the Zionist enterprise, by its very nature, involved tremendous difficulties. But if, ultimately, it were to turn out that the land of Israel was closed to the Jews and, at the same time, there was a practical alternative to it—there would then be no escaping the harsh conclusion: ultimately, the people of Israel did take priority over the land. Because of this Borochov drew up a second line of defense on behalf of the choice of the land of Israel. He wished to prove that even by the materialistic standards of the territorialists the land of Israel was preferable. In this connection, he sought to demonstrate that every territory that might be proposed to the people of Israel lacked the geographical, climatic, demographic, economic, and political conditions necessary for the establishment of a Jewish state. On the other hand, all of these conditions were present in their optimal form in the land of Israel. The obstacles were not to be overlooked, but they were relatively slight and could be overcome. If the positive factor were added to this, the decision that was bound to be reached was clear and unambiguous. We shall not describe Borochov's arguments on this point in detail. It is clear upon reading them today that they were not based upon a careful examination of the actual material conditions of which he spoke. His love for the land of Israel dictated both his selection of facts and the way he interpreted them. In this he unwittingly furnished additional evidence for the truth of his principal argument: the love for the land, felt by the national elite and its leadership, was very, very powerful.

We must, again, conclude by pointing out the typical ambivalence of this approach. Love for the land of Israel was a concrete, relevant factor, but its source was a religious and cultural way of life from which Borochov himself was distant. For him, the people's relationship to the land of Israel was not commanded by God; it was a fact of national psychology, a natural product of each individual's feeling of belonging to his people. The new, modern image of the land as a national home was thus sustained, in Borochov's thought, by the image it had had in the past, an image whose sentimental importance outweighed its actual content.

5

Before concluding our discussion of this issue, we shall describe one further attempt at providing a theoretical, scientific explanation for the necessity of holding fast to the land of Israel, this time on sociological and positivistic rather than on Marxist grounds. We refer to the writings of A. M. Berakhyahu.[12]

In two of his basic assumptions, Berakhyahu is quite close to Ahad Ha'Am. First, in the circumstances obtaining in modern times, the Jewish people requires a national political framework of its own, primarily in order to save it from the danger of assimilation. However, there was no possibility, at least not in the near future, that this framework would embrace all of the Jewish people. The state that was to arise, in which a minority of the Jewish people would live, would have to function as a focus of national identification for the majority of the people, that would continue to live in the diaspora. Secondly, national identification, in particular that of the Jews, who were still without a comprehensive, unifying political framework, was based upon historical tradition. Non-religious Jews were, indeed, moving away from the tradition that had united the people. In comparison with the European environment that had rejected them, however, they were still relatively conscious of the historic tradition that continued to bind them together. In order for them not to become estranged from themselves, they, too, needed a focus for positive identification, and it would be incumbent upon the state that was to arise to fulfil this function. The principal problem here would be that of having all of the people identify with a state in which only a minority of its number would dwell. The land of Israel alone could answer to this requirement.

In this connection, Berakhyahu proposes a distinction between a "state of Jews" and a "Jewish state." A "state of Jews"—that is, a state whose population was overwhelmingly Jewish and whose government was in the hands of Jews—could be established in any place open to massive Jewish immigration. Such a state, however, could not symbolize the national unity of the people of Israel; it would not yet be a "Jewish state." If such a state of Jews were to be established in some unoccupied territory, and especially if most of its population were not religious and did not keep to the traditional Jewish way of life, to most of the people it would constitute no more than another diaspora, albeit one with a unique political framework. For it to be the state of all the Jews, it must embody traditional historical content by means of which the people could identify itself as a unique and separate nation. With secularism becoming ever more prevalent, only a state of Jews established in the land of Israel could fulfill such a role: "That which must lie at the very foundation of the state of Jews to make it a Jewish state, so that both we and others will understand that the Hebrew people is a political entity, is tradition in the comprehensive, historical sense. Only a state of Jews in the land of Israel, in that land whose name testifies to its great significance in the consciousness and tradition of the people, in which the Hebrew people became a political entity and which it considered its land throughout its years of exile—only this may be considered a Jewish state. All those who remain outside of their land will be considered, by both themselves and by others, as living on the national periphery, and their center, the center of the people, will be that portion of the nation that dwells in the land. The political standing of the latter in the land of Israel will be considered as extending to the entire people, because the land itself is viewed as belonging to all of the people, and so had they related to it even before a state of Jews was established there once again. Only if they infuse new life into the land of Israel can the lives of the Jews, of the Hebrew people, be renewed. Only this can strengthen the bond uniting all segments of the people, complete and fulfill the essential nature of the Hebrew nation, raise its self-esteem and its worth in the eyes of other men, make it a full member of the society of the peoples of the world and put an end to the problem of the Jews and of Judaism."[13]

6

The above citation from Berakhyahu's writings clarifies two assumptions that underlie all of the preceding discussion, and it seems worthwhile, in concluding this chapter, to expand upon them. First, Berakhyahu provides an explanation for the fact that the arguments in favor of the land of Israel carried more weight precisely from the viewpoint of secular Zionism. While it may seem paradoxical, a closer look will confirm this statement. It is well to recall that even the "Mizrahi" movement, which represented religious Zionism, was temporarily attracted to the idea of seeking a "refuge for the night" in Uganda, which shows that the religious approach was not necessarily immune to seeking substitutes, albeit temporary, for the land of Israel. On the contrary—from the Mizrahi point of view, Uganda also provided a "refuge" from the pressure of its bitter controversy with ultra-orthodoxy, which opposed Zionism, seeing in it a brazen, secular attempt to hasten the Messianic age by independent initiative. Going to Uganda would prove that Zionism was not messianic but a pragmatic, national movement; all it set out to do was to provide relief for the concrete distress of the Jewish masses, and this could surely be no sin. On the other hand, the religious Zionists could simultaneously represent going to Uganda as a practical measure that would not entail a betrayal of the land of Israel. The religious bond with the land would still retain all its validity and power, and the faithful would continue to believe in its realization, whenever the time for it should come.

This view was certainly shortsighted. However, it does testify to a certain flexibility which the secular Zionist did not have. The distinctions made by religious Zionism between a pragmatic solution and the difference between a political and practical tie to the land on the one hand, and redemption and the people's eternal spiritual bond with the land of Israel on the other, were not real for the secularist. The practical solution, demographic, economic and political, was all there was to redemption, and the only ties one could have with any particular land were those to be formed by living there, or by an ardent desire to live there in the near future, in the way of a people dwelling upon its own soil. The secular Zionist thus could not avoid making an ultimate decision on the matter, and the secular "Zionists for Zion" understood this well. They sensed the full burden of the responsibility that rested upon them in making this decision. Uganda, for them, spelled unqualified betrayal of the land of Israel, and this meant breaking the most tangible bond they had with the historic tradition that identified the people of Israel as a nation. This clearsighted recognition explains the fanatical devotion of the "Zionists for Zion" to the land, and it was this that eventually tipped the scales in the controversy. Of all the thinkers surveyed above, Berakhyahu was the only one to point out that remaining faithful to the land of Israel was of fateful import precisely from the perspective of secular Zionism. It must find a way of spanning the gap between the modern image of the homeland as a territorial base and the traditional image of the land, for if it did not it would split the Jewish people in half, instead of uniting it. Ahad Ha'Am, Lilienblum and Borochov also seem to have been aware of this, however, and hence the sense of destiny that imbues all of their writings.

A second underlying assumption leads Berakhyahu to give explicit prominence to the fact that his discussion of the uniqueness of the people's bond with the land of Israel is written from the perspective of the exile. That is to say, he is concerned with a remote image which has to motivate members of the Jewish community to go to the land or to identify with it. As we study this image, therefore, we must bear in mind that the adherent of a movement whose goal was settling the land would not be influenced directly by promises of a life of plenty or of political power. These would be important considerations for him, the stuff of his great hopes, but in terms of his imagination, which must activate his sentiments, they would be no more than ideological terms. This is not true, however, of the image that is to be gathered from the sources, with all of its realms of meaning. This had great power to rouse both the emotions and the mind, and to attract the heart of those who suffered the sorrow of their people. Let us put ourselves in the place of a young Jew, sick with sorrow over the persecution and oppression of his people and dreaming of its renewed rise to power in its own homeland. What could the names "Uganda", "Argentina," or "America" have to say to him in the context of his national sensibilities? The answer is very simple. They might carry overtones of financial success or of escape from physical violence, but in national terms they were no more than three strange new names on the map of the Jewish diaspora. As a Jew he had no way of relating to them, and in this national context, going to a land that bore one of these foreign names meant no more than leaving one place of exile for another. The word "Israel," on the other hand, bore with it a tremendous tide of memories, which grew richer in proportion to the Zionist's knowledge of the Jewish heritage, but was meaningful even to the assimilated Jew who knew no more than the name. It signified an inner relationship, a homeland, a home, a place where one could belong, redemption from exile. It was all of these that the youth preparing himself to go up to the land most ardently desired. How could he compare the land called Israel, whose image called up a tangible vision of home before his eyes, to any other land? The territorialists argued that the name's effect was no more than "psychological," and what they said was true. But a person's decision to go and live in the land of Israel does belong to the realm of psychology. From the perspective of exile, it is the Jew's psychological ambience, his inner life, that determines the path he will choose. And this, indeed, is what determined the outcome of the controversy: the realization that there must be no break between the secular image of the land as a demographic and political base and the traditional image of the holy land. If these did not come together and sustain each other in the course of realizing the national goal, the Zionist movement would never succeed in infusing new life into the Jewish people.

Clearly, however, a change in perspective would reopen the question, and then the previous answers would no longer suffice. The pioneer arriving in the land of Israel was confronted, once he actually stood on the ancestral soil, with a new version of the problem, which was at the same time the task that he must fulfill: How was this real land of Israel, stretched out before his eyes, to be made to fit the traditional idealized image that had been formed in the exile?

PART IV

Building The Homeland

1

Confronting the Real Land

Religious Zionism's response to the question of the permissability of redemption through independent initiative, and that of secular Zionism to the question of the exclusive status of the land of Israel as the homeland of the Jewish people, reflected, as we have said, the nature of the national awakening as it took place in the exile; so things appeared, in other words, to those who had become convinced of the rightness of the Zionist idea on the basis of their experience of life in exile, in the context of their own Jewish education and upbringing. This was their response to the image of the land of Israel and to the symbolic significance that this image had from a distance. Their arrival in the land of Israel and their confrontation with the actual scene and with its social and cultural character, however, created a new state of affairs, putting the former image and its meanings to the test. Could it continue to stand in the face of one's experience of daily life in the land, in the here and now?

Moving from one land to another is always a trying experience, for one must uproot oneself from the known surroundings to which one is accustomed and reestablish oneself in a new, different and unknown place. Even if one does so because he had suffered in his old home, hoping thus to embark upon a happier life, the ordeals to be undergone are many. The change in scenery and climate, the unaccustomed conditions, the foreign society, the adoption of a new trade—even a young person cannot cope with all of these without enduring some measure of shock and tribulation. All the more difficult was the state of the new arrival in the land of Israel, considering the conditions that prevailed there in the late nineteenth and early twentieth centuries during the period of the first, second, and third *aliyot,* to which we now turn our attention. The differences between the externals of life in the land of Israel and in Europe were radical, and factors which today ease this transition did not then exist. The new arrival, previously accustomed to greenery, water in plenty, and shade, saw before him a desolate land, dry, unforested and exceedingly hot, everywhere exposed to the sun's fiery blaze. It was not a particularly inviting scene:

> O my land, my mother, why
> Is thy visage so scorched and sad?

131

> Memories of a foster-land
> Come unbeckoned into my heart.

Thus wrote Rachel.[1] Isaac Lamdan expressed himself even more bitterly and fiercely in his poem, "Massada":[2]

> But why did Hagar weep over Ishmael, because of his thirst
> when the water in the skin was finished?
> It was not she that should have wept—
>
> Where is Sarah to weep for Isaac her son
> who has been cast here, alone and forsaken
> upon the mercies of the desert?—
>
> (In the *Hamsin*)

Against his will, the settler recalls the land he left behind. That alien land grows dearer to his heart from afar, from the distant land that must become his home. Moreover, the physical reality of the land was a tangible manifestation of his whole new life situation. The new arrival was confronted with an unknown society whose ways were foreign to him; he had there no kinsman, no one to set him on his feet. For years afterward he still felt lonely and thought with yearning of friends and family he had left behind in the diaspora. Economic conditions were also difficult. Work sufficient to keep him was not easily to be found, and one who brought no funds with him from abroad might well go hungry. He suddenly realized that he was homeless in his own land, although he had perceived himself not as an emigre, moving from the land of his birth to a new destination, but rather as a traveler returning from foreign parts to his own home. There was thus something tragic about this meeting with the land, and the depth of his feelings of loneliness and alienation could not but give rise to the piercing question of whether this land before him was truly the land of Israel, the same land whose image had been before his eyes when he decided to make the journey?

Let us recall that the new settler at least did not set out on his journey in the way of a traveler to an unknown land. In a sense, he was already well acquainted with the land of Israel, for if he had not seen it in the flesh, his inner eye had shown it to him in the likeness that had taken shape from the "memories" formed and engraved upon his childish imagination as he read the sources, and from his hopes and the longings of his soul:

From his earliest youth, not a day passed that our friend Yitzhak did not call it to mind. The whole land appeared to him a place of blessing, and its inhabitants were blessed of God. Its villages lay in the shade of vines and olive trees, and all its fields were covered with crops; the trees were laden with fruit, flowers grew in the vales and the trees of its forests waved in the wind; its sky was all of blue, and its houses all filled with joy. All day long, its people plowed, seeded and planted, harvested their crops, their grapes and their olives, flailed corn and stamped the threshing floors, and in the evening each sat 'neath his vine and fig tree, with his wife, his sons and his daughters around him, rejoicing in their work and glad of their leisure, and recalling their past days in foreign lands as men in times of joy recall their days of sorrow and so doubly enjoy the goodness of the present. Yitzhak had an imagination, and he called forth his images from wherever he wished.[3]

"From wherever he wished", says Agnon, the teller of this tale, but we can easily discern the role played by the sources in Yitzhak's imagination, and, that played by the landscape around him, which sustained the tangible reality of the images. All that had delighted him in the scenery of his native land entered the picture of his hopes, while the cold and gloom made way for blue skies and a brilliant sun, bountiful produce, greenery and flowers. His native land was not his homeland, but it was nevertheless the framework of his childhood, of his home, and there was a deep personal relationship between him and the scenes that had sustained his earliest dreams. It was no wonder, then, that when he cast these scenes into the enchanted distance and called them from afar by the name of the land of Israel, he could identify these images as belonging to his homeland, for they really looked like his home.

A very characteristic example of this process is to be found in the poems of Hayim Nachman Bialik, who wrote no descriptions of the land of Israel after he actually experienced it, but made allusions to it while he still lived in exile. It seems most instructive to compare the description of the childhood surroundings of the blue-eyed youth in "The Scroll of Fire"[4] (which are meant to be scenes of the land of Israel) with the poet's lyrical description of his own childhood environment.[5] Bialik experienced the scenery of his childhood with great intensity. This was the surrounding that expressed what he was, the basic environment, in relation to which alone he identified himself. He certainly could not have called this scene, in foreign parts, his homeland. But it is no less typical that after he had settled in the homeland he could not describe its appearance out of a sense of personal identification with it, and that only from the perspective of exile could he take hold of his impressions of the landscape of his childhood, using the poetic images arising from the language of the sources, to shape an image of the homeland for himself. That is, the meeting between his unmediated experienced of the surrounding in which he was born and raised and the scriptural image, taking place in the dimension of poetic creativity, with its richness of vision, formulated a tangible, richly significant image of the homeland. But precisely for this reason, his confrontation with the land as it really was would be painful and unsettling. The reality was suddenly parted from the verbal image he had formulated, and a very important aspect of the character he had ascribed to the homeland remained attached to a landscape that was now clearly identifiable: that of "the foster land," which was entirely unlike the image of his true mother, though he knew in his heart that this indeed was she, and not that land in whose likeness and image he had previously drawn her. This, it would seem, explains the ambivalent responses we found in the poems of Rachel and of Isaac Lamdan. Rachel bears witness to this, sincerely and directly, when she refuses to accept the gap between the scenery of her hopes, formulated according to the image of her native land, and the actual appearance of the land of Israel:[6]

> O, my mother!
> Surely we shall grieve for you,
> Surely shall we demand recompense from God for your affliction—
> Those smitten by your fiery noontime, as of old,
> You shall yet succor with fragrance and shade.

Again, we must recall that the physical appearance of the land was not significant only for itself. It symbolized an entire life situation. This included its people, as they impressed their mark upon the surrounding scene; it included the land's cultural ambience, and the tangible opposition that could be felt between the latter and the historical memory compiled in the sources. The new arrival was greeted by much wasteland, little water, little shade, a blazing sun, and powerful light to which his eyes were unaccustomed. He also encountered strange people who did not understand him, and at times were hostile. In places whose names set his heart to pounding: Jerusalem, the Temple Mount, the Western Wall—he found churches or mosques, and if there were synagogues, their downtrodden state testified to oppression and spiritual descent. To all this was added the extreme tension prevailing between the settler who had come to the land of Israel because of his Zionist aspirations and the members of the existing Jewish community. The latter appeared to the Zionist newcomer to be living an utterly exilic existence, even more so than the Jewish community he had left behind in his *shtetl* in the diaspora. Their dress, their behavior, the ways in which they supported themselves, and their inner lives seemed like exaggerated, oppressive copies of all the defects that had spurred him to leave the exile and come to the land of Israel. It was a bitter, tragic paradox that he faced: the closer he came to the heart of the land of Israel, to its holy of holies—the more like the exile it appeared. This, incidentally, is the basic idea informing the plot of Agnon's *Only Yesterday,* from whose early chapters the passage cited above is drawn. Yitzhak Kummer, who comes to seek redemption in the homeland, turns out to have left the exile of Europe only to discover it anew in Jaffa and then in Jerusalem. He does not find his home, and each new exile is worse than the last.[7]

Having said all this, it must be stressed that the apparent opposition between former expectations and the encountered reality could not, by any means, cancel out the special significance that the land had precisely for the Jew who came to settle there. It was the land of Israel; it was Jerusalem; these were the remains of the delights that had been hers. Here the patriarchs had walked, the prophets had spoken their message and the Israelite kings had reigned. The harsh contrast between the dream and the reality thus took on a special significance. In no other place could such a multileveled tension exist between the Jew and the land wherein he sought his home, so that even the aura of foreignness that blanketed the land symbolized the fate of her people. It symbolized, too, the challenge that faced the settler who had come because of the Zionist ideal. His task was to overcome the contrast between the vision and the reality, to discover the true nature of the land of Israel and adapt himself to it, in such a way that the identification of vision and reality would symbolize his undertaking. At all events, his confrontation with the reality of the land gave rise to a difficult problem, and the struggle for a solution provided him with a lifework of multiple dimensions.

Let us recall that those whose motive for settling in the land of Israel was Zionist were not the first to be faced with this problem. We have already encountered it in previous chapters. The image of the land as it was formulated in the exile, especially in the kabbalistic literature, was one of a super-terrestrial entity which could not be reconciled with reality. Could it really be of this world? Could it possibly be a land like any other? And if one went and settled there—did he really reach that level of spirituality and holiness which he might reasonably have expected to attain? The pilgrimage of Rav Nachman of Bratslav showed up this problematic in sharp relief, as did that of several of his followers who went to settle in the land. The fact that they did not automatically achieve a spiritual ascent, but rather, given their physical and spiritual suffering, the reverse, gave rise to a great deal of inner struggle. They had to explain this awful contradiction if they were to be able to stand fast.[8]

The experience of these pilgrims and that of the settlers who came for Zionist reasons seems quite different, and in a sense the trials of the latter were more difficult. The kabbalist and the hasid were better prepared than the Zionist pioneer to understand the spiritual significance of the contrast between their vision of the land of Israel and the reality, and to formulate the behavioral response that this reality demanded. The contrast between the revealed, material aspects of life and its hidden spiritual dimensions was, after all, built into the foundations of the kabbalistic world view. Did it not follow from this same apprehension that the land of Israel itself, the holy land, should symbolize the exile, for as long as it persisted in its most radical form? For as long as the people were in exile the *Shekhinah,* God's indwelling, was banished as well, and the land of Israel was made the focal point of the struggle between holiness and the impurity that dominated the world. The behavioral response that this required was expressed in the divine service carried on in the holy places. This spiritual activity was meant ultimately to split open the sealed, external shell and reveal its glowing, inner essence. The sense of descent one experienced was a test, and he who withstood it ultimately would attain that great spiritual elevation that could be reached only in the land of Israel. But things would appear quite otherwise to him who had come to the land in order to make it his home in the physical, demographic, economic, social, and political sense. The settler was not indifferent to the image of the holy land that had been shaped by the sources. This image shed its light upon the idyllic perfection that he had imagined of the concrete land, creating in him a feeling of belonging. The land of Israel was his home by virtue of this image, and it is of immeasurable importance in this respect. We must realize, however, that a quality of special, intimate spirituality was ascribed precisely to the physical image of the land, upon which all of the settler's expectations were concentrated.

Ultimately, one did not go to the land because of its holiness, but, rather, it was its holiness that gave the land its unique distinction for the Jew seeking physical redemption. If this holiness could not be sensed, then, in the land's immediate physical presence, if one's feeling in the surroundings it provided was from the outset one of alienation—then the disappointment he experienced must be sevenfold in its intensity. The distinction between the revealed and the hidden could provide him neither aid nor comfort. It was, obviously, that which was manifest that he required, and divine service could no longer provide him with a means of discovering the land's concealed qualities, for the service he set out to perform was not divine service but physical labor. His disappointment was therefore all the greater, and the implements he needed to deal with it were not ready to hand; he would have to forge them in the course of the struggle, as he carried out what he had undertaken to do.

2

Despite the preceding comments, it would be inaccurate to say that the first meeting of the settler who had come for Zionist reasons, with the reality of the land of Israel, was always a disappointment. There are also memoirs attesting to meetings that affirmed and strengthened their authors' previous hopes. Some, too, show an unwillingness to admit disappointment, bearing witness to a deliberate effort of will to find what the heart had sought in the land of Israel. These testimonies are of great importance, and they may help us discover the way in which these settlers were able to confront their disappointments and overcome them, despite their severity.

We must point out, first of all, that the Zionist settlement movement was expressive of a vigorously active approach to life. When Agnon sought to convey the alienation experienced by newcomers to the land, he chose for the purpose a passive personality, psychologically and physically incapable of coping with his fate. He succeeded in this way in capturing a reality experienced by many of the new settlers. Most of them, however, responded differently. The very act of their coming to the land of Israel was in itself a way of rebelling against the life of exile. They had taken a bold initiative and, for them, the redemption was prefigured by their very decision to act. It symbolized potential ability of the Jewish people to solve the problems most critical to its existence by itelf, on its own initiative. One's personal decision to settle in the land was both a symbol and a realization of the national will. This single-minded perspective, to be sure, heightened the contrast between the settler's hopes of the land and the reality he found there. However, the pioneer who based his coming to the land on a decision to seize the initiative did not remain passive in the face of the reality he encountered nor in relation to himself. He did not accept his disappointment and feelings of alienation as unalterable givens of fate but began a determined effort to overcome them as soon as they were stirred wthin him. The disappointing reality had to be changed, and if he was to do this he had to formulate a correct psychological response to it. The transformation might not be easy, and its realization might take years. But the settler's refusal to accept the situation as he found it was clear from his very first step in the land. If he arrived prepared, with the implements he needed to establish himself and facilitate what he wished to accomplish, he was able to overcome his initial reaction fairly quickly. For someone arriving thus prepared, the desolation was a challenge rather than an obstacle, and he recognized, "beyond" the desert wastes, the landscape of his vision.

In the following typical memoir, Z. D. Levontin describes his first encounter with the bleak site upon which he was to erect the colony of Rishon LeZion:[9]

The place was desolate; there was not a house or even a booth or a hut, not a tree or a man in sight—thorns and thistles were all that grew upon the land round about us. The foxes, which were numerous in this desolate spot, were howling. I fired two or three shots with my rifle to scare them away. I spread out my cloak, and we lay down on the ground and rested to recoup our strength and await the arrival of our companions. A fresh breeze wafted down from the Judean Hills, good, healthy and restoring the soul. I nearly forgot the friends we were looking for, as I began to recall the prophetic stories connected with this place. I thought of Samson, the heroic warrior who had battled the Philistines, smiting them with the jawbone he held in his hand. I remembered the blood my forefathers had spilled here; perhaps I had spread my cloak upon their very graves. I felt a powerful love for the place, the love of a son who, after being banished from his father's home, returns there once more—but his father is no longer there . . . Tears fell from my eyes, and my heart and my soul, too, poured themselves out within me. This place was my home and the place where I would find my peace. And my cradle, too, the cradle of my childhood. I felt this even in the middle of the night. But my brothers— where were they? Would that bright morning really come, when the dispersed of our people would come here from the ends of the earth? Watchman, what of the night? The future still spread before me in mists of darkness. I would behold it, but not soon. There was still so much work ahead of us! We had to dig up the thornbushes, break the ground and remove the stones, plow and seed, root and plant, dig wells, level the land and divide up the plots, build our houses and make fast the doors. At the thought of all this work, my hair stood on end. Who would go with me? I recalled the meetings of the Lovers of Zion in Kremenzug and Kharkov, whence I had departed filled with such high hopes. I remembered the fiery speeches, the words each of them had spoken, and their faithful promises to aid me in my labors. But where were they now? I felt that tongue of flame that had consumed all of my wealth, leaving me as a brand plucked from the fire, and I began to think about how I was to live and support the members of my household, whom I had left behind in the land of my birth. Would my strength suffice to do the work demanded by this ideal, when my pockets were empty? Would my hands, which were accustomed to holding a pen and making accounts of credits and debits, be capable of taking up a plow and bringing forth bread from the soil, for myself, my wife and my children? Would I sacrifice these dear ones, too, upon the altar of this ideal? Did I have the right to do so? Would it be of any use? Would I be able to bear on one shoulder sheaves of wheat, and on the other the burden of this people that was with me, with all the trouble this would involve? As I was thus sunk in thought, my servant and dragoman, who had gotten up to recite the evening prayers, came and sat opposite me and said:

"I see your work, sir! How committed you are to it . . . and not for the sake of gaining any material reward . . . indeed . . . but . . . this place, upon which you intend to found a colony, is most dangerous . . ."

"And what is the nature of this danger?" I asked him.

"We Jerusalemites know all about it."

"Tell me, and I shall know, too."

"Look over there to the west, on the sand dunes," he answered, pointing in the direction of the sea and lowering his voice. "There dwell the marauding Beduins . . . and when you have built your houses and settled here . . . tens of them will come mounted on horses in the dead of night . . . plundering and murdering . . ."

"And as for us, what shall we do? Do you imagine that we shall sit with folded hands and not give battle in return?"

"You . . . but we are in exile," answered the interpreter, and he covered his face with his cloak.

"No, my brother, you Jerusalemites enslave yourselves; you do not wish to be free men, and that is why you are in exile. You do not care to understand that the laws of this land give you the right to live here as free people. But we have come here to enjoy the rights of the land, which neither discriminates nor differentiates between her inhabitants. And if men should rise against us with fists raised in malice, we will make them know that we, too, have fists, and rifles, spears and bayonets . . ."

The foxes cried bitterly, groaning and howling, and I fired another shot from my rifle. Then I raised a cloud of smoke from my pipe. The dew began to chill my bones, and I rose to walk around and warm my flesh. But the thorns and briars did not allow me to walk very far in the middle of the night, and I returned once more to the interpreter and said to him:

"Tomorrow, after we pitch our tents and divide the tasks among the members of our company, go into the city and buy me two good silken scarves, and hire two galloping Arabian steeds, for our own horses will be in use. When you return, we will travel west to the Beduin encampment, and I will introduce myself to the elder of the camp. You will present me to him as the head of the Jewish settlement, and I shall attempt to put the fear of me into him and his camp. We shall make a pact of love—of love based on fear and respect, to let them know that we will accept them only on terms of peace. And if they are for war—we too have strength."

"It is a good proposal," said the dragoman. "We will do as you say, and perhaps the Holy One will come to our aid."

So we passed the night, under the stars. I laid my head on the dragoman's shoulder and slept a little. At daybreak we saw our company encamped on another hill, about a bowshot's distance from us. We called them, and they came to us, and, singing, we pitched two or three tents on the hill where we had spent the night. We set about measuring out the site of the village in order to divide it into plots, determining the location of the well and performing various other such tasks. I called the place Rishon LeZion, and that has remained its name to this day.

An undercurrent of will, of initiative, flows through this description from its beginning. The speaker is not subdued by the desolation just as he is not defeated by the danger. He formulates his own response to the landscape, giving it meaning by activating the power of his memory, and even if he is disturbed by doubts, his reaction to an immediate, tangible danger readies him instantly for decisive action. The land of Israel for him—and this is the difference between him and his Jerusalemite dragoman—is his homeland, the foundation of his freedom. He feels himself at liberty to respond freely and to take the initiative, and thus he has come out of exile. At all events, his ability to act also enables him to interpret the reality of the land and to formulate, out of its desolate wastes, the true image of the homeland, that image that corresponds to his hopes and his vision.

If we now contrast this with another, completely different testimony, we will gain some idea of just how crucial was the settler's psychological preparedness to respond to his situation with initiative. Eliezer Ben-Yehuda came to the land of Israel with enthusiastic expectations. His image of himself, at the outset, was the same as Levontin's had been: that of a son returning to his birthplace.[10] However, he was stunned by the reality he encountered, and he was apparently unsuccessful in overcoming what he felt and directing his emotional reactions. His disappointment was crushing, shocking in its intensity. His feelings seem to flee before the alien circumstances like a broken, scattered army running from the enemy.[11]

In the first ports of Syria, Arab travellers began coming aboard our ship, and the nearer we came to the bay of Jaffa, the more numerous they became. Most of them were tall, strong young fellows, dressed in the style of the country, but in expensive, elegant attire, and they were all merry and joyful, jesting and riotous. I must admit that this first meeting with our Ishmaelite cousins was not a happy one for me. An oppressive feeling of dread, as though I were confronting a fortified rampart, suddenly filled my soul. I felt that they saw themselves citizens of that country which was the land of my fathers, while I, the descendant of those same fathers, was arriving in it as a stranger, a foreigner, the son of a foreign country and a foreign people. Here, in this very land of my fathers, I had neither political nor civil rights; I was a foreigner in it, a stranger! I was not prepared for this feeling; I had never imagined that I would respond thus to meeting my brother Esau. Suddenly, I broke. Something like feelings of regret began rising from the depths of my soul: perhaps all that I had undertaken to do was really vain and worthless; perhaps my dream of a revival of the people of Israel upon its ancestral soil was really no more than a delusion that had no place in reality, as Mr. Netter had said to me that day . . . Here was the reality, concrete and tangible! These were the citizens of the land; they dwelt there, they lived their lives there, while as for us, we were scattered in exile throughout all the countries of the earth, and in this land we had no more than a community small in number and lowly in character, poor and wretched both materially and spiritually . . . The last night before our arrival in Jaffa was a weary one for me. I could not sleep; I could not even lie down. Several times I rose from my berth and went to the upper deck of the ship. The sky was deep and pure, scattered with hundreds of thousands of sparkling, whispering stars. The whole natural world round about seemed asleep; there was only the sound of the paddle wheel as the ship calmly sliced through the quiet sea, and the whisper of the waves slapping it on either side seemed inconsonant with this mysterious silence. But within me was a raging tide; my emotions were seething, my thoughts in tumult. Now the sky was turning silvery. Dawn was breaking. Everyone began to wake. My wife and my Russian friend joined me on deck. All were gazing in the same direction, eastward. And now we could just make out a line at the end of the horizon. The line grew steadily broader. Yes! This was the coast of the land of our fathers! . . . And the feeling of dread grew yet stronger within me. Nothing else did I feel, no other thought was in my mind! I am afraid! . . . After about a quarter of an hour, my feet were standing upon the holy ground, the land of our fathers—yet in my heart was no feeling of joy, and in my head no thought, no idea whatsoever! My mind seemed to have emptied itself or turned to ice; it would not budge. Only one thing filled my heart—that same feeling of dread. I neither rent my garments, nor fell upon my face, nor embraced the stones, nor kissed the ground. I just stood there in astonishment. Dread! Dread! It was in this state of mind that I passed through the Jaffa Gate into the area enclosed by the walls, the holy city itself, the city of David, King of Israel, ruined and desolate, humbled unto the very netherworld; and no special feelings were roused within me. Even the two words, "David's Tower", spoken into our ears by our companions as we passed the citadel to the right of the Jaffa Gate, made no particularly strong impression upon me. If someone had told me beforehand that my entrance into Jerusalem would be so lacking in emotion, that it would not set my blood afire or astound all of my senses, I would surely have told him off for insulting me. Yet I must admit that this was actually the case. In almost total indifference, as though I were walking down the street in any of the cities of the world, I passed down the whole length of the way leading from the Jaffa Gate to the site of the Temple.

The first week of my living in Jerusalem was almost over, and I had already become somewhat accustomed to the drastic change that had come about in my life, to the tremendous fact that I was really and truly in the land of my fathers, that my feet walked the same ground that my ancestors had trod, that my eyes beheld the same sky, the same mountains and hills, valleys and plains as had theirs, that I was breathing the very air that my forefathers had breathed. But perhaps all this "wonder" on my part seems strange to the reader. After all, hundreds and even thousands of young Jews are arriving in the land of Israel, and the idea doesn't seem so amazing to them that they must allow themselves to become accustomed to it. But do not forget that this was in the year 5642 (1882), that is, some forty years ago! In those days the land of Israel was not yet the ordinary, everyday matter that it came to be later on. At that time, the land of Israel was almost legendary for most Jews, no more real, almost, than the kingdom of the children of Moses beyond the river Sambatyon, and people who had been there, lads and lasses, did not meet each other in the streets of the diaspora, as they do these days in almost every city and town. Even the name of the land of Israel was spoken by the Jews only in prayer or when reading from the holy books, and such like. And in this very land, which had seemed so distant, so imaginary, I, who just one month before had been in the center of the great, magnificent European world, now dwelt; it was now not only the land of my fathers, but the land where I lived! In the first two or three days, I was conscious of this wondrous change in my life every minute. Little by little, however, this feeling grew fainter, and by the end of the week there were already hours when I forgot that I was in the land of Israel.

The reader will note the powerful emotional upheavals that mark this testimony. The excited anticipation of arriving in the land of the fathers changes suddenly, as the journey nears its end and the atmosphere of the land's Arab populace begins to make itself felt, into a feeling of dread. The author's indifference, as he enters the walls, to the significance of the historical sites of the city of Jerusalem later turns into a feeling of wonder at the fact that his feet really are standing upon the ancestral soil, that he is breathing the same air as did his forefathers. And later, again, the sense of wonder dims and he forgets, except that this forgetting is engraved upon his memory and troubles him. But are these in fact emotional turnabouts? Precisely in his description of the moments when he is overwhelmed by feelings of dread, alienation and apathy, the writer seems most keenly to express the special significance of the initial confrontation with the land of Israel. This is because what we have here is not a simple, direct description of his emotional response, but, rather, a description of the way he saw this response from a distance, and this necessarily entails an evaluation of it as well. The perspective of time is, indeed, quite strongly felt; this is the testimony of a man recalling his experiences after forty years. His reflectiveness, however, is not only a function of his recollecting these events many years later; it is a dimension of the experience itself, and had been so, it would seem, at the time when it was happening.

The new arrival cannot gain an impression of the land of Israel without simultaneously examining and being struck by his impressions as well: Does he feel what a Jew ought to feel when he returns to his land? This anticipation that he must respond in a particular way is almost foredoomed to lead to disappointment. No actual impression can come up to the ideal emotion that he had prepared himself, in his dreams and hopes, to feel. On the other hand, however, what the person had anticipated feeling becomes an inseparable element of the experience of the encounter. It, too, is present in the confrontation and gives it an aura of extreme intensity, even if this takes the form of disappointment, dread, and indifference. These latter feelings are so marked in Ben-Yehuda's testimony precisely because of the presence of the dreamer's exaggerated expectations, experienced in the negative. The same is true of the apparent apathy he felt upon entering Jerusalem, to which he clearly could not remain indifferent. It troubled him, and this is what imbued his experience of the encounter with depth: for how can one actually feel what a Jew ought to feel as he first enters the gates of Jerusalem? However, his psychological reaction to his impressions is completely at odds with Levontin's. This kind of passivity, of emotional paralysis in the face of the reality of the land of Israel, transformed the gap between what he had anticipated and what he actually found into an existential problem which could have— and in Ben Yehuda's case, in fact, was—a spiritual crisis, and an ideological change of direction as well. Could the land of Israel really become a homeland for the dispersed people once more? Could the chasm of alienation that had formed between the people's memories of its past and the reality of the present be spanned?

Between these two extreme emotional reactions to the initial encounter with the land of Israel stands that of A. D. Gordon. His especial sensitivity to the appearance of the landscape and the way he viewed the relationship between man and nature led him to anticipate that the experience of his initial confrontation with the land of Israel, its scenery, its flora and fauna, and its socio-cultural ambience, would be an event of overwhelming importance to him. He viewed his coming as a return to his natural, original home, and during the sea voyage he thought of Judah Halevi yearning for Zion from the furthermost west. As he journeyed across the sea he did, indeed, sense a great elevation, infinite space, purity, a feeling that he was drawing near to the place he most deeply desired. It was precisely on this account that the alienation he felt upon his initial encounter was so painful and so shocking:[12]

And suddenly, from such purity, such space—I entered the dirty, Asiatic city of Jaffa, which echoes with talk of quite a different sort. This piercing transformation affected me severely. In fact, each time our ship had approached one of the port cities, such as Constantinople, Izmir or Alexandria, I had had an unpleasant feeling. These negative feelings were heightened by a further element: when we make the journey to the land of Israel, we come seeking a particular kind of impression, but whatever the reason for this may have been, when I arrived in the holy land I was far from feeling what Judah Halevi had felt; and later on, too, when I visited the agricultural colonies, I did not feel what every good Zionist ought to feel, or what his heart must feel even without his trying.

The natural scenery here (I am speaking of the colonies in Judea) is indeed astoundingly beautiful, yet I feel that this beauty lacks something; perhaps because there is just too much of it. I am not used to this kind of perspective; because of the transparency of the air, everything, even from a distance, appears with a startling clarity which pierces the unaccustomed eye, and the beauty of it thus seems unnatural, artificial. I am unused to this singularity of hue, to the unchanging nature of this beauty, which is never dulled, and to this calm, eternally undisturbed quiet. I am unused to this special, serious silence, which expresses the great thought and the great sorrow of the world. In the natural environs of the land of Israel I feel myself a wanted guest; if you like, perhaps even one most anxiously awaited, near and dear, but nevertheless a guest. To treat this natural scenery lightly would be impolite, and you would not permit yourself to do so; this is not the scenery of Russia, to which you had been accustomed and with which you had lived in spiritual intimacy. Not only does the natural world in Russia understand you, but you also understand it wholly, in all its simplicity and innocence; at times it rebukes you and at times it caresses—all with utter simplicity, like an innocent, naive, loving mother. Not so is the natural environment of the land of Israel. She, too, is loving and compassionate, and perhaps her love is the deeper. But she is infinitely elevated in her spiritual grandeur; the mark of the ideal is upon her brow, and there is silent sorrow in her gaze. Here you feel yourself embraced in the tender arms of a wise mother, eminent above all the rest, a princess, who looks upon you as a beloved son who has been raised in slavery and now returns to her bowed with affliction, devoid of education and culturally degraded, and she understands you well in her heart so full of wisdom, but you are incapable of understanding her.

Gordon reacts first with a feeling of letdown, although in the midst of this, facilitated precisely by his open, sober report of it, a set of concepts and images that will help him to overcome his disappointment begins to emerge. He must get to the root of his feeling, interpret it, and in this way conceptualize a different kind of emotional attitude toward the landscape. Gordon took the disappointment he felt as a sign that he must change something within himself in order to become worthy of the land of Israel, of this wise, proud, sorrowing mother. Accomplishing this, however, was no simple matter, for his sense of alienation did not fade after the initial encounter. It was not only the appearance of the landscape that was strange and remote; even harder to bear was the human milieu that had formed in the land of Israel:[13]

And it seems to you that the people who live here do not understand the natural phenomena of the land of Israel, so remote and so different from it are they! This natural world, astonishingly magnificent, filled with grandeur—and its inhabitant, a kind of filthy, degraded creature, whose life is contemptible. This absence of culture, this spiritual desolation all bear witness to the fact that the local populace has not raised itself to the spiritual level of the natural environment of the land of Israel.

Thus wrote Gordon in the same letter in which he described his initial encounter with the land. In a later passage from his writings, written after he had become integrated with and accustomed to life in the land, he expressed similar feelings from a perspective that exposed the cultural-historical significance of the spiritual alienation of the inhabitants of the land from its scenery, from the point of view, of course, of a Jew returning to his homeland:[14]

In the morning, on an empty stomach, a walk in the mountains. My mood was one of seeking calm without finding it, a mood which can be expressed by only one word, "woe", and to add any more to this would only detract from it. From mountain to valley and from valley to mountain— until I reached Mt. Tabor. Thoughts of the possibility that I might be attacked. A decision to give nothing willingly. What an indifference toward death, almost a desire to be killed. More fear of being plundered and beaten than of death. Shame of myself, and of the Jews before the Arabs. Awareness that I am approaching Tabor encourages me to go on. Hope that the mountain will repay me for all my physical and spiritual labors. The climb is difficult; my strength gone (I had eaten nothing, nor even drunk a cup of tea). A climb to the top in midday. What disillusion! The whole mountaintop is taken by monasteries, one French and one Greek. "Tabor and Hermon rejoice in Thy name . . ." Will Tabor really rejoice "in Thy name"? The beauty of the surroundings does not atone, and one practically does not perceive it. I will lift up my eyes unto the mountains; from whence shall my help come?

This passage from a composition written in diary form transmits in a telegraphic, impatient, almost strangled form the symbolic meaning of the landscape. Gordon's hopes of reaching home were not realized. His sense of degradation was heightened by a political dimension—the hatred of the Arabs—and a cultural/spiritual one—the occupation of Mt. Tabor by the monasteries. Gordon does not utter the terrible word, but it seems to hover over his description: exile. Precisely in the land of Israel, at home, one feels the exile with even greater intensity.

In this, Gordon's reaction was similar to that of Ben-Yehuda. Gordon, however, struggled against this response and did not let it subdue him even in moments of despair. Already in the letter describing his initial encounter with the land, he did not allow himself merely to be passive. He placed his will before his sensibilities and struggled to make his feelings follow his will to find in the the landscape he saw before him a scene that matched the image he bore in his soul. The landscape did not appear as he had anticipated it. The scenery of Russia now seemed to him to have been intimate, "motherly." Despite this, Gordon retraced his steps and began again to paint the portrait of the land, this time as that of a loving, wise mother, a princess, whose child cannot understand her, but who understands and takes pity upon him. With the passage of time, Gordon succeeded in coming closer to her and was able to become an understanding son to this knowing mother:[15]

The soul of the Jew is the offspring of the natural environment of the land of Israel. Clarity, the depth of an infinitely clear sky, a clear perspective, "mists of purity." Even the divine unknown seems to disappear because of this clarity, slipping from "limited, manifest light" into "infinite, hidden light." The peoples of the world understand neither this clear perspective nor this luminous unknown in the Jewish soul.*

We shall examine the theoretical significance of these characteristic lines in greater depth further on. What interests us here is the transformation that took place in Gordon's soul as it absorbed the impact of the landscape. In this passage, Gordon no longer feels remote and alienated in the face of the transparency and clarity, the intensity of the light that he encountered. Now he identifies with this open, clear light as a manifestation of the character of both the land and the people at once. Other peoples do not understand the powerful, open, unified simplicity of the Jewish soul, as Gordon himself initially found it difficult to comprehend the powerful, open simplicity of the land's scenery. Elsewhere in his writings, moreover, we find an answer to the bitter, gloomy diary passage cited above:[16]

. . .and this sky above, and this delicate silence, all this, all this—are they not within my own soul? But, especially, are they not manifestations of the soul of our people? Brother, be so good as to take up that most faithful album of the scenes of this natural landscape—our beloved Bible. I shall trace a few points in it, and you will see that by doing no more than putting my finger on one of them, I shall have touched upon one of the finest, most deeply concealed chords in your soul.

Gordon goes on to list the names of the biblical sites that are before his eyes, and the scenery of the land enlivens the biblical memory as the biblical memory imparts significance to the present, living landscape. If, when he lived in exile, he visualized the land of Israel by giving the landscape in which he grew up an "interpretation" drawn from the sources, now he accustoms himself to the reality of the land by way of Scripture, and it appears to him as though this landscape that he sees around him has suddenly risen from his own innermost self. He recalls this very landscape, which, if he had not seen it himself, his soul, cleaving to that of his people, had seen, and stored away in its inner recesses. Now, as his glance embraces both internal and external, past and present, the real encounter takes place. The banished son, who had forgotten himself in the servitude of life in exile, recalls and

*The expressions "Mists of purity", "limited manifest light" and "infinite hidden light" are, in fact, kabbalistic terms, which Gordon uses deliberately.

recognizes himself as he stands before his mother, recalls and recognizes his mother from the memories that have come to life within him.

3

In these last few lines, we have anticipated what is to come. The new arrival's confrontation with the real land of Israel brought on a crisis, and raised anew the question that had previously been laid to rest: Why set one's heart only upon the land of Israel? Or, is it really the land of Israel alone to which one must look? This question could no longer be answered solely on a theoretical, ideological level. The response had to come in the form of a full life, and the conceptual reply would accompany this vital activity, guiding and directing it and raising it to the people's conscious awareness. Gordon's thought is an outstanding example of this, and we shall return to it later on. Clearly, however, the individual's ability to provide such a response depended upon the strength of his will and the emotional resources that sustained it. Many new arrivals, among them persons of some note, failed in this great struggle. Those who succeeded had responded with activity, in settlement, building the society, educational, technological, and artistic creativity, and thought.

2

What Should the Homeland Be Like?

Overcoming the crisis of one's initial encounter with the land of Israel was a lifelong task. For the person who had come seeing himself as a pioneer, the journey itself was no more than the first stage in the realization of his ideal; its fulfillment would come about as he adapted himself to the reality of the homeland and molded its image to accord with his vision.

The struggle to accomplish this was difficult and complex, and fraught with contradictions. Conflicting impulses motivated the pioneer in his decision to come to the land, and the various streams within the Zionist movement had differing images of the desired future. The newly arrived settler sought to break away from his diaspora background and familiarize himself with the way life was lived in the homeland. He wanted to adapt to his new environmental and socio-cultural circumstances. At the same time, he was not content with the land as it was; neither its environmental nor its economic and social conditions were as he would have liked them to be. He had, therefore, both to adapt himself to the land and to change it if he was to make it into a homeland in the modern European sense of the word. There was, at the very least, a powerful tension between these two desires, though they also sustained one another: the pioneer's romantic yearning for the primordial root of his people's natural life, over against his desire to reconstitute a national entity founded upon the foremost achievements of modern culture.

This tension was given expression in the poetry of Avraham Shlonsky:

> Not like these is the descent of flocks over the slopes
> nor the lizard's or the hyena's lair;
> Not like these is the touch of the *hamsin*
> pressing down with its heavy hand.
> Thy feet are foreign, O man;
> Put off they shoes, man, and come,
> For barenecked and barefoot
> shall you make yourself known to the children of this fierce land.[1]

This is a romantic idealization of the scenery of the ancient homeland. As he strives to internalize the desolate landscape, however, the poet calls up his vision of the homeland rebuilt:

> Then give us dryness and desolation, and we shall bless,
> and answered him thistle and rock, Amen.
> And this was the blessing:
> We shall yet build you up!
> We shall yet build you up!
> And this the reply:
> Amen, Selah![2]

As we have said, these two goals sustain one another, despite the tension between them. The pioneer had decided to break with the exile and its heritage, and the antithesis of exile alternately took the shape of yearning for the scenery of the ancient land and aspiration for the modern future. In both these respects, that of the primordial past and that of the future as yet only intimated, the land of Israel symbolized a return to physical actuality, to life in the present, to certainty. We must note here that Shlonsky unified this dual image, imbuing the land of Israel with symbolic significance by using the traditional symbols in unconventional ways. In alluding to them while at the same time transforming their significance, he expressed his generation's desire to break away from the exile, without cutting itself off from its people's historic continuity. Shlonsky himself saw this as "returning to its simple meaning" what exilic thought had distorted by its demands. From an abstract spirituality, we now return to physical actuality, and it is this actuality that we wish the symbol to signify. The following poem expresses this very strongly and bluntly:

> Dress me, my own right mother, in a magnificent coat of many colors
> And at the hour of morning service carry me to work.
> Light wraps my land like a prayer shawl.
> The houses stand upright like frontlets.
> And the roads, paved by laboring hands, run down like the straps of
>   tefilin.
> Thus shall the fine city offer her morning prayer to her creator;
> And among the creators, your son Avraham, paving poet in Israel.[3]

In these lines the poet uses a series of traditional symbols, while rebelliously transforming their significance. They are brought back to their "simple" physical meaning. The pioneer who paves the roads and builds the houses is the creator to whom the city prays. A new land is coming to life, one that responds to the will of its builders. Even so, however, the pioneer poet will not relinquish the traditional symbols. His refusal stems, it would seem, from his realization that only by their means can he preserve the continuity of national consciousness that identifies the land of Israel as the homeland of the ancient people now renewing itself.

Shlonsky's poems are a radical expression of the pioneering vision that saw the ancestral soil being turned into a homeland in the secular-romantic sense. Over against this, religious Zionism posed a vision of its own, and a similar tension was present within this as well. The romantic motif expressed in Shlonsky's works in his yearning for the ancient landscape came out in religious Zionist thought in its yearning for the golden age of the ancient kingdom of Israel, the days of David and Solomon. His desire to internalize the scenery of the real, tangible land of Israel is also present in religious Zionist thought, and the latter, too, is imbued with yearning for a full national revival. Instead of laying hold of the natural and physical for their own sakes, however, religious Zionism sought out the symbols of messianic redemption, which allude to a spiritual reality that lies beyond. One returned to the homeland in order thence to reach the realm of the holy.

2

The present discussion goes beyond the limits of Jewish thought about the image of the land of Israel and its symbolic significance. It touches upon every aspect of the Zionist idea. How was the Jewish people that would rise again in its land to appear? What would its demographic, economic, and political character be like? And what were to be its social customs, its moral values, and the forms in which its spiritual creativity would be expressed? The land itself constituted the foundation for all of these things, and it was ever reflected in them, particularly in the creative products of its philosophy, its art and its science, functioning both as matters for research and for visions of the future, and as symbol. Indeed, in this symbolic function the words "land of Israel" now expressed the whole Zionist endeavor in progress toward realization.

In the secular Zionist view, the principal vehicle by which the image of the land of Israel was to be interpreted was that of culture.[4] The revival of the Jewish people in its land would be realized through the revival of its unique culture, the creative outpouring of the people. What distinguished the culture of one people from that of another? According to secular Zionism, this was a matter of framework and of belonging; it made no initial commitments with regard to any defined contents or commonly accepted ways of life. A culture was distinguished by the people's shared relationship to the land in which they dwelt, by the language they spoke, their link with the same historical continuity and their drawing upon the same literary sources. For the people of Israel, this meant that their culture must be based upon the land of Israel; it must be a Hebrew culture, drawing upon the sources of Hebrew literature, particularly the Bible, and bound to the history of the Jewish people. This shared relationship to the same framework of belonging would, indeed, surely lead to a certain commonality of content and way of life. However, these could not be defined in advance, much less be considered obligatory. They would take shape as part of the process. Judaism, according to this way of thinking was all that the Jews created freely on the basis of shared conditions of living.

The land itself had an important role to play in the realization of this conception. One had to relate to it consciously and intentionally, daily and hourly, and from several different perspectives. The land brought the people together; it constituted the base for all of their activity and provided the material resource upon which they drew and, conversely, it thence became the object of a rich artistic figuration. Of course, the same can be said of the relationship of any cultured people to its land.⁵ In this sense, the ideas we are examining are, in fact, an aspect of the Jewish people's effort to establish itself as a "normal" people. We must bear in mind, however, that for as long as the effort to take possession of the land of Israel and develop the possibilities it embodied continued, the land itself could never be put out of mind. It was not a matter of course, as England is to the English or France to the French. It had continually to be studied, and one could not desist from this enquiry without causing harm. If the Zionist wished to realize his ideal he had, therefore, consciously and intensively to live the fact that he was in the land of Israel. It was the land of Israel to which he brought new settlers, whose earth he plowed and sowed, whose pathways he explored and whose historical remains he researched. The fact that he was doing all of these things in the land of Israel heightened their significance—that is to say, even as it became a homeland, it remained a land of destiny.

Moreover, in the land of Israel the pioneering settler confronted the history and culture of his people in a new way. The land gave history and culture a dimension of tangibility, physicality, and contemporary relevance. In this we are referring first and foremost to the Bible, which now reasserted itself to the pioneer as a book created in the land and testifying to the role that land had played in the life of the people, and which had now to be reinterpreted in light of the newly-discovered traces it had left there. Suddenly, the tales of Scripture acquired a tangible reality they had never had in exile. Their literal, historical meanings slipped into focus as one identified the places in which the events they described took place; back in their original settings, they assumed flesh-and-blood reality. Conversely, the land, too, appeared differently as one called to mind what had occurred in each particular place. This was the significance of the pioneers' renewed encounter with history and with the sources. But the Bible was also an avenue for a renewed encounter with the Hebrew tongue. This was now the language of the homeland, a language of life in the world and not only of prayer and religious thought. (This symbolism was emphasized by the settlers' adoption of the Sefardic pronunciation in place of the European, Ashkenazi accent, which was identified with the exile. One had to go back to the source, to strip off the garb of exile and put on that of the homeland). In all of these three respects, then, going back to the land of Israel was a return to the people's point of origin, its place of birth. The people's way of life would be reconstituted right from the beginning, and this time it would grow in the natural way.

It is no wonder, then, that the land of Israel played a principal role in the new settlers' creative expressions, in thought, literature, poetry, the plastic arts, folksong, music and dance. In this pioneering period, creative expression in all of the art forms centered around the subject of return to the homeland. The young artists wrote of the land of Israel, put its scenery into verse, sang of its rebuilding, composed on the theme of its fields, and danced their efforts to strike roots in the soil. They aspired to create a unique, Israeli style. The culture created in the land of Israel by the Zionist movement was thus stamped all over with the impress of the land. Its task, first and foremost, was to mold the countryside directly, by building settlements, paving roads, drying the swamps, planting forests, plowing fields and sowing them; thereafter, it had to internalize this renewed landscape by means of art and ideas. In both these respects it was a culture that belonged to the land of Israel, and not only because it was created there; the land was its content and determined its style.

To explore this subject thoroughly, we would have to devote a detailed discussion to each of the areas noted above. What ideas guided the physical molding of the landscape? What governed the way the land of Israel appeared in literature, in art, and in music? The material for study here is very rich, and it is difficult to generalize about it. At all events, the Zionist enterprise shaped and interpreted the land's image, in every form of creative expression, in accordance with its secular-nationalist conception. We may say, moreover, that since the land's physical reality was still rather visionary, this image could still reflect characteristics relating to the people's religious and spiritual heritage, though their interpretation may have changed. The ancient past has a part in the image of the future. In the painter's hues of brilliant blue or the musician's tones, transcendent memories and hopes are yet intimated. The general trend, however, is clear: all of the meanings must be compressed into the tangible symbol. They must take shape in the open, physical world.

3

Up to a certain point, religious Zionism sought to make its own conception approximate this image of the homeland, but also drew back from it. The land of Israel, even as it became a physical homeland, had to remain the holy land. Here, too, we are clearly exceeding the confines of our discussion of the image of the land itself, for what is involved is the goal of the whole Zionist enterprise and, in particular, the character that renewed Jewish life in the land of Israel was to take. Religious Zionism took exception, practically speaking, to the assumption that underlay the "land of Israel" orientation in secular Zionism's concept of culture; it could not accept the idea that culture is wholly the creation of a people's natural powers working in relation to the natural conditions of its land. Here is a typical religious response to this hypothesis:

And these new arrivals, who have lately come and proclaimed that the Torah has no connection with the land, and that in returning to Zion they attain no more than a safe shelter and the realization of man's materialistic purpose: "From the earth you were taken, and to the earth you shall return," have frozen the soul of the people of Israel, by denying the holy quality that is within it.

These lines are, in fact, founded precisely upon the assumption that there is an essential bond between the people and its land, so that they cannot be parted even in exile:

On that ancient day when the Holy One, Blessed be He, created His world, from the very beginning He marked out a special land for the people that was to become the bearer of the divine faith, the source of the prophets who would come forth to set the seal of their great spirit upon the whole nation, which nation would then set the seal of its spiritual ideals and concepts upon all the nations of the world. This land, by its splendid beauty and the power of its glory, the transparency of its air, the majesty of its mountains, the blue of the sky spread above it and the holy splendor wafting over its clear heavens, will arouse within its inhabitants a sense of the divine, so that their soul would burst out of its hidden prison. It would forget the world and all of the universe; it would forget all trial and tribulation and make its nest among the stars. From the perspective of this correct conception, our sages well discussed the matter and concluded that "Dwelling in the land of Israel is as important as fulfilling all of the mitzvot" (*Sifre* to the Torah portion *Re'eh*), for its qualities are important factors in conditioning the soul and in training the people through fulfilment of the *mitzvot*. . . The good, temperate climate of the plains, the air of the mountains that runs through the land between the two valleys, cold in the rainy season and temperate and pleasant in summer, and the climate of the Jordan valley, hot throughout most of the seasons of the year. He who enjoys all this effulgence perfects his abilities to study and to act, which are so necessary for the performance of each and every commandment.[7]

It is instructive that in describing the essential bond between the people and its land, it is precisely the effect of being physically present in the natural environment of the land that is emphasized in this passage. In this, these lines approach the lyrical attitude that characterized the pioneering settlers. Here, however, the physical landscape has transcendent, symbolic significance, and it brings about the people's elevation to a spiritual dimension. The scenery conditions the soul to fulfill the commandments which depend upon the land, and to its rise to a supernal, spiritual life. This, then, is the heart of the matter: that which embraces people and land and joins them into an indivisible unity is the Torah. Or, in the words of the writer cited above, "When He gave the people of Israel His Torah, and when He preordained the order of the world, the Holy One, Blessed be He, deliberately saw to it that the greater part of the commandments be made to obtain in the land of our fathers above; and at one and the same time, He gave them a deed to the land as well, and His commitment to its fulfilment is engraved in the Book of the Covenant. Ever since that time, the Torah constitutes a 'means for taking possession of the land' in the hands of every member of the people of Israel, wherever he may be. Ever since then, the people of Israel and its land have joined together. This threefold cord shall never be sundered; and no vessel shall succeed in making a spiritual separation between these joined parts, which would, ultimately, lead to despair and a split which could never be joined. These three are one, in every time and in every place."[8] True, the Bible played a role in the bonding between people and land in the secular view as well. There, however, the Bible was seen as having been created by the people in its land, and it was in this sense that it testified to the bond between the people's culture and the land of Israel. In the religious view, it was the supernatural Torah that bound the people to its land. In the same way, the concept of the national homeland, too, was defined by the commandments given in the Torah.

This was clearly a comprehensive counter argument to the secularists' conception of a "land of Israel" culture. All that was accomplished in the land of Israel had to be done in accordance with the Torah. The framework of belonging of which we spoke above, comprising land, language, literature and history, was not enough. Halakhah was the main thing, and a Hebrew, land of Israel culture based on literature and history would not be truly Jewish unless the halakhah determined its way of life. The opposition between these two conceptions found expression in a series of bitter disputes between religious and secular Zionism. They differed over the nation's educational system, over the place that was to be accorded the plastic arts, over the status of the rabbinical courts, and over the constitution of the national leadership. In all of these controversies, the two sides were, in fact, struggling over the image that Jewish life was to have in the land of Israel, and so, too, over the image of the land itself. In the context of our discussion, however, particular importance attaches to one dispute which, chronologically, preceded all the rest—that which was waged over the question of the seventh year, the *shmittah*.[9] Did the commandment to let the fields lie fallow in the seventh year have to be kept in the new agricultural settlements that had been erected upon the soil of the land? This practical question was filled with spiritual significance for all parties to the dispute. On the one hand, keeping the commandment of *shmittah* would clearly attest to the settlers' respect for the Torah, for this was one of the most important of the commandments whose fulfilment depends upon the land. It expressed the relationship, mediated by the Torah, by which the land of Israel as a homeland was kept sacrosanct to the Jewish people. On the other hand, strict observance of this commandment might deal the new Jewish agricultural enterprise an economic blow that it could not survive. In other words, if one kept this commandment, it would be tantamount to admitting that settlement, in the nationalist sense, was of no real value. The nationalist and religious ideals were thus in direct conflict here, and since the matter was of practical importance, a decision on the issue could not be avoided. The extreme secularists had no trouble deciding which way they would go. For them, the values of Judaism were embodied in settlement itself, and to do anything that might obstruct it was thus out of the question. For the extremists on the religious side, too, the decision was simple and clear-cut. Keeping the Torah was their supreme value, and if establishing settlements by independent national initiative could not be done without breaking the commandments, it was clear that no such settlements must be erected. The religious Zionists, however, were caught in the middle, torn and indecisive. Their basic assumption was that the two ideals were, by their very essence, complementary, and they therefore had to find a way of establishing the pioneering agricultural enterprise upon a firm religious base without breaking the commandments. They did, indeed, reach a technical compromise, but the basic problem remained unsolved.

The *shmittah* controversy thus expressed the internal tension inherent in religious Zionism, and the way it was solved only showed that a unity between the religious and the nationalist ideals could exist only on the philosophical level, or in the hoped-for, utopian future. In the present, however, as the religious Zionists sought to take part in realizing the movement's nationalist goals, the two ideals were in continual conflict. How were they to cope with this? How was the endeavor, which would in the process of its unfolding mold the image of the land, to be directed? Two approaches to this issue took shape. The first began by recognizing that the Torah must direct the people's actions in circumstances not determined by it alone. There are natural and historical factors which the halakhah must accept as they are, and it must teach the people how to live with them in accordance with the Torah's commandments. According to this conception, the people's historical and cultural circumstances and the natural conditions of the land are independent, substantive elements in the national culture, and the possibilities for changing them are determined by the internal, natural laws that govern them, and not directly by the halakhah. The compatibility of the Torah with life was not a predetermined given; rather, it had the nature of a demand that had to be fulfilled again and again from time to time. The return to Zion demanded such a readjustment, and this time it would involve some far-reaching changes, for settling the land meant that the people must also incorporate some of the achievements of Western, secular culture. A religious thinker who came to the conclusion that the Torah favored the Zionist idea in general had to be bold enough to apply this overall demand to the details of how the commandments were to be fulfilled. Only then would the land of Israel, rebuilt as a modern national home, be graced with the sanctity of the commandments, and only thus would the link between present and past be preserved. This view continued in the tradition of Maimonides' conception of the halakhah, and Rabbi Haim Hirshenson was its most consistent representative.[10]

The second approach presupposed an original, fixed identity between Torah, people and land—that is to say, the nature of the people and that of the land were reflected in one another, and became identical in practice when the people observed the commandments that depended upon being in the land. In exile, the nature of the people had become distorted, and the land, whose sons were far away, lay desolate. When the people returned to its land, both would reassume their true nature, and the original culture of the people of Israel would flourish once more. The culture that was to be renewed by Zionism thus had a special land of Israel character to it, and there was even a unique quality about the religious learning that took place and the legal decisions that were made there. This approach comes quite close to the cultural ideal of secular Zionism in this respect. By their very proximity, however, their internal contradictions stand revealed. The compatibility between the nature of the people and that of the land was embodied in the supernatural Torah, and this meant that the two were not subject to any independent, internal laws. They were emanations from above, from the spiritual dimension, the infinite outpouring of divine life. That being the case, the identity between the nature of the people and that of the land would not show itself through the nation's material culture as such. It would come about as a result of their elevation to a spiritual dimension. Only when the Torah absolutely determined all of the circumstances of life would the redemption come. And this process, even if it began within history, which appeared to progress according to its own laws, would be completed only beyond history, by an event which superseded these seemingly independent laws. Only then would the true image of the Land of Israel be revealed. This view continued the tradition of Judah Halevi and the kabbalists, and its most outstanding representative was Rabbi Abraham Isaac HaKohen Kook.

The first approach is what underlies the practical halakhic solutions that enabled the religious Zionists to cooperate with their secular counterparts in building the land of Israel. In general, however, we may say that religious Zionism took this path reluctantly, as a strained compromise between its two ideals; that is to say, it never fully accepted the view upon which it was founded. It was the second approach—which gained the religious factions unqualified ideological acceptance—that view which had painted its utopian vision of an ideal land of Israel above the visible horizon of the historical Zionist enterprise.

In the following two chapters, the conflict between the more naturalist, secularist conception which saw the land of Israel as destined to become the Jewish people's homeland, and that which saw it as a homeland which was destined to become something much greater, will be explored in greater depth by means of a comparison between two wide-ranging doctrines which emerged within Zionist thought as it developed in the land of Israel, namely, those of A. D. Gordon and of Rav Kook. These two thinkers were not typical; in the great spiritual force that marked their works they were even extraordinary. Nor did they represent perspectives foreign to one another; on the contrary, there is a great deal that brings them together. Their very proximity, however, only served to emphasize the opposing streams that surged through Zionist thought as it sought to realize its ideals. The two thinkers we are about to study represent spiritual trends which, in spite of their differences, approached one another, and in spite of their proximity, opposed one another.

3

A. D. Gordon:
A Homeland That Is a Land of Destiny

A. D. Gordon, in his ideological approach, drew upon sources that he had studied and pondered while still in exile. Gordon came to the land of Israel at the age of forty-eight, and although at that time he had not yet formulated his ideas in writing or, it would seem, even in his mind, the learning upon which it was based was already complete, and he added very little more to it after his *aliyah*. What did this basis consist of? First, the traditional Jewish sources. We must bear in mind that Gordon had considered himself an "Orthodox Jew,"[1] up until his *aliyah*, and he continued to do so during his first years in the land. Only gradually was his Orthodox religiosity (which, even while he lived abroad, had been far from rigid) replaced by a pioneering way of life, imbued with a religious spirit. At all events, as a religious Jew he was well versed in the sources, and in addition to the Bible, the traditional commentaries and the Talmud, he had also studied hasidic literature and the ethical writings of the *Musar* movement, whose influence is quite obvious in his writings.

As we have said, Gordon was far from being rigidly Orthodox. Along with his traditional education he had applied himself, on his own, to secular learning, and he was proficient in contemporary Russian and German philosophical literature. Of the important thinkers of his day, the influence of Kant, Schopenhauer, Nietzsche, Marx, and Tolstoy is especially noticeable in his works. These, then, are the sources upon which he built.[2] As he put together his doctrine, after coming to live in the land of Israel, he drew upon these ideas as though they were original with him, not realizing that they were borrowed from external sources. He had to put his entire intellectual background to use in order to cope with the personal and communal difficulties that life in the land of Israel presented, and it was these that served as both stimulus to thought and its organizing principle. In this sense, the whole body of his thought may be seen as a "land of Israel philosophy." It reflected, in the course of its development and the way in which it was expressed, how *aliyah* could be a life-long endeavor. Moreover, it may in itself be seen as one of the dimensions of this endeavor. *Aliyah,* coming to

live in the land, was of spiritual significance. It was only natural, then, that
the image of the land of Israel, with its many facets of meaning, should be
central to his thought. What was the land of Israel, physically, ecologically,
historically, socially and culturally? And what should it be?

For Gordon the process of putting together his direct impressions of the
landscape, from his first view in Jaffa until the last years of his life, was like
trying to accustom oneself to the appearance of a person, with whom one
had once been intimate, after long years of separation. What did it express?
What kind of inner life did it reflect? It was not easy for him to "solve" the
"riddle" of the landscape, but in his last years he was able to sum up what he
perceived in it, as though he were seeing his own life in that of a close friend:

> The soul of the Jew is the offspring of the natural environment of the land
> of Israel. Clarity, the depth of an infinitely clear sky, a clear perspective,
> mists of purity. Even the divine unknown seems to disappear in this clar-
> ity, slipping from limited, manifest light into infinite, hidden light. The
> peoples of the world understand neither this clear perspective nor this
> luminous unknown in the Jewish soul.[3]

These lines are brief and tightly composed, but behind them lies a world of
experience and thought: Gordon's encounter with the scenery and historic
sites of the land and with its inhabitants, Jew and Arab; the experience of his
working the land, and of creating a new Jewish society. All these experiences were tested in the crucible of a mind whose historical memories were
like personal recollections, drawing upon philosophical ideas which had
been fused with Jewish and secular sources in a fierce blaze of original,
personal creativity. In the paragraphs that follow we shall attempt to understand these principles, and some of the ideas to which they led.

2

We must begin with Gordon's views on the relationship between man and
nature.[4] Returning to the land of Israel, we recall, meant returning to the
homeland in this primal sense as well: the people of Israel, which had lived
in exile cut off from the unmediated contact with nature that could be offered
only by work, would once more lead a natural life. It would again live in its
own land. Gordon put this Zionist aspiration into comprehensive ideological
terms. Man is a creature of nature; he is in the continuous chain of development from the inanimate to the vegetable, from the vegetable to the
animate. The creation of man marked a turning point in the process of
natural evolution. Consciousness, which is present in animals only indis-
tinctly, became totally focussed in man. He was distinguished by a special
mental power whose function differed from that of his other faculties; and by
means of this power he could set himself apart from nature and even attempt
to subdue it, to direct it to serve his needs and draw from it more than it

would have bequeathed him without his intervention. Even so, however, he remained a creature of nature. The fact of his birth, the whole gamut of his faculties, including that of consciousness—all were nature's gifts. His physical and mental qualities were natural, and he thus remained dependent upon nature for his existence, comfort, and development. Thus, his efforts to break away from nature in order to dominate it involved an internal contradiction, for he was in fact seeking to subjugate and exploit the inner source of his own being. In this way, he became alienated from himself.

It seemed to Gordon that human culture reflected an increasingly stronger process of alienation, which had reached its most radical expression in the modern industrialized city. Here, man's break with nature and his exploitation of it reached their peak, as did the corruption and deterioration of human nature. The situation of man in modern culture could thus be described as one of exile, and that of the people of Israel was doubly so. If Zionism wanted to redeem the people of Israel, it had to restore it to a natural way of life, and to propose a comprehensive solution not only to its national problem but also to the problem of mankind. It must be emphasized, however, that Gordon was not offering man a way back. There was no going back in the natural world. Cultural development was essential to man, and his redemption would come about not through a return to a pre-cultural state, but rather by a further development of culture. Until then, man had developed the possibilities inherent in his consciousness in a one-sided, perverted way. From now on, he had to develop the possibilities present in another faculty of his soul, a faculty which Gordon called "chavaya" (immediate experience). This meant that man must make a fundamental change in his goals, in his relations with his fellow man, and so, too, in the way he made use of nature. He had to follow nature and to be responsible for it, rather than merely following his own egotistical interests. If man were to behave in this way he would create a new kind of culture, and thus would arrive at a stage of development that transcended his present form of existence.[5]

These things of course all demand detailed study in their own right. For our purposes, however, they are important in that they form a basis for understanding Gordon's conception of the bond between any people and its land. Gordon assumed the existence of a *natural* bond between people and land, formed by continuous, organic growth. A people is a unified group of persons sharing a natural place of origin, and they are thus molded by the distinctive qualities of the region in which they grow up.[6] The natural world contains complete life-systems which comprehend the full continuity leading from the inanimate through the vegetable and the animal up to man. These systems differ from one another by virtue of the unique conditions prevailing in the areas in which they developed, and these differences can be seen in the attributes of each of the strata they comprised. The homeland can thus be defined as the natural place in which a people developed. That quality which distinguishes its natural scenery, the inanimate objects and the plant and animal life it contains, also mark the men who grew up there—that is to say, peoples are organic units of nature, and they join together to form mankind in the same way that they come together within themselves: organicly; not by obliterating their uniqueness but, rather, by sustaining it. Thus, each people's relationship to its homeland is the natural, primary, and continuous foundation of its existence.

One more presupposition must be added here to complete our sketch of the philosophical basis of Gordon's thought, as it relates to our survey: Gordon saw religion as the functional, substantive relationship of man to the Infinite Source of all being and of his own self. For the Infinite, when conceived as a unity, is God.[7] However, if this relationship is to be functional and substantial, it must be mediated by the things with which man is in direct contact. The Infinite presents itself to each man in the image of his immediate surroundings. It is by his relationship with these surroundings that man expresses his relationship with God. This is the basis of both the unity of all religions and the uniqueness of each. Each person and each people lives their unique relationships with God by way of their particular environments. Thus, conversely, any person's relationship with his people has a religious quality about it. There is no original religion, according to Gordon, which is not national in its essence, and there is no nationality that is not imbued with religion. In other words, Gordon saw the national-religious character of Judaism as a model applicable to other peoples as well, and this model influenced his understanding of the bond that linked each people to its land.

3

Gordon explained the bond between the people of Israel and its land on the basis of the above assumptions. It was a natural tie that could neither be severed nor replaced by another. The people of Israel had grown up organically within the natural environment of the land of Israel, and the impress of this fact was stamped firmly upon it, in terms of both heredity and heritage. A historic tie born of political possession alone could be broken if that possession came to an end. If the people of Israel's link with its land had been no more than historico-political, if it had stemmed only from the fact that at a certain time in the past the people had ruled this territory and established its kingdom there, then it would by now have forgotten the land and assimilated into other peoples. But what was involved here was a natural bond, sunk deeply into the fixed character of the people, and this could never be erased or forgotten. To be sure, individuals and even whole segments of the people might attempt to do so. The suffering of the exile pressured them strongly in this direction, for they were tempted by the opportunity that merging with the surrounding populace offered them to lead a life of affluence. In Gordon's opinion, however, these efforts to assimilate could never entirely succeed, for they forced a perversion of the Jew's own true, original nature.[8] It was no wonder, then, that the assimilating society sensed the alien's strangeness and rejected him.

Paradoxically, moreover, the people's own natural character might show even in the ways in which its members sought to assimilate. Even as they fled, even as they tried to conceal themselves, they revealed their true nature, though it might be distorted on the way. One way or another, they never really forgot the land of Israel; their bond with it always remained. They continued to draw upon their recollections of it and upon what they had created while living there. Their ability to draw upon this heritage was, of course, limited, for their national life had dried up and withered in the course of the exile. It followed from Gordon's assumptions, however, that only a return to the land of Israel could reverse this process of deterioration. The people must renew its direct contact with its own particular natural environment. Just as an uprooted plant can renew its growth only in that soil to which it is suited, so an exiled people can renew itself ony by returning to its natural homeland. We must stress once more that Gordon was not referring to a reconstitution of the people's political framework. He was speaking of living in the land of Israel, and first and foremost of the labor that would enable the people to be sustained by its own soil, with its copious natural produce.

These assumptions were seriously challenged, practically and ideologically, by the opposition of the land's Arab inhabitants to Jewish settlement there. Gordon had personal experience of the violent manifestations of this hostility.[9] How was it to be evaluated, and how was one to respond to it? Did it not question the right of the Jewish people to return to its land, and rightly so? Let us state, first, that Gordon was sensitive to the problem of the rights of the Arab population. They must not be oppressed or deprived of what belonged to them. The creative work generated by a movement of national revival should benefit its participants, but also all those who came in contact with it. Zionism, too, was a creative movement; it had no interest in conquest or in the expulsion of others, and the good things that it would bring about could and must benefit all of the land's inhabitants. However, Gordon's recognition of the rights of the Palestinian Arabs did not, as he saw it, weaken in the slightest the primary, natural right of the people of Israel to its land. To be more precise, the Jews' right derived from a factual bond that had never entirely been sundered. If one examined the problem in light of this *national* tie, it was clear that the people of Israel, and only this people, belonged to this land. It had grown up there, and it bore the mark of the land's natural environment upon its character—unlike the Arabs, whose birthplace as a people lay in another land with different natural traits. The right of the Jews to return from their exile was thus no more than the realization of an existing bond. But what was the practical significance of this statement? Gordon demanded neither international political recognition of this right nor the establishment of a political framework for possessing the land. For him, the people's right to the land of Israel would be fulfilled by going to live there. It was the fact of their living there that would determine the outcome. If the people of Israel went to live in its land, and if it lived there in the full sense of the word—by making its desolate wastes fertile once more, growing crops in abundance, establishing a new society and creating a culture—the land of Israel would belong to it. If it failed in this endeavor, then political recognition or even political possession would never make Israel its land. The land would belong to those who worked it. In fact, then, the two peoples would have to compete for the land of Israel, trying to settle its empty wastes and build up their societies; and, again, it would be positive activity that determined the outcome. That people which concentrated its energy upon destroying what the other had built would ultimately destroy the foundations of its own existence, for it would not live its own life, and it would create nothing. The Jews, therefore, had to defend themselves against attack, but they must not reply with violent attacks of their own. The human rights of the Arabs must be honored, and the Jews must refrain, as far as possible, from injuring or oppressing them. Primarily, however, they must concentrate upon their own activity, whose justice would be proven by its achievements.

4

We said above that the natural bond of the people of Israel with its land found expression through the people's native qualities even while it was in exile. This statement must be clarified. A generalized characterization may already be inferred from the brief quotation cited: "The nations," Gordon wrote, "understand neither this clear perspective nor this luminous unknown in the Jewish soul." This "clear perspective" and "luminous unknown" were qualities of the scenery of the land as it was reflected in the soul of the Jew. These things are explained in greater detail in several places in Gordon's works, but particularly in one essay in which he attempted to capture, as far as possible, the essential uniqueness of Judaism, by juxtaposing it with and distinguishing it from Christianity:

Generally speaking, two main paths, two ways of the soul's being, are to be seen here: In one type of soul, all of the spheres—thought, emotion, the limited will and the sublime will, and each of the particular powers of each of these spheres—are like governments in their own right, like many governments belonging to a single union, that exist alongside one another without having much influence upon one another, to the point that they are, at times, like utterly different streams. One or several of these streams may flow in positively, while others may flow toward negation. On the other hand, there is a kind of soul in which all of the spheres, and all the particular powers of each sphere, are tightly bound to one another, so that it may be likened to a centralized government—wherever the center may be—and thus when one of the spheres becomes dominant all the others are drawn after it, whether positively or toward negation. This, we may say, is the difference between Israel and the European peoples, and it is this that we must understand first of all if we are to grasp the difference between Judaism and Christianity. The basic quality of the people of Israel is unity; it is faithful to itself with all of its being, right to the very end, whether for better or for worse. Emotion, thought, action, the limited will and the sublime will, all the powers of body and soul—all are one unity, whether it tend toward light and goodness, or toward darkness and evil . . . When thought becomes dominant in the Jew his mind rules over all, governing his emotions, his acts, and all of his being as well; when his emotions dominate, they rule over all. It is so, too, when his limited will becomes dominant, or when all the powers of his soul, all of his being, are in a state of perfect harmony—that is to say, when the overall spirit of life, the sublime will, dominates. We may say that in light of this basic quality of the people of Israel, all the more outstanding things that have characterized the life of this people from the day it came into being—and its lesser, more ordinary characteristics as well—become clear.[10]

This quality of unity in the soul of the Jew, especially when it emerges under the dominance of the "sublime will"—that is to say, when the Jew unifies his life in relation to the infinite divine unity of the universe, is the same as that "clear perspective" and the "luminous unknown" of which we spoke above; and it is this that has its origin in the natural environment of the land of Israel. In another place Gordon makes this link explicit:

It seems that here (in the land of Israel) the essence of the sublime efflu-ence, which pours down from the upper worlds into the soul of man, but especially into the soul of the Jew who is the offspring of this natural environment, is entirely other, entirely different from what it is in the lands of exile. In the language of the soul—but only in the language of the soul—I would say that the soul here conceives differently, in different terms, of the infinite itself, truth itself, holiness, beauty, majesty, the es-sence of all of the spheres, and that they come together in different combi-nations. And thus each of the multiple emotions, tendencies, lusts and powers of the soul has a different luminosity here, a different coloring, a different richness, a different profundity, a different clarity and a different mystery from that which it had in those other lands, and all of these together form different combinations. It thus follows as a matter of course that each of the powers active in the soul: will, intelligence, understand-ing, emotion, imagination and the "hidden intelligence" (or the sphere of the unknown) acts together with the others differently here, with a differ-ent character and a different power; and the place occupied by each and the relationships between them all are also different . . .[11]

Only in the land of Israel, then, does the soul of the Jew regain its original character. Only there does that quality of sublime will which is unique to it dominate the soul of the Jew.

We must emphasize that it is a natural quality of which Gordon is speaking and not a particular world view or way of life. It can appear in a variety of ways, subject to external influences or voluntary psychological or spiritual fluctuations. Nevertheless, it is a wellspring of creativity which, although it may appear in various guises, is clearly unique in character. Moreover, a fundamental, realistic understanding of a people's character can be gained only through study of its creative works; and if this character derives from the people's natural environment and is accurately reflected in the qualities of that land, then, clearly, the most impressive, outstanding testimony to the nature of both people and land, and the relationship between them, will be found in those works that the people produced when it dwelt upon its own soil. It may be said that these creative works *are* the link between people and land—that is, they embody the living encounter, as it takes place. It is no wonder, then, that even in the exile these works bore within them the presence of the land of Israel. They *were* the homeland—or rather, they were the mirror held up by the homeland, in which the people could recognize itself even in exile. Gordon was speaking, of course, of the Bible:

Here I sit, as I write these lines, on top of a high mountain, on the tip of a rock. My vision encompasses great distances, and my soul far, far more. All about me are mountains and hills, valleys and ravines, rocks and boulders of every kind, dimension and color, the green of crops and grass, the black of plowed fields, the brown of boulders and rocks, the blue of the mountaintops, shrouded in mist—all this presents itself to my sight by turns. It is a grand and glorious sight. The profound, mighty, luminous features of Galilee are those of a giant, in force and in spirit. And these heavens above, and this delicate silence, all this, all this—are they not within my own soul? But, especially, are they not manifestations of the soul of our people? Brother, be so good as to take up that most faithful album of the scenes of this natural landscape—our beloved Bible. I shall trace a few points in it, and you will see that by doing no more than putting my finger on one of them I shall have touched upon one of the finest, most deeply concealed chords in your soul. Here to my right, not far away, is Mt. Tabor, fair and tall among the mountains, head and shoulders above its brothers, round of face and sincere and soft of feature, it is the family's soldier of valor and its "precious stone." And here to my left, far in the distance, is Mt. Hermon, a proud grandfather, most eminent and lofty, covered in everlasting snow and surrounded by clouds of glory, spreading itself out broadly—it is the prince of mountains. And before me, to the east, are the mountains of Gilead, elevated and mighty, guarding as a rampart the lovely, modest Sea of Galilee and the fertile, pleasant Vale of Genossar, lying like twins, broad and ample as the daughters of kings, at the foot of the mountain upon which I sit. And all that is around me, near and far; all this great family of mountains and hills, large and small, those that hold their heads erect, and those whose heads are bent or lowered, with towns, villages and farms jutting out from among their folds—all these, though we do not know all of their names—do they not speak from within our soul, like feelings we had forgotten, or like sequestered thoughts, great and wonderful, struggling to be born? But lo, these feel-

ings are once more being renewed, these thoughts are steadily coming to
light. Here, to my left, is the settlement of Migdal, lying on the slope of the
hill like a baby in its cradle. And there, strong young people busy themselves in the valley, giving new life to the stones and making the soil bear
its fruit, and who knows what strength they sow there, what heart and
what soul . . . ?[12]

Looking down from his mountaintop over the land of Israel, Gordon saw at
once both the past, still living in memory, and the future that was being born.
Where was the point at which past and future joined? According to Gordon,
it was in the soul that recognized itself in the scenery of the land. But the
soul's recognition of itself in the landscape came about by means of the
Bible. The Bible here functioned as a spiritual lens for perceiving the landscape, or for perceiving the inner nature of the people, which was provided a
visible image by the landscape.

The lengthy citation quoted above is highly important for our understanding of the process by which Gordon's theory of the land of Israel took shape
in his works. It describes the fascinating meeting between his rich landscape
of memories and the tangible presence of the scenery of the land and how
these two direct and define one another, to the point that they actually
become one. We have already seen, in the preceding chapter, how Gordon
struggled to identify with the landscape. In the letter that follows, he tells of
this struggle once more, but now he has accepted and become reconciled
with what he sees:

Not for nothing, however, did I spend those years in Judea. For something
like this happened to me in Judea as well, so that I had already learnt
about it there. The soul of man is strange and wonderful, and at times it
has desires that are odd and difficult to understand. At times, for example,
it longs for the dark, melancholy and chill days of winter, for snow, frost
and ice, for rivers frozen as though covered in glass, for dark blizzards
that cast dread, gloom and silent melancholy over the destiny and future
of man; and it happens, too, that it takes a desire to spread out limitlessly,
to reach out to infinity—it must have space, distances like those of the
great sea, like the heavens above the earth. At that time, the first days
after my arrival in the land of Israel, there arose in me a strange feeling, or
rather, a peculiar admixture of two opposing feelings, which was difficult
for me to explain. On the one hand it was as though I were alarmed or
dismayed by these broad, broad distances, so naked in the glare of the
powerful light that poured down upon them, revealing everything to you
as far as your eyes can see, with a cruel clarity, as though it were saying:
"Nothing is concealed from my eyes!" But on the other hand, just because
my eyes could see so far my glance came up against the mountains opposite, which seemed to fence it in, preventing it from making its way further
and further. In this state, it was not long before my soul began to argue
with me, raising doubts about the virtues of the land of Israel: "This land is
small and narrow; there, beyond the mountains, one almost comes to the
end of it—the bed is too short for a person to stretch himself!" . . . And if
you should ask her, for example, "What does what lies beyond the moun-

tains have to do with you?" she will not answer you, she will neither consent nor obey; she will only fulminate and groan with melancholy, she will not let you rest. But what the mind would not do, life, nature and work did. To the extent that my hands grew accustomed to labor, that my eyes and ears learned to see and hear and my heart to understand what is in it, my soul, too, learned to leap upon the mountains and to skip upon the hills, to rise, to soar—to spread out the expanses it had not known, to embrace all the land round about, the world and all that is in it, and to see itself embraced in the arms of the whole universe.[13]

Life, nature, and work accomplished much. Gordon gradually penetrated the landscape to its very depths, learning to sense it from within. From this description, however, it is already quite apparent that it was not only life, nature and work that brought this about, but also the Bible. Using scriptural language to describe the countryside followed naturally from his sense of belonging, his act of recall, and the way he imbued the landscape with meaning. This, indeed, becomes quite clear from the continuation of the same passage:

> And now, when I arrived in Galilee, I felt almost pressured; my heart was nearly beset with onerous thoughts. But then my soul roused itself and drew courage, and in one leap rose up to the mountains. And here there was space, and how wonderful it was! What a multitude of sights, forms and colors, what richness, and what depth! What a closeness of the soul to the land, to the heavens and all that is in them! Then I recalled that in these parts, in that vale to the south, Elijah of Gilead rose up to heaven in a storm. Yes, it could not have been otherwise. Elijah had to rise up to heaven here, alive, and it had to be in a storm! And then I recalled: "And behold, a ladder was set up on the earth and the top of it reached to heaven." And what is it that we seek? Is it not a place for the ladder?[14]

It is in this context that we must view what Gordon said earlier about the sublime effluence pouring down to the land of Israel and especially into the soul of the Jew, and so arrive at a correct understanding of these ideas. Encountering the scenery of the land of Israel from a Scriptural perspective gave new life to the Bible. The past approached the present, living once more in the depths of the soul, and the landscape thus became imbued with meaning drawn from the depths of the memories it had revived. Is it any wonder that Gordon spoke of the Bible not only, nor even primarily, as a book? Before it is a book the Bible is an internal spiritual experience. Scripture is concealed deep within every Jew, so that he discovers himself as he reads it, always expressing, when he speaks in its words, more than it actually says. This amazing fact is explained, so it would seem, by the direct, unmediated experience of the Bible provided him by the scenery of the land and by the experience of the landscape provided him by the Bible. A few lines that Gordon wrote in connection with the right of the people of Israel to its land will help to demonstrate this, and to close the circle of our discussion of this subject:

We have a deed to the land of Israel, which has never ceased, and shall never cease, to be valid; this is the Bible; and not only the Bible, and not because our right to the land was promised therein, but because it was in the land of Israel that we created the Bible . . . Works like these, the creation of the Bible alone, give us an eternal right to go on creating it . . . However, a right that comes into being by force of the Bible must be claimed by force of the Bible—that is to say, by that sublime rousing of the spirit, by that spiritual and physical devotion, by all those sublime powers that would bear witness to the fact that our ability to create works like these has not ceased to exist within us up to this day.[15]

5

The preceding citation from Gordon's works shows that he understood the people's relationship to the Land of Israel, mediated by the Bible, as being religious in nature, but in the special sense in which he meant this. A typical allusion to the nature of this special interpretation is to be found in the paragraph's opening sentence:

And not because our right to the land was promised therein, but because it was in the land of Israel that we created the Bible . . .

The religious dimension does not come from without; it flows from within—that is to say, in Gordon's view the divine was not external to nature. It was the "concealed intellect" at work in nature, a voluntary, purposeful, beneficial power permeating nature and making it flow to infinity, beyond the limits of any existing achievement. Every new creation demonstrated this divinity, for it brought forth something that had not yet existed and so bore witness to the infinite potential that transcended all existing achievements. A creation like the Bible was an even greater testimony to this potential. It demonstrated the divine by way of the people's creative enterprise in its land. This, then, is the key to a correct understanding of the above citation in its entirety. Gordon does not accept the idea of the divine promise in its literal sense, according to which a supernatural God promised the land to the people. The promise, to him, was what the people created in its land by means of the divine power coursing through it, and its realization lay in the people's continuing thus to reveal the divine, in their continuing the unique, sublime creative work that could be carried out in the land of Israel alone.

These things can fully be understood only in the context of Gordon's overall concept of religion. Religion, as we have said, is each man's relationship to his own infinite source. A person's experience of his own selfhood in relation to the whole universe that surrounds him is religious in nature. It is an individual experience, but it is also more than that. A person's relationship to the infinite source progressively broadens to encompass every sphere of existence. In religious experience, one feels oneself together with the other; he grasps how firmly he is bound to that which lies beyond himself and then gives himself over to it. Neither is this some abstract act of the intellect. A religious experience involves the activity of all of one's physical and spiritual powers: will, thought, imagination, emotion and feeling. These do not operate over against some abstract concept of an infinite universe; rather, they relate to the real presence of specific objects that lead on to one another, spreading out in ever-widening circles that reach beyond the horizon of the direct experience of man.

In other words, the religious relationship must be mediated by the specific, unique substances that present themselves to man in his surrounding, through his family, his community, and his people, and through the unique natural environment of his land. This is the reason for the unrepeatable individuality of every religious experience. It is this same specificity that underlies the uniqueness of every faith that expresses the shared experience of a community of people. The religions are differentiated by the individual experience of each people, through its history and the natural environment of its land. Since the broadest natural and cultural unit of commonality is that of the people, every consolidated religion must be national in character, just as every nationality has its unique religious dimension. And since the unique character of each people is molded by the natural environment of its homeland, every national religion is bound to the land from which it sprang. A people's relationship to its homeland is thus religious in nature insofar as it conceives of its way of relating to the universal infinite by means of its land. This conception, moreover, is expressed in the sacred texts of each and every people.

In sum, Scripture expresses the most sublime, religious aspect of the people of Israel's relationship to its land. This religious dimension is unique, as the individual character of every national religion is unique. Israel's relationship to its land is singular in character, but so are all religious relationships. From the point of view of its relationship to its own, specific way of being, every people is unique.[16] The people of Israel, however, was distinguished by its quality of sublime unity, and since this quality flowed from the natural environment of its land, it would seem that the relationship of the people of Israel to itself and its land was, nevertheless, unique in a special way, which found expression in its aspiration to sanctify every aspect of its national life in the land.

6

The perfect unity of the Divine, the people, and the land, as Gordon saw it, stands out clearly from all of this. In formulating his philosophy of pioneering Zionism, he had taken an ancient conception, one that had been thoroughly expounded in the Kabbalah, and reconstructed it. We must, however, immediately point out the reversal in perspective that gives away Gordon's pioneering, Zionist outlook. Gordon saw the Divine effluence, which, in the kabbalistic view, poured down from the supernal spheres of the spirit into the grim natural world, as welling up from the natural world toward the supernal spheres of spiritual creativity. The land was the primary element; being cut off from it meant detachment from the source of being and of creativity. In order to cleave to the divine, one had to cleave to the land, so as to draw from it the abundance that sustained the people, both physically and spiritually.

The clearest expression of this approach is to be found in Gordon's theory of *avodah,* labor. *Avodah* in the religious sense—the service of God—was the juncture between God and man. By serving God with the intention of his heart, man was able to cleave unto his Creator, and this service, according to the Kabbalah, united all of reality and drew down over it the divine effluence. Gordon used this model in developing his theory of labor.[17] *Avodah* united all of reality; by means of it man attached himself to the Divine and drew the goodly stream down into the world. Gordon was using the word, however, in its original sense—to signify the labor of the farmer in his field or the craftsman in his workshop, physical labor that provided man's primary needs and, with this as its base, all creative work that was done for its own sake—that is, for the sake of broadening the horizons of human life. This kind of labor joined man with nature, so that the powers of both flowed together, strengthening the stream of plenty welling up into the world. This, according to Gordon, was the true way for man to cleave unto the Divine, thus becoming a channel for spreading the stream of life over the world, and a vehicle for its elevation. The Zionist idea, which taught that the Jewish people would be revitalized and redeemed by going back to a life of labor upon its own soil, thus acquired a "cosmic" religious significance in Gordon's thought. Redemption would mean a return to the source of life and creativity in the most comprehensive and basic sense; it would renew the pepole's life by revitalizing that of each and every one of its individual members. This, it would seem, it what he had in mind when he wrote that "a right that comes into being by force of the Bible must be claimed by force of the Bible—that is to say, by that sublime rousing of the spirit, by that spiritual and physical devotion, by all those sublime powers that would bear witness to the fact that our ability to create works like these has not ceased to exist within us up to this day."[18] We must, however, stress over and over that the sublime powers of which Gordon spoke spring from the depths of natural, physical, and spiritual life. In applying this conception to the land of Israel, he meant that the significance of the land was embodied in the land itself, in the quality of the landscape, its particular mountains and valleys, the blue of its skies, the blaze of its sun, its heat and vegetation, and the way life was lived upon its soil. In order to relate to it and to experience its full significance, one had to be there, to feel it in every cell of one's body and with all the powers of one's soul, to work its soil and make it bloom. The kabbalistic system of symbols by which the land was interpreted was thus brought back to its literal meaning and reinterpreted in the opposite direction, in order to make sense of the physical entity itself. Gordon had re-created it in inverse form as a result of his real, powerful contact with the physical substance of the symbols—the physical land.

4

Rav Kook:
A Land of Destiny That Is a Homeland

Rav Kook's ideas carried on the same line of thought that we met with in the works of Judah Halevi and the kabbalists, the Maharal of Prague and Rav Nachman of Bratslav. The particular form this took with Rav Kook, however, came in response to the situation of the Jewish people in the twentieth century. His understanding of the land of Israel, too, drew upon *The Kuzari* and the Zoharic and Lurianic Kabbalah, but it expressed the people's struggle to realize the vision of the return to Zion, and the conflict between his own religious-nationalist viewpoint and that of the Orthodox anti-Zionists on the one hand and the secular Zionists on the other.

The experience of being in the land of Israel, as expressed in Rav Kook's thought, in fact, partook of both these dimensions: the people was returning to its national homeland in the Zionist sense, socially, culturally and politically, but it was also going back to the primal wellspring of sanctity. It was the unity of these two aspects of experience that led Rav Kook to distinguish so radically between the nature of the land of Israel and that of other lands. Neither the kabbalistic works that preceded him, nor even the secular Zionist thinkers, including those who were absolutely opposed to exchanging the land of Israel for any other land, would seem to have drawn so radical a distinction. The line of thought leading from Halevi and the kabbalists to the works of Rav Kook is well expressed in the following citation:

> When the divided world shows itself to man with more power than the supernal world of unity, then materialism overpowers spirituality, and the lusts of the body stand in the forefront of what man does with his life, and the world lies in great darkness. But when the unified world is the more powerfully visible, then man's spiritual desires and his finer aspirations grow stronger, and the world becomes ever more light.
>
> It is *the air of the land of Israel* that makes one wise, that illuminates the soul to enlighten that element which is derived from the world of unity. In the land of Israel, one draws upon the light of Jewish wisdom, upon that quality of spiritual life which is unique to the people of Israel, upon the Jewish world-view and way of life, which are essentially derived from the dominance of the world of unity over the divided world. And it is on this

basis that *idolatry is blotted out,* together with all of the ambitions and the
other phenomena which accompany it.

In the impure lands of the gentiles, the world view of unity is impercep-
tible, and the divided world rules with force; its solipsistic, separated,
divided and alienated world-view dominates all aspects of life, and with all
one's efforts to take a breath of Israel's way and become enlightened to
the mystery of the unified world, the air of the gentile lands holds him
back. The impure soil that is everywhere outside the land of Israel is thus
suffused with the stench of idolatry, and the Jews there are worshippers of
idols in purity. The only way in which we may escape the disgrace of
idolatry is for the Jewish people to gather in the land of Israel, as it is
written, "to give you the land of Canaan, to be your God." (Lev. 25:)38)

The lands of darkness may be capable of sustaining the trivial discussions brought up by the world's divisiveness, but enlightened wisdom is to
be found only in the land of light; *there is no Torah like that of the Land of
Israel.*[1]

This brief citation contains, as we shall see, a precis of Rav Kook's ideas
regarding the unique nature of the land of Israel. In the context of our
discussion, however, we must take special note of the sharp distinction it
makes between the land of Israel and other lands. The difference between
them is existential. The other lands push their inhabitants to lead a materialistic life, into separating the material from the spiritual and, ultimately,
into impurity and idol-worship. The land of Israel, on the other hand, pushes
its inhabitants toward the spiritual life, toward uniting the material and the
spiritual and toward holiness and worship of the true God. This distinction
between the land of Israel and the other lands parallels a like distinction, also
on the qualitative level, between the people of Israel and the other nations.
The other lands are thus essentially antithetical to the character of the Jewish people, and the land of Israel alone is truly suited to it. This land is called
by the name of Israel not only because it is the people's inheritance, but also
because, by its very essence, it is uniquely destined for this people.
Moreover, we must note the fact that Rav Kook believed that being physically present in the land had a direct, immediate effect. Inhaling the air of the
land (and breathing was of particular importance, since in this way the
external environment entered into the body and touched the inner recesses
of one's nature) influenced one's way of being: "it is *the air of the land of
Israel* that makes one wise, that illuminates the soul to enlighten that element which is derived from the world of unity," as the atmosphere of other
lands leads to materialism and spiritual descent. It would thus seem that the
external influence of living elsewhere could never entirely be overcome.
Relative purity could be maintained by means of careful and loving observance of the commandments, but even the faithful were like "worshippers of
idols in purity" if they lived in exile!

As we have noted, we have met with this distinction before, in the Kabbalah. Rav Kook's conclusion, however, is immeasurably more radical than

that of his predecessors; his "renunciation of the exile" in the secular Zionist sense was the more extreme precisely because of its kabbalistic transformation. Jewish existence in exile was fundamentally false and distorted. The situation of exile was absolutely intolerable, for even the inner soul of the Jewish people was defiled by its very presence in the lands of the gentiles. Israel could be saved only by a total return to its own land!

In some of Rav Kook's other essays we find that that exile did, nevertheless, fulfill a historic function. It was not only a punishment for sin; but rather, as such, it must be seen as a necessary descent so that the people could rise from the depths to complete restoration. This idea, too, was drawn from the Lurianic Kabbalah,[2] which spoke of the world being emanated from the Divine Infinite through a series of "falls" into the depths of material existence, from which the process of restoration, which had the nature of "repentance" or "redemption", must begin. This was because it was by means of falling and breaking that all aspects of existence became clearly and distinctly visible. Thus, there was an aspect of progress to the very fall itself. This was particularly true of the history of the people of Israel.[3] When, in the period of the First Temple the people dwelt upon its own soil, the "Divine Idea" was revealed in Israel. It worked on the national level, through the full compass of the people's sacral and governmental institutions. However, it did not yet show itself in the minute details of the lives of individuals. And so idol worship was able to penetrate their lives, and the kingdom was destroyed. In Second Temple days, when sovereign glory and national independence never reached the level of the First Temple period, the process of creating the halakhah as we know it, touching upon all of the daily activities of each individual, was begun, and it was completed in the exile. It was then that what Rav Kook called the "Religious Idea" appeared, a reduction of the "Divine Idea," as a result of the limited scope of expression possible in exilic life. Independent Jewish life was restricted to the realm of ritual, where it broke down into a plethora of rules and minutiae. In the previous citation, we found that even that limited realm was tainted by the materialism of the lands of the gentiles, but from the present essay we learn that this development was, nevertheless, a form of progress. The restriction in scope brought with it a deepening on the individual level. This was the greatest achievement of the halakhah as it took shape in the *Shulkhan Arukh*. However, Rav Kook saw this as a dialectical process with both positive and negative aspects. The price exacted by this progress had been very great, and it was not to be paid any longer, once the exile had fulfilled its function. Now the people of Israel must demonstrate its special quality throughout the full scope of its national life, and this was impossible in exile.

It is at this point that we may appreciate the full dimension with which Rav Kook endowed the Zionist motif of the "renunciation of exile": The essence of exile is restriction. In exile, the people of Israel cannot develop a full national life with its own multi-faceted economy and society, culture and polity. The people of Israel must regain the "full stature" of a living people dwelling upon its own soil. Only then would its unique spirit be revealed, leaving behind the level of the restricted "religious idea" for that of the "Divine Idea", ever broadening outward to infinity. The closing sentence of the citation quoted above clearly expresses this idea: "The lands of darkness may be capable of sustaining the trivial discussions brought up by the world's divisiveness, but enlightened wisdom is to be found only in the land of light; *there is no Torah like that of the land of Israel.*

As we have said, what we have here is a combination of two motifs into a single consistent, radical philosophical unity: the kabbalistic motif of the uniquely holy status of the land of Israel which, in Rav Kook's thought, has become the higher, absolute reason for Zionism's exclusive choice of the land of Israel and none other; and the Zionist aspiration for a national life that was full in every respect: economic, social, cultural and political. In Rav Kook's thought, this aspiration, whose fulfilment was denied the people of Israel while it was in exile, became a necessary, condition for the people's spiritual perfection even in the land of Israel. Without this national scope and these earthbound institutions, the people of Israel could never attain a full spiritual life, for this could not come to full expression in thought or inner feeling alone. It had to be expressed through the full cultural creativity and mode of living characteristic of a people restored to its own soil.

Having concluded the importance of these two motifs, we must examine their development in the thought of Rav Kook. How did he experience the existential uniqueness of the land of Israel, and how was the Zionist normalization of national life there to affect the chosen people's realization of its unique spiritual quality?

2

The key to understanding these two issues and the relationship between them is to be found in an additional distinction, paralleling those he made between the people of Israel and the gentiles and between the land of Israel and the lands of the gentiles, which Rav Kook makes between the Torah of the land of Israel and the Torah of exile. This distinction is already implicit in the concluding sentence quoted a second time above. It is further developed in the following lines:

> The Oral Torah is sustained in secret by heaven, but openly by the land; and so the land of Israel must be restored, and all of the Jewish people must live there in accordance with the prescription laid down for it by Scripture: Temple and kingdom, priesthood and prophets, judges and officers with all their trappings—then shall the Oral Torah come to life with all the splendor of its glory; it will bloom and hoist its banner aloft, and, having risen to its full stature, join together with the Written Torah.

In the exile, these two realms were separated from one another. The Written Torah rose to the heights of sanctity, while the Oral Torah fell to the lowest depths. Even so, the latter is still sustained in secret by the light of the Written Torah, from the accretions of the past, which suffice to keep it alive in a limited way; but it sinks lower and lower every day—until that day breaks, may it come speedily, when the light of life will descend from the treasury of eternal redemption; then the people of Israel will act with valor; it will plant itself anew in its land and prosper amid all the beauty of its biblical order. Then the Oral Torah will spring up anew from its deepest roots. It will rise higher and higher, and the light of the Written Torah will again shine its beams upon it, renewed each day. The two lovers will unite in their chamber, under their canopy. And the light of the soul of the eternal God, which is revealed when the people of Israel is revived and its horn is raised aloft, will shine with the light of the seven days of creation, the light of the sun and the moon shining together, and their light will be direct, penetrating and continuous, from the one to the other, and it will respond to land and people with the full splendor of life: and "the light of the moon shall be as the light of the sun, and the light of the sun shall be sevenfold as the light of the seven days, in the day that the Lord bindeth up the wounds of His people, and healeth the stroke of their wound." (Isaiah 26:30)[4]

The distinction between the Torah of the land of Israel and that of the exile is developed in this passage in the language of kabbalistic symbolism. The Written and the Oral Torahs symbolize two *sefirot* in the Divine emanations, paralleled by the symbols of the light of the sun and that of the moon, which shall both rise together at the time of the redemption.[5] However, these symbols also have an immediate significance to the present life circumstances of the people of Israel. The Oral Torah—and it is this, and not the Written Torah, which serves as the source for legal decisions in everyday life, drew upon the same authority, derived from the revelation of God's presence, that was embodied in the Written Torah, which was given to Israel by God Himself at Sinai. However, the relationship between the Written and Oral Torahs was not apparent in exile. What Rav Kook meant by this, it would seem, is the simple fact that the sages, who studied the Oral Torah and made the legal decisions upon which it was built, did not function as prophets; they did not draw their authority directly from divine revelation, as Moses had done in bringing the word of God directly from Him to the people. The sages simply worked with a continuing tradition of Torah learning, applying it to the people's changing social circumstances. Rav Kook's statement that in the exile the Oral Torah drew upon the Written Torah only in secret, though it drew openly upon the land, would seem to mean this: The sage, as he expanded upon the Torah by learning it and making legal decisions, did so in relation to the physical conditions of his time and place. As these conditions changed and new questions arose, his task was to provide the people with the Torah that they required. Clearly, then, the extent to which the Oral Torah could be expanded depended upon the extent to which it was actually possible, in terms of the prevailing physical conditions, to apply the law to the way of life and the deeds of the people of Israel. If their physical lives were restricted in scope, then the innovations they could make in the Oral Torah would also be limited; and, conversely, if they had a broad scope for living, the innovations they could make would be so much the greater. The unique, primary position occupied by the Torah as it was interpreted in the land of Israel, in contrast to that which it occupied in exile, followed from this. In exile, the people's life was restricted, so that whole branches of the halakhah could never be interpreted and applied there. In the land of Israel, particularly when its "Temple and kingdom, priesthood and prophets, judges and officers with all their trappings" were established there, the laws relevant to all of these functions could be interpreted and applied.

These things are clearly drawn from the same distinction that we noted previously, from a Zionist perspective, between the existential circumstances of the land of Israel and those of the exile; or, to be more precise, this is the halakhic conclusion which Rav Kook drew from this distinction. It is also clear, however, that there is more to the difference between the Torah of the land of Israel and that of exile. Rav Kook also develops his kabbalistic motif in a radical direction. The Torah of the land of Israel will express a higher, more openly apparent level of spiritual authority. It is the Oral Torah, of course, that serves as the source upon which legal decision-making is based in the land of Israel as well, but the relationship between it and the Written Torah will here be open and direct. It would seem no exaggeration to say, as the subsequent portion of the citation implies, that this in itself allows one an experience of redemption; that is to say, it is life in accordance with the halakhah of the land of Israel, with its special status and authority, that will give us a taste of the special flavor of life in the redeemed land. By living in accordance with the Torah of the land of Israel, we experience the existential significance of being in the land.

3

Before examining in greater detail the nature of this experience of being in the land that is brought about by its special Torah, we must appreciate the importance of the very statement that there is a special spiritual significance to being in the land of Israel:

> That conception of the land of Israel, which sees it as no more than a tool to keep the people together, or even for sustaining the Jewish ideal in exile by preserving its character and strengthening the people in their faith, their piety and their constancy in observing the commandments that must be practiced daily in the proper way, is sterile, for this foundation is weak in comparison with the land's towering holiness. The Jewish ideal of the exile will be truly fortified only when it is firmly implanted in the land of Israel, and it is ever the hope of the land of Israel which endows it with all

of its unique characteristics. The anticipation of redemption is the force which keeps exilic Judaism alive, and the Judaism of the land of Israel is salvation itself.[6]

In other words, simply to be in the land of Israel, if one can come to know its inner essence, is already to experience the redemption.

From the following citation, we come closer to understanding this astonishing statement:

> When one distances himself from the secret knowledge, his recognition of the holiness of the land of Israel becomes obscured. When one is alienated from the mystery of God, the supernal qualities of the vale of divine life become trifling matters which do not penetrate the depths of the soul. Then, as a matter of course, the soul of the people and that of the individual will lack their mightier force, and exile will appear attractive in its own character; for a person who apprehends only that surface which is open to view will not feel that he lacks anything fundamental in that he has neither land nor kingdom, nor any of those elements that will pertain to the people once it is restored; and this in itself attests to the want of understanding attributable to this spineless way of thinking. We do not reject any kind of world view or understanding that is founded upon sincerity, feelings of belief and some kind of fear of God; we reject only that aspect which would deny the mysteries and their great influence upon the spirit of the nation. This way of thinking is disastrous, and we must fight against it, with wisdom and understanding, in sanctity and with valor.[7]

According to the "secret knowledge", the mystical theory of the kabbalists, the land of Israel exists on a supernal plane. It symbolizes the *sefirah* of *malkhut*,[8] and this, in and of itself, makes its spiritual significance so much the greater. A person who lives in the land of Israel and is versed in the "secret knowledge" thus experiences this symbol in both the tangible and the abstract realms at one and the same time. His experience is one of closeness to God, that same inner intimacy which will be brought about by the redemption. Does this mean that one can truly experience the land of Israel only if he possesses the unique religious consciousness of the mystic, that this experience has no clear "objective" expression, so that a person who has never felt it in his inner life will never know or understand it? From the above citation, one might indeed think that Rav Kook held such a view, but this would appear to be rather too hasty a conclusion. We must examine the citation in its broader context, and this will bring us back to our discussion of the unique status of the Torah of the land of Israel.

To live in accordance with the Oral Law without an understanding of the "secret knowledge" is, as we learned above, to live a religious life that is right and proper, but hollow. It lacks an inner dimension, and it is their inner dimension that makes the commandments significant. A person who performs the commandments in this way is obeying the law, but he is not expressing himself actively and creatively. And if he does not express himself by way of the commandments his obedience draws him no closer to his commanding God. One's inner, spiritual nature must be roused by the commandments if obedience to them is to be a freely forthcoming act of the human will. True fulfilment of the commandments is founded upon an inner awakening. And it would seem from the preceding discussion that such perfect performance of the commandments cannot occur in exile; it is possible only in the land of Israel. In this we are, indeed, still in the subjective realm of the internal experience of the mystic, but it will now take just one more step for us to make the connection between this and the objective expression we seek, which will appear in the status of the halakhah. In exile, the fact that the connection between the Oral and the Written Law is concealed means not only that a person who accepts the joke of halakhah is not acting upon the authority of direct prophetic revelation, but also that as he moves from the level of spiritual meaning to the level of the actual legal decisions upon which he bases his actions, he is not operating on the basis of halakhah. It is, after all, well known that in exile, too, there are mystics, well aware of the importance of the "secret knowledge", who were much occupied with making kabbalistic interpretations of the mitzvot and carrying them out with "devotion" and "mystical intent", in the sense accorded these terms by the "secret knowledge". Why then did they not, in Rav Kook's opinion, reach the level of holiness abscribed to the land of Israel? His answer would appear to be this: the mystics of the exile were not able to link their actions, on the halakhic level, to their "secret knowledge"; or, in broader, more general terms, in the exile a person operating on the basis on halakhah cannot draw the correction between the legal decisions upon which he acts and the realm of aggadah. These two realms, that of aggadah, of ideas and spiritual vision, and that of halakhah, molding one's behavior in the every day world, stand alongside one another, but the aggadah has no direct involvement in determining the halakhah. In other words, the legal decision which directly shapes one's everyday behavior, and thus determines the objective reality of Jewish life in the exile, is not drawn directly from the realm of the higher meanings of the commandment-symbols. Rather, it flows directly from and in accordance with the rules of formalistic legal deliberation. This is not true, however, of the Torah of the Land of Israel. The reappearance of the Written law within the Oral law, the reemergence of prophetic authority in the legal decision, means that the aggadah, drawing upon the depths of the "secret knowledge," upon the realm of the significance of the commandments, will directly shape legal decision-making and so determine everyday behavior. This means that Jewish life, in its *objective* appearance, is essentially different in the land of Israel than it was in exile, since in the former the halakhah operates on qualitatively different levels of authority and significance than it did in the latter. The special spirituality of the land of Israel is thus to be experienced through the Torah of the land of Israel, which reveals directly that which the

Torah of exile, by its limited dimensions and the gray, earthly formalism of its legal decisions, conceals. It is no wonder, then, that the Jew yearning for redemption at times feels that the exilic halakhah is permeated by the essence of exile, that it seems to him to block off the stream of his life and spiritual creativity which, welling up in his inner soul, can never be fulfilled. There were great souls in the securlar community who were led by this feeling to reject religion entirely.[9] They were mistaken, however, in seeing the Torah of exile as the only authentic version of the Torah. In fact, the only fully authentic Torah is that of the land of Israel, and the reality that is can shape there, and nowhere else, is the only fully authentic Jewish life.

Rav Kook was speaking, first and foremost, of the commandments that can be carried out only in the land of Israel. It is easy to see that the Jew who lives in the land of Israel and can fulfil these (and they constitute quite a large proportion of the body of commandments as a whole) lives a quantitatively fuller and more perfect Jewish life than his fellow in the Diaspora. A look at the following passage, however, will show us that Rev Kook expanded much further upon this theme of the unity between the spiritual/religious and the secular Zionist motifs in modern Jewish thought. The Jewish reality of the land of Israel would be complete only when the commandments that applied to the full scope of the people's national life, restored to all of its relevant institutions, were drawn directly from the realm of their symbolic significance, that of the aggadah, of the "secret knowledge" and of prophecy.

> The essential form of the order of a society organized in accordance with the divine way, the form that is most in keeping with life, stretching it forth from purity and exaltation toward freedom and the concentration of those means by which freedom becomes a truly good gift to man, lies in the system of commandments that depends upon our being in the land; that is, those involved with the Temple and the whole order of the Jewish kingdom and all that attaches to these; and those involved with the unique quality of prophecy, so necessary to the people if it is to fulfill its character. The people continually await the restoration of this quality unto it in luminous form, so as to make it abound once more with all the good that it had in the past and to restore to it the great strength that it will need for the future and for the numerous new things that this will bring about in the world and in human life. The future never ceases to demand of the present that it fulfil its function, and the present is filled with importance insofar as it knows that it is necessary for the future; it does not become insignificant in the face of the future because of this—rather, it is filled with its own character and individuality, and its involvement in man's aspiration for the future and in the exalted status of the latter rejuvenates it and adds to its vital strength.
>
> Thus, the memories stored up in those little things we do in remembrance of the commandments that depend upon our being in the land are full of vitality for us, whether we do these things because of tradition or scribal emendations, because of teachings handed down by our ancient forefathers or because they comprise a remnant of the primary obligation that the Torah requires us to fulfil, according to the various, conflicting

ways in which the practical requirements of the legal wisdom of our people are understood. These things seem all dried up to us now; externally, they appear trivial, but they are full of vitality and importance within. We get around the requirement to keep the seventh year by selling the land to a gentile, and we observe the requirement to give tithes of our produce to the priests and levites by means of a practice involving no great loss to the donor, nor any great profit to him who receives them; and so we make our blessings and separate these portions, and redeem the second tithe that should have been eaten in holiness in that central, sacred and vital city, the place that was chosen by God, the heart of the people's life in every respect—"so shall we render for bullocks the offering of our lips" (Hos. 14:3), substituting an outpouring of words for vital ways of life, for a living social order filled with splendor and beauty, song and melody, strength and delight. But these tiny seeds conceal within them a great power to grow—toward all that for which they long, from within the past in which they are planted—and to send up new shoots in the future. All these patterns are contained within them, and so they act subtly upon the soul that observes them, to kindle the sacred flame of love of the land by means of these small shares of holiness, by means of the divine, religious, national and moral benefit bound up with each of these minor deeds, and so they educate the people in its days of lowliness for the spirit of greatness which they are to take on. The community of Israel and its sons, who are called its builders, have been wise enough to observe these commandments, and not to desist from their active fulfilment both in the lands in which they wandered, as far as this was possible, and in a more significant and widespread form as they somehow make their return to the place where they belong, their own national possession.

The unique splendor, beauty and glory of the commandments that depend upon being in the land, as we, the vanguard that is building up the land of our fathers and creating a stronger, brighter future and hope for the generation to come, fulfill them in the land of Israel, reveals itself to us in the power of the inner longing coursing through our souls to restore our people to its full character in the land of our fathers, with all the points and lines that are its essential nature, that reveal and emphasize that this is our own people in its original, exalted form, body, soul and spirit; and thus we hope to renew our days as of old, as in ancient times. For lo, our people has slept through a very long and difficult exile. For all this time, our national powers have remained swallowed up within us; externally everything has become old and wrinkled, but inwardly the dew of life has continued to flow. Just as the whole range of commandments that must be observed in everyday life went with us into exile and there preserved for us the order of our lives and the mark of our spirit, in accordance with our inner nature, and now has brought us to these first days of the period of our enlightenment to a life of desire for the revival of our people in our own land, so may the commandments that depend upon our being in the land, whose nature was determined to accord with the perfect form of our national life, bring about its exaltation. And the more we study the nature of these commandments that depend upon our being in the land, and the more we see how far away from us they are, how much stronger and healthier the conditions in which we live would have to be for these commandments to be observed, so there will grow within us the desire to keep, with love and devotion, that portion of them which we can fulfil in remembrance of the rest, in remembrance of our sacred past, as a memento of the perfect life into which we shall come when perfect salvation comes to our people upon our soil, so that we shall be redeemed eternally; and as we keep these commandments now, we enrich the soul of our people with a sacred flame which will become a holy fire, filled with vitality, when its time comes.

As we now observe the commandments of *terumah* and tithing, even though we do not have the real foundations upon which these commandments are built, "no priest at his service, and no levite upon his dais", this vision stands before us, and we are filled with an exalted spirit of song, soaring like an eagle, as we see the light of those happy days that await our people upon our blessed soil: here stands the Temple upon its foundation, to the honor and glory of all peoples and kingdoms, and here we joyfully bear the sheaves brought forth by the land of our delight, coming, our spirit filled with true freedom and pure trust, unto threshing-floors and wine-presses filled with grain and wine, our hearts glad over the goodness of this land of delight, and here before us appear the priests, holy men, servants of the Temple of the Lord God of Israel, their hearts filled with love and mercy, their faces drenched with the holy spirit, and we recall all the exaltation of the holy feelings that welled up within us upon seeing their faces when we made our pilgrimages, when we saw them at their service in our Temple, the pinnacle of our glory and the delight of our eyes. How beautiful and pleasant they are to us; and now here is our threshing-floor, filled with God's blessing, the produce brought forth by the land of delight which we have inherited from our forefathers, and some of these people, men of the spirit, are here with us, and we are glad to give them their share joyfully; and, discovering within ourselves an exalted spirit, we rise up together with our donation to the same spiritual height to which these holy men themselves are elevated, and our souls are satisfied with the choicest fruits of heaven. And here are the levites, those good and gentle men, who conquered our hearts with the sweetness of their song in our sacred halls on the festivals, when we made our pilgrimage to see the splendid glory of the Temple of God in Jerusalem, to see the face of the Lord God of Israel. Their noble, exultant faces call to mind their sacred song, and flowing with rivers of spiritual delight, we give them their share—the tithes—with hearts full of gladness and joy. We shall see them again on the mountain of the Lord in the near future, and how shall our hearts swell to see these priests of the Lord and these levites at their holy service and at their wonderful singing. "Happy is the people that is in such a case. Yea, happy is the people whose God is the Lord." (Ps. 144:15)

We long for these ancient, perfect things, and this is a divine yearning, a secret desire, filled with a potent vitality welling up from the source of eternal life: kingdom and Temple, priesthood and prophecy, which stamp their imprint upon every other aspect of our life, in relation to which we have no less to boast of than any other people. A good complement of material strength, human morality, national honor, wealth spread among the whole population and breadth in our lives are demanded of us by this quality of our people's life, and this may be ornamented by the spiritual pearls, more fine and wondrous than any man upon the face of the earth, that are to be found within the soul of our people, to perfect its beauty and add to its inner courage and might, and to its outer glory and splendour. This ideology of ours, of the perfection of our lives, which is so distant and wondrous to us, is also close and real within the fullness of our people's soul, as long as we are not busy with putting it out of our minds and as long as we listen to our inner voice, which draws us on to make room for the memories that keep this vision alive even in its days of lowliness, when "this voice is as of a ghost out of the ground." (Is. 29:4).

The Temple: this is the foundation of that ancient religious cult which shall be ever new, which swore to strike down idolatry with all of its abominations, and provided mankind with a pure and exalted base upon which to erect its spiritual life; from which light and freedom went out to grow and develop in the course of the history of mankind; they become ever weaker as they move further from the source from which they came, but they will again grow strong insofar as they return to the source whence they sprang. A healthy mankind, when it recognizes the splendor of the divine, will remain in its presence as a weaned child with its mother; it will forget its elevation, its light and its might and all of its speculations, and it will know that its natural feeling, which enlightens more than any other kind of wisdom, is precious to it, when it is erected upon the firm foundation of man's psychological nature and adorned with the crown of consciousness, which rises ever higher and higher and will remain ever concealed, making every soul long for it; and it will eternally send forth its beams, to make every being rise up to the heights of its splendor; it will bring the divine beauty and splendor into its soul; man's longing for relationship to God and actual closeness to Him will become overwhelming, and every aspect of thought and morality will shed its light upon this venerable emotion. It is well for mankind to see itself, in one place in all the world, with the innocence of its childhood, the vitality of its youthful strength and the splendid joy of the elevation of its common soul, stamped with the form of this ancient, marvellous people, its grandfather Israel; there shall be no end to the joyous song that will break out over all the world as it awakens to gaze up at this exalted vision of the renewal of the ancient wellspring of divine song, which lies within Israel when it is at the height of its glory. Only a fool or a person with no heart, and the voice of such a one will be indistinguishable at the time when this great light shall come to life, would want to put the flimsy cosmetics of modern culture, riddled with emptiness and superficiality, hate, competition and every kind of sickness and insanity, in place of this surge of ancient, healthy vitality, borne gloriously aloft to the heights of heaven. Rather, all will rejoice at this luminous and natural sight, with all of its ancient innocence; just then will it stream with the rainbow colors of its lights and scatter them over Israel and over a great multitude.[10]

4

The long passage reproduced above incorporates all of the theological assumptions that we have discussed up to now and explains how Rav Kook was able to feel something of the redemptive experience of the land of Israel even upon his arrival there, at a time when the Zionist enterprise was still in its initial stages. The redemption, indeed, had not yet come to pass. The perfect Jewish life of which he spoke, molded by the Torah of the land of Israel, did not yet exist. Even the unique authority that would be accorded the Torah of the land of Israel was as yet no more than a hope. But Rav Kook was able to feel, in the present, that this longed-for reality was very close at hand, and that something of it had already begun to spread abroad in the air of the land. It was like the first rays of light breaking forth on the eastern horizon before sunrise. A person who dwelt in the land of Israel and was participating in its restoration, and living, as far as he could, in accordance with the commandments to which dwelling in and building up the land obliged him, had already begun to enter into the unique reality of the land of Israel—that of the redemption. His visionary future already exerted its influence upon his life in the present. Even having understood this, however, a further question, one vital to understanding Rav Kook's synthesis between the spiritual-religious and the geo-political perceptions of the redemption, remains to be answered: How does the unique experience of physical presence in the land of Israel come to expression in real life? How does the unique nature of the land of Israel express itself in the immediate, tangible dimension of the relationship between man and his environment? Zionism was meant to revitalize the people of Israel, economically, socially and politically. For this purpose it required a land, but if it was precisely *this* land that was required, then it must be because its physical, geographical character had some unique quality.

Moreover, if the people's physical revitalization was to lay the foundation for its spiritual perfection, and this too required the land of Israel, then it would seem that the special flavor of life there ought to be perceptible already in the physical dimension. The emanations of the spiritual must illuminate the matter of the everyday world, as the glow of the candle's flame shines out from within the wax that sustains it as well. It is easy enough to say, in halakhic terms that only in the land of Israel is one bound by the commandments that relate to tilling the soil or to the worship of God in His Temple, or that only in the land of Israel, in a time when the Temple stands upon its mount, does the people's highest court enjoy full authority. All of this, of course, is true, but its significance is no more than formal and legal, and to Rav Kook's way of thinking it did not suffice. The land must have some special, essential quality, for why else would the halakhah declare that only there could all these reforms in the people's life come about? Must there not be something in the land's very nature, in its material reality, that would explain this? A person who desired the people's physical restoration, who wished to live like all other peoples in its own homeland, but still in accordance with its own unique character, must answer this question.

We must note, first of all, that a thinker like Rav Kook, who saw the world around him as a unity, could not agree to separating the halakhic vessel from the reality to which it gave shape. It was only by means of the halakhah of the land of Israel that the land's essential character came to light, as is clear from the long passage quoted above. Thus, it might well be that a person who lived in the land but did not keep the commandments would not sense its unique quality; moreover, a person who did keep the commandments but did not see the coming redemption, or keep, in deed or intent the commandment to dwell in the land and build it into a homeland for the people—he, too, might not perceive this unique quality. It is the people's active anticipation of the realization of its prophetic vision that shines through it like the flame glowing from within the candle's waxy stem, so that one who did not participate in this expectation would find that the unique flavor of the land's physical character, too, was concealed from his senses. And if, nevertheless, there was some worth to living in the land even without keeping the commandments, especially if one worked toward its restoration, how much more was this true of those who both kept the commandments and took part in rebuilding the land. For them, the land had a different quality; there was an aspect of spirituality even to its physical dimension, and it was this quality which, in fact, constituted the bridge between the symbol and its meaning. This was not merely a matter of rational understanding; it was a sensual, emotional experience. Clearly, one could never fully convey the nature of this quality, but only testify to its existence; its true flavor could be gathered only through immediate experience:

> We are commanded to bite deeply into the delightful sweetness of the land of Israel's glorious, invigorating holiness. "That ye may suck, and be satisfied with the breast of her consolations; that ye may drink deeply with delight of the abundance of her glory." (Is. 66:11) And we must announce to the entire world, to those who languish pitifully in dark exile, that the channel through which course the full life, the abundant light and the pleasant holiness of our lovely land has begun to open up. "The flowers appear on the earth; the time of singing is come, and the voice of the turtledove is heard in our land." (Song of Songs 2:) Our pleasant land seeks out her children; she is spreading out her arms to them in love. With her love, she covereth all transgressions (Prov. 10:12). Come back, come back, you cast-away, dispersed children, to your mother's bosom. Remember once more the God of life who fathered you, remember the pleasant sweetness of the power of His love, as it was in the home of our mother and in her chamber; now does He begin to reveal it to us. And while, with the onset of this revelation, we may see only fragile beams of light, their radiance will burst forth very soon over the full breadth of our land; God is with us.[11]

This citation opens with a description of how one may tangibly perceive the holiness of the land. From this feeling, spreading sensually like the taste of a sweet fruit, Rav Kook passes spontaneously into a description of the land as a loving mother. For him, this is no mere metaphor. The face of the land, its physical image, is that of a mother. A sympathetic heart beats within her. A Jew returning to the land feels, by his physical contact with it, her loving embrace. In the flavor of its crops and its waters, he senses her consolations, which are directed exclusively toward him. This sense that in the physical contact between man and land their inner souls are responding to one another—this only the land of Israel can give to the Jew, and this sense alone is a sufficient foundation for the true revival, both physical and spiritual, of the people's national life.

5

On this point, Rav Kook's conception of the land of Israel comes close to that of A. D. Gordon. This proximity shows itself, too, in their views on the people of Israel and how it may be redeemed. They both see an inner compatibility between the people and its land, and both feel that only there can the people live a full Jewish life. Both lay hold of the physical foundation of the land in order to discover the spiritual significance it bears within it. They felt that nationalism, working itself out upon a specific piece of land, was vital to the development of a full, healthy spiritual life. The land of Israel thus became, for both of them, a bridge between the people's physical and its spiritual revival. Their very proximity, however, lays bare the disparity that propelled them in opposing directions as they took their respective parts in the effort to realize the Zionist vision. Gordon's conception began with the people's natural, physical foundation, working toward a perfect spiritual life that was to be sustained by its source, which was, for him, nature. Rav Kook's conception begins with the people's spiritual foundation, and he works toward the realization of that spirit in the formulation of a physical life ever drawing upon its source, which was, for him, the Divine Infinite as revealed in the Torah.

What separates Rav Kook from A. D. Gordon in relation to the way they understood the experience of the land of Israel can be seen quite clearly in the way each understood the concept of *avodah,* of service or work. Both saw *avodah* as facilitating the Jew's entrance into the unique reality of the land of Israel, and it may be said of both that this concept was central to their ideas. The way one really entered into the reality of the land of Israel was by performing the commandments that could be fulfilled there alone, and it was the performance of these commandments that constituted *avodah.* But when A. D. Gordon said "work", he was speaking, at least initially, of working the soil, of dwelling in the land in the physical sense. By working the soil, one could commune with the natural environment of the land. As one brought forth its streams of produce, this material plenty came to underlie an abundant flow of spiritual creativity. To Gordon, this kind of "work," in and of itself, constituted divine service. When Rav Kook spoke of "divine service," however, he meant the commandments that were ordained by the Torah. To be sure, dwelling in the land of Israel was also the fulfillment of a commandment, and to perform all the commandments that it involved was to take part in divine service. But this was because they were commandments to start with, and it was as such that they then went on to reveal what was unique about the land's natural environment . . .

Zionism was thus the common thread running through these two conceptions, paralleling and reflecting each other as they flowed in contrary directions. The visionary and practical interpretations that each gave to their shared endeavor to revitalize the Jewish people in the land of Israel led the one to strive for a cooperative workers' society, and the other to seek the establishment of a Torah state. It is no wonder, then, that the tension between these opposing factors grew progressively greater in the ideas of those who followed them, the secular Zionists on the one hand and the religious Zionists on the other. But neither could let go of the common geographical, settlement-political thread which constituted, for both, a defining element not only in their proposals on the practical level, but also for their experiences and their ideologies. The two had need of each other, both theoretically and practically. This fact lies at the root of the dialectical understanding of the land of Israel to be found in the body of ideas that has accompanied the Zionist enterprise to this day.

5

The Right of the People of Israel to Its Land

In concluding this part of our discussion, we must examine a moral and political issue which has plagued the Zionist endeavor with increasing insistence over the course of its realization: what right, morally speaking, does the people of Israel have to return to its land after an exile lasting hundreds of years? Is it not, in so doing, plundering those who have in the meantime made the land of Israel their home? From the perspective of exile, this question did not appear to require serious discussion. From there, as we have seen, debate within the movement centered around the question of why it should cling stubbornly to the land of Israel and reject all offers of alternative territories. The territorialists did, indeed, submit the fact that the land of Israel was not entirely vacant and open for Jewish settlement as a supporting argument. In this context, however, it was less an ethical problem than a practical obstacle. The adherents of Hibbat Zion and of early Zionism generally were of the impression that the land of Israel was open to a national settlement movement and lay waiting for the return of its sons.

What about the existing Arab population? First of all, it was few in number and took up no more than a small part of the area of the land and, secondly, it did not define itself as a separate people that considered the land of Israel to be its national home. Moreover, the early Zionists supposed that the Arab population, whether Moslem or Christian, must, on the basis of its religion, recognize the bond between the people of Israel and its land. Since the Arabs, too, were Semites—and so, in a way, "relatives" of the Jews— they would give the returning Jews a brotherly welcome; moreover, the Jewish settlement movement would be only to their advantage, since it would bring them the blessings of Western civilization.[1]

These suppositions remained prevalent even after the violent opposition of a portion of the Arab population to Zionism had made itself felt. The Zionist leadership claimed, not without foundation, that this opposition did not embrace the majority of the people, and that it was not backed by a national movement resembling those of Europe in political and sociological terms. The violence was a product of the negative, ulterior motives of a thin crust of the population which was inciting the Arab masses in order to exploit them for its own benefit. On the contrary, the true interest of the Arab peasants and laborers lay in supporting Zionism, which was developing the country's economy and bringing about progress on the societal level. In any case, the Jews' movement to settle in the land of Israel was being carried out in ways that were both legal and ethical. It did not infringe upon the human rights of the Arabs, and it brought them, from the very beginning, a good deal of material benefit.[2] Nevertheless, Zionism could not ignore the political, nationalist nature of the dispute indefinitely, and in any case, it was viewed as such by the mandatory authorities and by the other peoples involved. The Zionist movement was now required to defend its rights before international institutions. And as the struggle gradually grew more heated and claimed more and more victims, it turned into an internal question as well, and a serious controversy within the Zionist movement grew up around it. The practical solutions that were proposed had to be supported by certain ethical, legal, and political assumptions, and these had to be developed and defended. Thus, a fairly broad literature came into being around this subject, and it is relevant to our discussion of the image and significance of the land of Israel as a homeland for the Jewish people. We must recall, too, that this question was of great importance in shaping the nationalist/Zionist consciousness of the generation that grew up in the land of Israel. This generation's own experience of the realization of Zionism was increasingly pervaded by the violent struggle that the Jews had to wage, against the Arabs on the one hand and the British on the other, over the fulfillment of their national right to the land. Its view of the land was thus increasingly colored by this struggle, which ever and again raised the question of the Jewish right for public debate.

2

This kind of question is generally answered simply by affirming the existing bond between the people and its land. If it has been answered in several different ways, then, this is because the various streams within Zionism differ from one another in their understanding of this bond, and each has defended the people's right in terms drawn from its own comprehensive vision.

Religious Zionism's response was framed in terms of the Divine promise and the covenant. The land of Israel was destined for the Jewish people by the will of God. The Torah testifies to this explicitly, promising that the land's predestination for the people of Israel shall remain eternally valid. Can other peoples understand and accept this kind of claim? The Religious Zionist thinkers would appear to answer in the affirmative. Christianity and Islam, the faiths of the peoples who govern the fate of the land of Israel, hold the Jewish Torah sacred and see it as a revelation of the divine word. The fact that the land of Israel is holy to them as well only confirms that they hold the Jewish Torah to be true, and if they accept its attestation to the land's holiness, then they must also accept its attestation to the bond between land and people. Moreover, the fate of the land parallels that of the people. The land was laid waste when its people went into exile, and so it remained. For hundreds of years no people had succeeded in taking national possession of it and freeing it from its desolation. On the contrary, its deterioration grew ever more severe. Only with the onset of the new wave of Jewish settlement did the land begin to rise up out of its desolation and reveal its excellent qualities. This was conclusive evidence that the land was destined for the people of Israel and had awaited only its return. All things considered, the people could, on the basis of their religious bond with the land, claim a right to it that was eternal and absolute.[3]

This is a very simple answer. Therein lies its power, but also its weakness, for it leans towards oversimplification. Does the divine promise really cancel out the human and ethical problem? Or, alternatively, does it really provide an answer to it? We must, indeed, stress that religious Zionist thought was no different from the ideologies of secular Zionism in its emphasis that the return to Zion must be carried out in peaceful ways, on the basis of international agreement and the legal purchase of properties. Moreover, it opposed any infringement of the moral rights of the Arabs. However, the possibility that any other national claim could stand before the Jewish people's right to its land appears totally absurd from this perspective. The usual legal, political and moral categories are simply irrelevant where the bond between the chosen people and the holy land is concerned.

3

The answers that sprang from within the bounds of secular Zionist thought were, naturally, more complicated and fraught with tension. On the one hand, they had to rest upon religious underpinnings, for the historic bond of the people to its land had for generations been religious in character. On the other hand, they had, by their very nature, to refer to the legal and political categories accepted in contemporary international relations. Secular Zionism's aspiration, after all, was to make the land of Israel a national home in the secular sense, and to bring the people of Israel into the modern "family of nations." The tension between these two elements is, indeed, especially striking in the ideas of several thinkers who would not give up the values of religion as they shaped their worldviews, even though they had left religious orthodoxy behind in favor of a more humanistic perspective. Thus, Gordon's hypothesis that there is an essential, natural bond between the people of Israel and its land was in fact a reformulation of this religious understanding. The people's right, in his view, grew out of this same existential, organic connection. A people must not be separated from the land in which it grew up, just as a tree must not be parted from the soil in which it is rooted. The people of Israel was the natural fruit of the land. Not so the Arabs; their habitation of the land of Israel was neither essential nor natural but coincidental. Their natural homeland lay in Arabia. The right of the Arabs to the land of Israel thus bore no comparison with that of the Jews. The Arabs' right had come into being by means of their conquest, while that of the Jews was natural and organic. In so saying, Gordon was not, indeed, questioning the personal right of the Arab peasant to dwell upon the land that he had received from his forefathers. He saw this, however, as a private, human right, and not as a national one. Only the Jewish people had a national, natural right to the land of Israel.

We must note here that Gordon's conception of the "national right" of the Jews had no political overtones. He was, after all, opposed to political government of any form. The heart of the matter, to him, was the question of which people would *live* in the land of Israel. In other words, he was asking which people would prove capable, on the national level, of being materially and spiritually productive there, and not which people would rule the land. And if the question was one of how the people was to live, then so must be the answer, which would come in the form of actual deeds, of creativity. The people that would strike its roots deepest in this soil and bring forth the most bread from it, that would establish a thriving society and create a culture of its own—that people would be the one to call Israel its home. It was a rivalry of this kind, played out in peace and creativity, that would determine the struggle's outcome. The Jews must not, therefore, be dismayed by the violent deeds of the Arabs, nor must they respond to them with violence on their own part. They must defend themselves, refrain from any acts of injustice and pursue their creative work. In the long run, the national conscience would test the inner justice of the Zionist cause by the moral purity with which it was carried out, with regard, among other things, to its relations with the rival people. This, too, would be a factor in shaping the image of the homeland.[4]

In Martin Buber's theory of Zionism, which in several ways is close to that of Gordon, a further religious and spiritual dimension was added to the discussion. In Buber's opinion the bond between the Jews and the land of Israel cannot be compared with that of other peoples with their respective lands. The unresolved situation existing between the people of Israel and its land is extraordinary and unrepeatable, and only by considering it from the perspective of its uniqueness may we judge it rightly. Buber was speaking not only of the special fate of the people of Israel, which had preserved itself and its bond with the land despite centuries of exile, but also of the essential uniqueness this people had about it, which explained how this unusual history had come to pass. The power that had kept the people of Israel in existence in the circumstances of its exile was the universal role for which it was destined as a nation, and it was this that had preserved its tie with the land of Israel. Other peoples might have formed themselves upon their ancestral soil, but they had distintegrated once they were parted from it. For the people of Israel, however, the soil from which it sprang was not merely a land of national origin, but rather a land of destiny; there alone could it fulfill its national mission. It was this, in Buber's opinion, that made Zionism necessary, but the latter must define its purpose in accordance with this universal destiny. If it did so, it would thus justify its claim to Zion; but if it did not, if it laid claim to the land of Israel in the same way that other peoples "claimed" the lands in which they lived, it would not be justified, for the condition upon which the claims of the other peoples rested, the fact that they actually did live in their lands, did not exist in this case. In other words, the Jews' universal ethical-religious mission, which has meaning for all peoples, is the source of the validity of Zionism's claim to the land of Israel. It is a matter of relevance to all of humankind, and not only to the Jewish national interest. The return to Zion constitutes the rectification of a historic injustice, but at the same time it is a condition for and symbol of the redemption of all of mankind. All this would be true, of course, only if Zionism actually realized a social and moral vision that transcended the solution of its own, individual national problem.[5]

It is a matter of course that Buber's conception would not have the people of Israel take possession of its land in the same way that another people might. Neither conquest nor seizure of political authority nor, assuredly, the dispossession of another people would befit it. The Jews' return to their homeland, carried out for the sake of realizing their universal mission, would stand or fall by the moral purity with which they accomplished it. For this reason, Buber concluded that Zionism must recognize not only the personal rights of the land's Arab inhabitants, but also the national rights of the Arab people to the land. This did not, of course, mean that the Jews must forego their own right, but that each side must retrain itself and make concessions to the other so that both might have the minimum they needed to maintain themselves as free peoples. Two peoples would live in the land of Israel, and both would see it as their home; and it was precisely in this way that the universal vision of Zionism would meet its test.[6]

4

Gordon's and Buber's ideas were outstanding in the history of Zionist thought, but they represented the views of individuals. The outlook that came to be accepted by the various streams of secular Zionism (and we must stress that sharing this same basis did not stop them from reaching different and even opposing political conclusions) rested upon their conception of the land of Israel as providing the foundation for a secular national culture. Their affirmation of the people's historic and cultural bond with the land was expressed in their claim to a historic and cultural right to it, and thus, indeed, was coined their slogan that the Jews had a "historic right" to the land of Israel.[7]

What, then, is the nature of the historic right of a people to its land? Let us note once more that secular Zionism's point of departure was its aspiration to "normalize" the people of Israel. Like all other peoples, it must buttress its freedom by possessing its own land. If this be the case, then, counter to the orthodox religious conception and to that of Martin Buber, the discussion of its right must be framed precisely in those legal and ethical categories that would be used in considering the right of any other people to its land—despite the fact that the circumstances of the Jewish people were extraordinary. The most basic axiom, then, was that every people had a right to exist and to be independent, and since national possession of a tract of land was necessary for free existence, each people had a right to live in its own homeland. The people of Israel was no exception to this rule, even though it had been excluded from its application for many generations. It asked for itself no more than what was considered the natural right of all peoples, but it was justified in insisting that it receive no less. The fact that even in modern times it had found no rest in the lands wherein it dwelt meant that the other peoples bore a weighty moral obligation towards it. It thus had a right, in general terms, to demand its own homeland. But what gave it the right to demand precisely the land of Israel, and no other? If we examine this matter systematically, we must conclude, first, that this question would have arisen sooner or later in connection with *any* land that the Jewish people sought to make its national possession. There simply are no countries in the world that are both suitable for colonization and completely empty of inhabitants. But the Jews required the land of Israel because it was their historic homeland, and their consciousness of this bond had given them a consciousness of their right to it as well. Secular Zionism did, indeed, base its discussion upon a sense that the people's national bond with the land was coterminous with its national right. In so doing, it was applying an extremely common argument for a people's possession of its land to the quite uncommon circumstances of the people of Israel.

A particular land is always ascribed to a particular nation after the fact. The people has a right of possession to that land in which it has already dwelt for many generations. The fact that it dwells there is precisely what creates its right. Being in a certain place and creating a national culture there are what enable the people to possess its land. When a people actually does dwell continuously upon its own soil, it usually would not occur to anyone to question its right to that land. That right is a fact, a historic fact. Any people's claim to have a national right to a particular land is thus historic, in the sense that its members must say that they have a right to live there because they and their forefathers have always lived there. What Zionism did was to make the same claim for the Jewish people: it had a right to the land of Israel because its bond with this land had remained unbroken for generations. It was by force of this continuous relationship with the land that it had remained a people.

We must not err, then, by thinking that the Jewish people's claim that it had a historic right to its land rested upon the fact that its forefathers had dwelt there in the distant past. It was based upon their statement that the bond between this people and its land had never been disrupted. Even if the people had perforce lived for generations in exile and its land had been conquered by others, it had never relinquished its desire and hope to return there and wrest it from foreign domination. The Jews had never accorded this foreign domination legitimacy, even though it had gone on for so long, and they had never considered exile a natural way of life for them. Their unending protest against the conquest of the land and their efforts to maintain a Jewish presence there confirmed that their right of possession had never been disrupted or replaced by legitimate possession by any other people. Of course, this was evidently an extraordinary situation nevertheless. In general, as we have said, it is because a people has dwelt continuously in its land that its right of possession is never in doubt. The people of Israel was exiled from its land, and the fact that the land had not remained empty of inhabitants in the meantime could not be ignored. While the right of other peoples might be taken as a matter of course, that of the Jews, at any rate, required explanation. How had their historic right continued to exist despite the fact that they had been so far away for so long, and why should the new, foreign population that had sprung up in the land not be recognized as having a national right of possession of its own?

Part of the answer is already apparent from what we said above: the people of Israel had left its land under duress and then had been unable to return. It had not relinquished its right, and a right of possession, as long as it has not been surrendered in despair, ever remains in force. The fact that a Jewish community, however small and impoverished it might have been, had remained in the land of Israel whenever even the most minimal conditions for its subsistence had existed expressed the people's continuing refusal to submit to the conquest and surrender its right. Moreover, no other separate national entity based on this land alone had come into being in the land of Israel. That is to say, foreign conquest had not turned into the establishment of a new nation. The Arabs who lived in the land belonged, in terms of their national affiliation, to the greater Arab people, for whom the land of Israel was but one of many conquests. Under its domination, the land of Israel did not even have a separate political status; it was merely a province within a greater mass of conquered land. The Arab population that had settled there, too, was extremely small and mean. It never produced anything of note on the demographic, economic, social or cultural and spiritual level. On the contrary, the land of Israel lay desolate under its rules. As the generations passed, its ruin only grew ever more complete. It regressed from an agricultural point of view; its arable foundation degenerated, its soil was laid waste and its population dwindled. Furthermore, the Arabs who lived in the land of Israel never demanded national self-definition before the Zionist settlement program was begun. Their claim arose only after and in response to the Jewish settlement movement, and their motives in raising it were negative. That is to say, the movement representing itself as laying claim to a Palestinian Arab nationality is younger than Zionism, and its driving force is not any positive aspiration to establish itself as a nation, but rather a negative impulse to thwart Zionism. The fact that it does nothing on behalf of the lower classes of the Arab population bears witness to this. All of its activity is centered around its violent efforts to destroy the positive achievements of the Jewish settlement movement.

Thus, the national right of possession of the Jewish people was not nullified by the exile, and the foreign conquest created no rival right of possession. But does the return of the Jews to their land not, nevertheless, involve an injustice to the exsting Arab population? Several answers to this question have been submitted. Some completely deny that the Jewish settlement movement involves any kind of injustice. On the contrary, Zionism has benefited the interests of the Arab population and, in any case, there is plenty of room in the land of Israel for millions of Jews to be absorbed without any detriment to the rights of the Arabs. Others would admit that although this may be true, the Jewish settlement movement does limit the ability of the Arab population to express itself in national terms. Although the latter may not have defined itself as a separate people in the distant past, it ought not in principle to be denied the right to do so now. Even so, however, it must be recalled that Arab nationalism has elsewhere come to full expression in the form of several large states, while the Jewish people has but the one land of Israel. It is just, therefore, in demanding this limitation of the Arabs' national right, for its own right antedates theirs historically and outweighs it morally.[8]

The following points summarize the argument of these secular Zionists: (1) the historic right of the Jews to their land, based, like the right of any other people to its land, upon the continuity of their bond with it, precedes and outweighs the claims of any other people purporting to hold a rival right to the same land; (2) Zionism involves no injustice to any other people or populace. The ways in which it has been realized are ethical and legal and based upon a just national demand. If it limits the Arabs' potential claim to a rival right, it does so with justice; (3) Zionism has a right to the moral and political support of the other nations of the world, because it aims to rectify a historic wrong committed by these peoples against the Jews. As one strives to realize the Zionist goal, he is supporting the cause of justice in international relations.

Despite the recourse these responses have to the relative categories of international morality and justice, instead of the absolute categories put forward by the religious Zionists, the conclusions cited above reflect an unwavering certainty. This is, indeed, characteristic of all the various streams within the Zionist movement, including those that have sought compromise even to the extent of recognizing a national right on the part of the Arab population. The use of humanistic, ethical arguments does, indeed, presuppose a willingness at the outset to listen to the claims of the other side; it does not automatically foreclose the possibility of recognizing the relative justice of such claims. The various factions were thus able to arrive at several different and even opposing political solutions on the basis of this same conception of the historic right of the Jews to the land. Some cling to an absolute, uncompromising demand that the whole land of Israel, on both sides of the Jordan, be recognized as the exclusive homeland of the Jewish people.[9] Others were prepared to come to terms with the Arab national movement, either by erecting a binational state[10] or by partitioning the land.[11] The differences between these political solutions stemmed from various practical and moral considerations which were unrelated to the arguments by which their adherents justified the Jews' historic right to their land, and there is, therefore, no need for us to go into them in detail. It may be said that where it came to the validity and justice of this historic right, the various streams within the secular Zionist movement were in full agreement.

5

In concluding this discussion, let us examine the relationships among the three responses to the challenge of Arab nationalism: that of religious Zionism, that represented by the views of Gordon and Buber, and that of secular Zionism. The differences clearly stem from qualitative differences in their respective worldviews. However, the contrasts seem asymmetrical. Gordon and Buber, for example, could accept all the claims of the secularists, and on that basis arrive at practical conclusions which appeared no different from those of the latter. However, they added a further argument, a moral and spiritual one, to the secularists' claim to a historic right to the land, one which the latter could not support from the perspective of their worldview and even, at times, found repelling. They would have no more of the Jewish boast of a universal mission; their whole desire was for the people of Israel finally to look after itself and further its own national interest like any other people. For thinkers like Gordon and Buber, however, it was precisely this universal spiritual and moral vision that was the soul of the Zionist endeavor. When they wanted to defend their people's right to resettle in its land, they did so by affirming the moral value, in terms of their own vision, of what they were doing. It was because of this moral value that the Jews had a right to return to their land, and it was this, too, that should determine the way they acted towards the Arab population.

More or less the same thing can be said of the relationship between those who held these latter two views and the adherents of the orthodox religious outlook. Here, too, we are faced with a contrast which appears, at the outset, to work in one direction only. The religious Zionists did not reject the claims of those who supported the other two views; they simply had no need of them. Their own argument appeared to them to have absolute validity. Why, then, should they supplement the absolute with the merely relative? It was the adherents of the other views who could not agree to this absolute claim. Or, to be more precise, only the secularists actually rejected it outright, since the concept of a "divine promise" had no meaning for them; those who held the second view did partially accept it, but they interpreted it differently, in a way that sat better with their humanist-secularist worldview. What was really at issue, then, was how the principal content of the Jewish religion was to be understood and, again, the essential disagreement between these views did not necessarily express itself in differing political conclusions as to how the Jewish settlers were to relate to the Arabs. Even the Orthodox could still, from their standpoint, come out in favor of reasonable political compromise.[12] The essential differences between these factions related to the way of life the Jews were to create in the land of Israel, and to the network of relationships they would develop with the Arabs upon this foundation.

If we now examine these arguments to determine their viability in debate with the opponents of Zionism, we shall find that the secularist outlook was the most convincing. The reason why is simple: the secularists used the same terminology used by other modern national movements. Any possibility of achieving mutual understanding between the national movement of the Jews and that of other peoples had to be founded upon a secular ideological system that broke out of the closed circle of religious conflict among Judaism, Christianity and Islam. In other words, Zionism is the more understandable and acceptable to other peoples insofar as its demands center around those conditions and frameworks with which secular national movements normally are concerned, and insofar as it attempts to explain even what is extraordinary about the Jewish people and its fate in the terms used by modern, secular nationalism. It was, indeed, the secularists who succeeded in responding directly to the arguments raised by the opponents of Zionism. Even if they did not succeed in persuading the other side, the replies they submitted were at least framed in the same terms as their opponents' challenge, and so could constitute their part of a dialogue.

Those who held the second view were also able to elicit a positive echo within an elite circle of humanist religious intellectuals, who, though they belonged to rival faiths, held religious opinions which were far from dogmatic. But the proponents of the orthodox outlook, though they may have won their antagonists' respect for the personal authenticity of their beliefs, never even began to confront the rival claims. They had no place in the dialogue that was so essential to Zionism as it struggled to bring the Jewish people back into the family of nations and rescue it from its isolation.

Secular Zionism was the strongest of the three in debating with the movement's secular opponents, then, precisely because it had internalized the nationalistic ideals of modern secular culture and spoke in the latter's own terms. Its weakness, however, showed itself internally, in the educational realm. Its claims that the Jewish people had a historic right to its land was based on a bond that had for generations been sustained by religious symbols. The Israel to which the people had felt itself linked for all those generations was its divinely predestined land, sanctified by the holiness of the commandments. To be sure, this detracted not a whit from the secular claim to a historic right to the land. The religious bond of the Jews to the land of Israel was, in and of itself, national in character. It was thus only right and proper for the Zionist movement to base the arguments that it put before the various international forums upon the fact that the Jewish people had maintained a continuous national relationship with its land. Internally, however, this argument gave rise to a different problem: could this bond be maintained even without relating to the religious symbols that had expressed it in the past? As the people renewed its ties with the land by means of the settlement movement, without recourse to the sanctity of the commandments, would it still be the same Israel to which previous generations had seen themselves bound? Would the people still be the same people, and the land the same land? This was not a question of right, but rather of the bond from which that right was derived or, to put it another way, of the degree to which the Jews maintained the devotion and loyalty by which a people affirms its moral claims on the factual level.

It would appear no coincidence that the secularists tended more and more to emphasize the actual existence of Zionist Jewish settlements in the land in their polemic statements. The arguments based upon the past, important as they were, were no more than prologue. They were also confirmed practically and concretely by the new facts being created in the present. Zionism could point to some impressive achievements. It could claim quite early that it had done more for the land of Israel in a few decades than had the Arabs in the hundreds of years in which they had dwelt and ruled there. Before the founding of the state, when the Jews were still a minority of the population, they could not, indeed, support their demand for the creation of a dominant Jewish majority there without emphasizing the convincing testimony of the past in their arguments. Even then, however, it was the success of the settlement movement in redeeming the land from its desolation and increasing its ability to absorb new settlers that was seen as providing decisive evidence of the seriousness of the Zionist claims and their superiority over those of the Arab nationalists. Zionism had stamped a lasting imprint upon the physical appearance of the land. Its presence there had persuasive power. It was only natural that the secularists should have increasingly shifted their emphasis from past to present as these achievements become the more impressive. This, too, was an expression of their effort to "normalize" the people; in resting their claims upon their actual presence in the homeland they were like all the other peoples who had lived for generations in their own lands. The trouble with this argument is that the actual presence of these other peoples in their lands also embodies the historical dimension of their national lives; and for this reason, too, they usually do not need to confront a total denial of their right to live there. But the Jewish community in the land of Israel did not embody the historical dimension of the Jewish people's national life in the same way, and it *was* faced with a total denial of its right to live in the land. The inner certainty and will power with which this community affirmed its presence there was thus of decisive importance, and the problem of its relationship to the past rises to trouble it over and over again.

It is extremely doubtful that the secular perspective will suffice to meet this inner problem. Both the orthodox and the secular outlooks then, have been found wanting, the one in the Jewish people's debate with the other nations and the other in its own internal debate with itself, and the conflict between the two is the source of the ambivalent, crisis-torn attitude of the generation born in the land of Israel toward its homeland. This generation's relationship with its land was to have been stable, evolving as a matter of course; it was to have been "normal." But suddenly it seemed that this relationship was still problematic, though in a different way. Precisely because those born there no longer saw their country as a land of destiny, their right to have it as a homeland appeared more and more in doubt.

Conclusion
Is Man Nothing but the Shape of His Native Land?

The significance of the land of Israel as a spiritual and religious symbol was renewed and reaffirmed in the works of Gordon and Rav Kook. For them, the people's living memories, laden with historical events and religious thought, added a transcendent dimension to the tangible reality of the land; and the tangible was bound to what it concealed by a powerful love, as the body is bound to the soul. Most important, the way of life they would have the people follow in the land, as set forth in their philosophies and demonstrated in the example they set in their own lives, would express this religious significance actively, in deeds. It was meant to create a dimension of spirituality that could exist only in a society of Jews living in the land of Israel.

If the truth be told, Gordon's ideas were unusual in secular Zionist circles. They did, indeed, express feelings that were dimly present in the hearts of many. However, the worldview that Gordon shaped out of these feelings was not that of the majority of the secular Zionist community, and the example of his life embodied a requirement that went against the will of this majority. The pioneering Zionist community had broken with religion, and it rejected the religious concepts of the land as a religious symbol as well, for it saw the ghost of the exile lurking in this concept. Its whole ambition was to grasp the tangible reality of the land. This was its vision of redemption; and the very concept of redemption, whose "great hope" originates in religion, was nevertheless interpreted as a natural process involving the "normalization" of the people. The people of Israel would be defined by its land, and the land would be its homeland in the simple, or perhaps even simplistic, sense of the word—the land of one's birth. If the land of Israel still had something of the symbolic, it was in the process of restoring the significance to the symbolizing physical self. The country in its physical manifestation represents the hoped for, longed for land. It must be, more than it is at present, firm ground under our feet, abundant air for breathing freely, heavens high enough for one to stand straight beneath them. Land which brings forth bread. Why Eretz Israel, specifically? Because it is, in fact, the homeland. It is the beginning of national life, and it binds to itself all who are born there. A man does not change his homeland, just as he does not change his parents. These are the facts which establish his identity.

Scrutiny will show that this approach had already appeared at the start of the Hibbat Zion period. As a nationalist movement paralleling the European nationalist movements of the nineteenth century, Hibbat Zion defined the relationship of the people of Israel to its land as resembling that of other nations to their lands. It is the homeland, and as such Israel has a right to it. And what does the word homeland mean in this context? It is the land in which the nation was born. However, it would seem that this claim did not exactly fit the biblical narrative. According to the testimony of the Bible, the people of Israel became a nation in the desert, on their way to inherit their land—that is, the people of Israel entered their land as conquerors, and took it from the indigenous nations living there. However, there were indications that the influence of modern nationalism led them contrary to this traditional understanding of the biblical evidence. First, there is a question as to the act itself—the dispossession of nations with a natural right to it. Though this problem was of no contemporary relevance at the time, it might, potentially, point to a moral flaw in the people's historic bond with its land. Secondly, if the people of Israel was not born in this land, then the latter could not be its homeland in the same sense as seemed so firmly implanted in the consciousness of other peoples in modern times.

The early Zionists' wish for the people of Israel to be like other peoples led them to expect its historic bond with its land to look different from this; the land of Israel must be its homeland in exactly the same way as England was for the English and France for the French. We should not be surprised, then, to find already in the literature produced by the Hibbat Zion movement,[1] that its adherents made ideological and even scholarly efforts to prove that the traditional understanding of the biblical testimony was incorrect; that it was a distortion that had developed in the course of the exile. The Jews were, in fact, the people born in the land of Israel, and the Bible was their national creation, composed while they dwelt upon their own soil. The seven nations had wrested the land from its natural masters, and some of them—but only some—had been exiled. The majority had continued, though oppressed, to dwell in the land. Joshua thus did not conquer a foreign territory, but rather restored the land to its original owners. One way or another, these theories held that the land of Israel was, in fact, the natural homeland of the Jewish people. This people was born there, and its national character was stamped with the impress of the landscape. Only when it returned there could it develop in accord with its own nature.

Such theories were neither strange nor extraordinary to Zionist thought; they had their adherents among those who molded the more mature stages of Zionist theory as well. The most famous example of this occurs in the thought of David Ben-Gurion,[2] but there are others. Even thinkers who did not go as far as to alter the accepted version of Jewish history, however, tended to emphasize the period when they dwelt in their homeland. They felt that the people had produced the best of its national works while upon its own soil. The Jewish national character had been formulated there, and there was thus a natural bond between the people and its land. We have already seen examples of this in the ideas of Gordon and Rav Kook, which were typical in this respect. One might even say that it was in this that Gordon and Kook expressed their participation in the experience and outlook by which Zionism may be identified as a secular national movement. This should help us understand the tension so strongly present in their ideas: in their attempt to bridge the gap between traditional ideas and modern reality, they refused to relinquish the image of the land of destiny, but they held fast to the image of the homeland as well, and sought to unify these two images. Most of the ideologues of pioneering Zionism, however, sought to free themselves of this tension. Having taken the initial bond of the people to its land from the tradition, they interpreted it contrary to that tradition, as no more than that of any people with its homeland.

It is difficult to free oneself all at once from a whole heritage of symbols. Even as they aspired to shape the land of Israel into their homeland, the pioneers retained no small degree of the burden with which the experience of exile had left them. The land of Israel was still a land of destiny—it was destined to become their homeland. Even after he had come there, the pioneer still felt an unbridged emotional distance between himself and his land, and the destiny of which he dreamed was expressed in the idealization of his wish to reach the very heart of its elusive physical reality:

> Not the mists of tomorrow—but today, already here, in hand,
> Today, concrete, hot and powerful;
> To drink our fill of this single, short day,
> Here upon this earth of ours.
>
> (Rachel—"Here upon the earth")

It was especially in relation to its ideas about the kind of education the youth was to receive in the land of Israel that Zionist ideology developed this motif. It must be recalled, however, that Zionism held this field to be of essential importance. All of Zionist ideology was focused upon its educational endeavor, for this was seen as the single guarantor of its continuation into the future, and of the fulfillment of its goals. Since it was working toward a vision that would be fulfilled only in the future, Zionism saw the formation of the character of the next generation as crucial to its success or failure as a movement; in a way, this *was* the goal it sought. The first generation of immigrants had been born in exile, and it must ever remain, however much it wished otherwise, the "generation of the wilderness." Only the next generation, all of whose members would be born in the homeland, would truly be able to live in the redemptive reality. For them, the land of Israel would be their natural homeland. They would grow up there, gazing upon its scenery and drawing their sustenance from its soil. The land would be their most basic experience. It would be no exaggeration to say that the generation of immigrants saw in the generation to come, that which would grow up in the land of Israel, the aim of all its endeavors, and it therefore devoted the best part of its thinking to education.

This desire to strike roots in the land and to fulfill its aspirations by shaping the character of the next generation became the cornerstone of the nationalist, Zionist educational program that was formulated in the land of Israel. Love of the homeland was placed above all else, and the need to focus the attention of the youth upon their presence in the land of Israel was the guiding force behind a multifaceted program of educational and social activities: the land of Israel had to be the axis upon which all educational activity turned. It was the principal subject about which the pupil's senses were to be roused, his emotions stirred, and his mind piqued, drawing together all scholarly, productive, and creative activity in the educational realm. How was this to be accomplished? First, the pupils would tour the country as often as possible, and on foot, not by vehicle. In this way they would be exposed to the landscape, its sights and sounds, its smells and flavor, the feel of the ground under their tramping feet, and the wind and dust blowing about their bodies. Thus they would begin: by absorbing the land of Israel through their senses, through physical contact. The most powerful experience of their childhood and youth would take place against this backdrop, and thus a deep foundation of early memories, images, and sights would be laid within their psyches. The land of Israel would be an integral part of their personal biographies. They would live it together with the other formative experiences of their childhood and youth. Academic activities, too, were bent to the same purpose. The land of Israel would provide the principal content for several of the subjects the pupils studied: topography, geography, climate, flora, and fauna. It would also be the principal subject taught in the humanities: Jewish history would be taught mainly insofar as it related to the land of Israel. The pupil would discover the remains that testified to the life and struggles of the Jewish people in its land; he would learn about his people's bond with the land and about the movements that had sought to redeem it from exile. This was, in fact, the basic outline of Jewish history as it was understood by the Zionist educators. The same was true of the Bible. Scripture would be studied in relation to the testimony offered by the landscape. The youth would hike with the Bible open in their hands. The study of Hebrew literature, too, concentrated primarily upon the "rejection of the exile" and upon the various writers' fierce yearnings for the land of Israel. Education in the productive and creative fields was also, of course, bound up with the land. Farming, which created a primal bond between worker and soil, was placed high on the list of educational priorities. Through poetry, art and music, the pupils would absorb the sights, images, memories and sounds of the land of Israel. In this way, their roots in the land would grow deep, involving all of their being.[3]

What, then, did the homeland signify, according to this educational perspective? It was the person's place of birth, which stamped its imprint upon his physical and psychological character. This natural given, of course, had to be firmed up and complemented by means of education. The bond between a person and the landscape into which he was born, however, was essential and organic, not incidental, and as his personality developed it would come in a way to mirror the natural environment into which he was born:

> Man is nothing but the soil of a small country,
> nothing but the shape of his native landscape,
> nothing but what his ears recorded
> when they were new and really heard,
> what his eyes saw, before they had their fill of seeing—
> everything a wondering child comes across
> on the dew-softened paths,
> stumbling over every lump of earth, every old stone,
> while in a hidden place in his soul, unknown to him,
> there's an altar set up
> from which the smoke of his sacrifice rises each day
> to the kingdom of the sky, to the stars,
> to the houses of the Zodiac.
> But when the days become many, and in the war of being
> the scroll of his Book of Life is being interpreted—
> then comes, one by one, each letter with its interpretation
> and each symbol revealing past and future
> that was inscribed in it when it was first opened.
> A man is nothing but the landscape of his homeland.

> Saul Tchernichovsky, "Man is Nothing But . . ."
> Translated by Robert Mezey (Poems from the Hebrew N.Y. 1923)

This poem, which was much studied and quoted in the schools, could have served as a motto for the educational endeavors of that generation whose members' lives embodied their efforts to transform the land of destiny into a homeland.

2

With this, the body of Jewish thought about the land of Israel that had drawn directly upon the experience and heritage of the exile would seem to have reached its final incarnation. The great wave now broke upon the shore with all the force of its yearning, spreading the quintessential power of its desire before those who were to realize it by their success in altering the direction of their lives. The immigrant generation wanted its children's perspective to be directly counter to its own, and this was, indeed, the strongest bond linking the ideas of the generation that grew up in the land of Israel with those of its parents. The new generation was meant to fulfill the dream that had hovered over the years of exile. But did this common aspiration have the power to link the new reality that was developing in the land of Israel with the dream that had produced it? If we are to respond to this question, we must study the thinking of the first generation born in the land of Israel, insofar as it has been given literary expression.

Let us state at the outset that the answer to be proposed here will necessarily be only partial. We are still at the beginning of the road, and still involved in the struggle of building it. Moreover, the literature of this generation is still almost entirely experiential, fictional and poetic. Its philosophical dimension has barely begun to develop. The paragraphs that follow will thus perforce be based upon personal experience and upon an analysis of the experiences expressed in the literary works of several of the most prominent writers produced by that generation, called by its parents and educators "the generation in its land."

How, then, does this generation, in its deeds and creative works, relate to the land? If we are to generalize, we may say that there are two contradictory answers to this question. The first is positive. The young people of this generation have displayed warm, emotional feelings toward their land. They love its scenery, its mountains and valleys, its flora and fauna. They love being surrounded by this countryside, describing it and sensing it about them. Several behavior patterns will attest to this. First, there are the organized field trips in which Israeli youth frequently participate. Anyone sensitive to the ambience of these trips can see that they are not merely another form of entertainment. There is something ceremonial, serious, and elevated about the way the participants go about their preparations and about the trip itself, a kind of psychological attitude and devotion that give it an almost ritual character. In other words, the field trip is an act of symbolic significance; by means of it one accomplishes a higher purpose. It is the culmination of a process, the fulfilment of a hope. It embodies something of the whole meaning of life. This is especially true of trips to certain places of particular significance such as Massada.

However, any trip that takes its participants some distance from the towns and into the heart of the ancient countryside has the same air about it. And this does not just happen by itself; it is the product of a well-established tradition, which began with the hikes organized by the youth movements and the Palmach in the period before the founding of the state and has continued, in a more institutionalized form, to our own time with the hikes and field schools organized by the Society for the Protection of Nature, the educational activities of the Israel Army unit devoted to increasing knowledge of the land, and, to a lesser degree, with the field trips run by the schools and youth movements. The fact that the annual march to Jerusalem has attained the status of a popular holiday and has taken the place of the Independence Day military parade shows how deep this tradition runs among the people. In other words, Israelis feel that their encounter with the physical environment of the land is of great significance. The element in their life experience that it embodies is fundamental in the Israeli ethos. And if this element expresses itself on the popular level in the field trip, it emerges amongst an elite of the youth in pursuits that demand even greater continuity and commitment on their part. We are speaking here of those areas of learning which have to do with the physical features of the land, the most notable among them being that of archaeology. It is no exaggeration to say that in Israel archaeology has become far more than the occupation of a circle of professionals. There is a large group of active, interested amateurs who respond to the achievements of the professionals not only with enthusiasm, but also with expert understanding and sympathetic participation in their experience. The same is true of the natural sciences involving study of the minerals, flora, and fauna of the land; these, too, evoke an interest that transcends mere scientific curiosity. They are a channel for the expression of love of the physical land.

Let us, finally, call up the evidence of *belles lettres* in support of our argument. We must note here once again that the writers of the second and third *aliyot* displayed, from the outset, an ambivalent attitude toward the landscape. By the contradictory sentiments that their encounter with it generated, they expressed their simultaneous attachment to two different homelands, that which they had left behind and that to which they had come. This is not true, however, of the descriptions of their native scenery penned by the writers and poets born in the land of Israel. On the contrary, these portrayals are the most impressive of their literary achievements, distinguished not only by their sensitivity and delicacy, but also by their direct personal identification. They write as though the landscape were, for them, the most sensitive and sometimes the exclusive reflection of the inner convolutions of the psyche.

Most outstanding in this respect are the works of S. Yizhar, rightly considered the greatest of the first generation of native-born Israeli writers. Descriptions of the landscape form the greater part of the content of his stories, and in several of them, such as "The Edge of the Negev," the countryside is, in fact, his principal hero, the plot consisting of a series of events that take place within it. Even in some of his other stories, however, he spends less time describing the characters themselves than he does describing their feelings about the landscape. As they hover on the edge of failure in forming relationships with others, the countryside is always their last refuge. It is to the land that they return in order to find the meaning of life and a sure feeling of belonging.[4] There is thus a strong religious element in the way Yizhar's heroes relate to the landscape. They yearn to unite with it, to be caught up in it to the point of annulling their own being, and this super awareness of it on their part rises at times to an altitude of mute prayer. It is worth emphasizing, moreover, that their bond with the land, in its physical uniqueness, is stronger, more imbued with a sense of belonging and more spiritually significant than is their relationship with their people. The land of Israel symbolizes the purpose of their own lives, though nothing explicit is ever said of the nature of this purpose, or of a world view by means of which one might venture to interpret the symbol. Yizhar's heroes seem to prefer hiding behind the symbol, because they do not understand its significance. They believe, nevertheless, that it does have meaning, hidden deep within the endless abundance of visual images. But it is within the tangible, not beyond or above it.

Yizhar's stories—and in this he is typical of his generation—are journeys of love and devotion into the Israeli countryside. They clearly and unambiguously bear out our previous statement that these members of the generation born and raised in the land of Israel love their land and feel that they belong to it.

3

Just as we can muster testimony in support of a positive reply to the question we raised, however, we can also bring evidence to the contrary. Insofar as we approach it with a view to the native-born generation's consciousness of the quality of its attachment, we find that its relationship to its homeland is weak and easily undermined. To prove this, we might point to the number of emigrants who leave every year, among whom are many native-born Israelis, and even quite a few who had received the finest of nationalist-Zionist education. However, emigration is the product of a combination of factors, and proves, at best, that love of the homeland is not always the decisive factor in a person's choice of his way in life. We must find a more direct expression of this failing, but we need look no further than the stormy debates about "our right to the land of Israel" which broke out after the Six-Day War and have raged ever since. What is astonishing about these controversies is that intelligent young people, educated in Israeli schools and youth movements, should prove so weak in their ability to explain their national right to live in their land. When the question of the right of the Jews as against that of the Arabs is put to them bluntly and directly, their response is generally one of mute confusion. A perusal of *The Seventh Day,* a book containing the most intimate and instructive testimony that Israeli youth has given about itself in recent years, shows how deep this confusion runs. After numerous discussions with young people, high school and university students, and soldiers, I have come to the conclusion that this phenomenon is common to almost all of them, and particularly pronounced among the elite.

Does this confusion also express itself in their organized activity on behalf of the common good? Does it weaken their readiness and desire to devote themselves to defending and building up the land? Apparently not. Native-born young people bear the main burden of defending the country, and many individuals have shown themselves ready to serve with devotion and sacrifice not inferior to that of their parents. Moreover, among the most willing to make such sacrifices are quite a few of those who are the most troubled and confused by this issue—that is to say, the most sensitive and thoughtful of the youth. Even so, we must not belittle the potential danger inherent in this bewilderment. When people are involved in a war for survival such considerations are swept aside. But when they address themselves to the political struggle, which will demand the ability to persuade others on the moral and ideological level, and even more so when they think about choosing a way in life that will contribute to building up the land, this spiritual weakness may be laid bare.

Let us return to the literary expression of this relationship. We have already met with that aspect of Yizhar's stories which reveals the native-born Israeli's love for the physical environment of his land. These same stories, however, provide us with a most instructive insight into the spiritual confusion of Yizhar's heroes. The most outstanding feature of his main characters is their inability to identify with the community of their people in the land, even though they act in its name and at its command. They are individualists, and while they may not rebel openly against this community, they live inwardly in continual opposition to it, yearning to flee. The countryside is their home in their most difficult hours, but they seek it out as a refuge from the community, whose demands upon them oppose the inner flow of their own feelings. In other words, the land itself is dear to their hearts, but they do not understand the tie that binds their community—their people—to the land, for any sense of the brotherly attachment that members of a people feel for each other is foreign to them. Yizhar's greatest work, *Days of Ziklag*, is a monumental expression of this inner tension. In it, we meet a unit of fighters in the War of Independence, struggling bitterly to hold an outpost in the Negev. The theme of the story is thus nothing less than the Jewish people's struggle to hold onto the right to live in its homeland. The heroes' loyalty and dedication in battle is exemplary. What takes place in their thoughts and their conversations with one another, however, reveals the insoluble dilemma with which they live. Along with page upon page of sensitive, astonishingly beautiful and loving descriptions of the landscape, we find page upon page of internal brooding and dialogue expressing the characters' alienation from their parents' nationalistic aspirations and endeavors on behalf of the Zionist cause. This dilemma is left still unsolved in works dealing directly with the moral problem of the Jewish people's right to the land as against that of the Arabs, such as *The Story of Hirbet Hizeh*. It is characteristic of Yizhar's heroes that they cannot resolve the matter, and so, ultimately, they are swept along with the aspirations that their people has established in common—as long as these stay powerful enough to keep them going.

4

Despite the paradox created by the juxtaposition of these two contradictory responses, they are not mutually exclusive; on the contrary, they support one another. First, the spiritual confusion felt by these young people would seem, in a way, to be the obverse side of their love for the landscape. Their ascription of an indecipherable symbolic meaning to the landscape expresses an inarticulate feeling that something is missing from their lives, and they do not know what can take its place. In other words, their love for the countryside is a product of their yearning to make up for an intellectual and spiritual vacuum which no physical landscape can ever fill. Yizhar's stories reflect the imbalance between this intense, overwhelming longing and the ability of the objects that he describes to fulfill it; we see this, among other things, in his excess of verbiage. His words rush in pursuit of something that remains elusive, trying to exhaust the inexhaustible, and despite their amazing multitude they return empty-handed to their author. The main thing remains beyond his grasp, lurking silently in the mysterious landscape which persists in concealing the depths of its meaning.

We shall return to this issue later. First, however, let us go back to the status of archaeology in Israeli culture. What people seem to be seeking in archaeology is the embodiment of some spiritual meaning in the physical landscape, for archaeology preserves the past not in the treasury of memory, but in tangible form. When one's true cultural bond with the past, that built of a heritage of values and modes of living, becomes weak, one naturally wishes to hold onto its tangible, physical remains. A person acting upon this impulse, however, knows deep in his heart that he is deluding himself. The traces left by the past do not preserve its vitality. The corpse of history, disintegrating into these crumbled remains, cannot take the place of its soul, which lies concealed in the recesses of the people's cultural memory, though the scholar may sublimate his desire for it by satisfying his scientific curiosity. Archaeology thus cannot fulfill the longing that impels its amateur enthusiasts to pursue it. At best it provides them with a poor substitute for that which they seek. The same is true of the study of the land's flora and fauna. These subjects are certainly interesting in and of themselves, but if the student has an ulterior, non-intrinsic motive for pursuing them as well, it will not be fulfilled. Ultimately, no kind of learning related to Israel's physical aspect can take the place of the cultural and historical tie that binds a people to its land. And it is this that we sense in Yizhar's stories. Yizhar's relationship to the landscape is, as we have said, almost religious, but it is not by chance that his prayerful journeys into the depths of the enchanted countryside, with its shadowy evenings and dark nights, end in disappointment. He is driven to seek out the landscape, but it eludes his verbal embrace, for where the tangible symbol should link up with the meaning it represents, there is only a vacuum. A landscape can, indeed, symbolize a spiritual presence that transcends it, but it cannot take the place of that presence. From the visible landscape it is, indeed, impossible to arrive at any kind of spiritual significance—the place to look for that is in the cultural heritage of the people.

The confusion of the young people is thus expressed in love. There is, similarly, love mixed in with their confusion. Native-born Israelis tend to define their national identity by the place where they were born and raised. When asked about their national identity, most will thus answer that they are Israelis. But Israel is their land and state, not their people. If we go on to inquire about the difference between Israelis and Jews, they will respond with bewilderment, for most of them would intend no such distinction. No more than a few would say that they do not see themselves as Jews. Most would reply that when they define themselves as Israelis, they mean that they are Israeli Jews. They would not abandon their national bond with the Jews of the diaspora, at the very least for practical reasons: without their aid, Israel could not survive. We would soon find, however, that this feeling of a national bond with the Jews of the diaspora is conditional; it depends upon the latter's potential candidacy for *aliyah* and upon their willingness to extend material assistance to the state of Israel. In other words, this feeling, too, has its roots in a sense of affiliation with the state rather than with the Jewish people. Beyond the horizon of their relationship to the state, their sense of belonging to the Jewish people seems rather vague.

What unites a people, apart from its state? This, then, is why the young people cling so strongly to the land they can touch and to the concrete political framework of the state. Furthermore, though it may sound paradoxical, this confident trust in land and state to define their national relationship with the Jews of the diaspora is but the obverse side of their bewilderment in facing up to the Arab challenge. The link between these two issues is simple: only as a member of the Jewish people does the native-born Israeli youth have a historical bond with the land of Israel, which makes it his national home. But since his relationship to his people is so vague, he is as sure of his "Israeliness" when he encounters the Jew who lives abroad as he is confused over his right to the land when he encounters the Arab who lives there just as he does.

We may note here that this combination of bewilderment and certainty shows just how different the emotional and spiritual world of Israeli youth is from that of their parents. When their parents demanded that every Jew come to live in the land of Israel they justified it on the basis of the fact that they themselves had made *aliyah*. This demand, however, was a product of their prior identification with the Jewish people, and not a condition upon which their willingness to identify with it rested; and since their sense of identification with their people was clear from the outset, the parents had no doubts about the right of the Jews to return to their land. They, who in childhood had never seen the land of Israel, who had not grown up there and absorbed the shapes and forms of its landscape from their earliest youth, were more certain of their national right to live there than their children, who were born in the land! Does this have to do simply with the alienation that commonly separates one generation from the next? It has, perhaps, come to have something to do with this, but if we study the problem carefully, we must note that it did not arise from any intentional rebellion on the part of the youth. On the contrary, it is a product of a kind of continuity between the generations, for the young people born in the land became estranged from their parents precisely because they accepted in good faith the educational message which their parents had transmitted to them. They wanted to be what their parents had hoped they would become: the fulfillment of the dream that had drawn them from the exile.

In other words, the alienation of the youth is the product of an educational success story. The childrens' fulfillment of their parents' dream removed them from the historical and cultural continuity within which their parents had lived. With their own hands, the parents had borne their children toward a future from which their own part could no longer be seen, at least not openly. What had motivated them to come to the land? What had sustained their dream? The children had not experienced these things. They had experienced only their parents' devotion to the visible land, their longing to strike deep roots in its soil, their desire for it to become their homeland. This, the children knew, was meant to be of great significance. But what was that significance? They could no more than dimly sense how they missed it.

5

If the goals of Zionism had been realized quickly; if all or most of the Jewish people had come to settle in their land within one generation and had succeeded in winning the recognition of their neighbors, then, perhaps, the transition from the traditional image of the destined land to that of the national home would have been completed without there having been any consciousness of a crisis. First, there would have been no barrier between one's identification with the Jewish people and one's identification with the state. The people would have been here and now, just as the land is. Secondly, if the whole people were living "normally" in its land, a national tradition might have been created within the space of one generation; it would, indeed, most likely have been poor and superficial in character, but it could at least have formulated a new image for the homeland of a people newly revitalized. Even then, it would surely have been difficult to create a new culture without drawing sufficiently upon the people's historical tradition, but there would at least have been no dilemma regarding their right to the land. But Zionism, despite its impressive achievements, is still far from completing its task. Most of the Jewish people has not gathered in its land. Many still look upon the land from the perspective of exile, and in Israel itself the process of rebuilding is nowhere near the end of its difficulties Zionism needs a sense of continuity to be able to complete the realization of its goals, and this is not possible without some kind of continuity in the will of the nation and in its vision. This is the source of the young people's sense of crisis and confusion.

The need to continue the pursuit of the Zionist endeavor over several generations thus exposed the error made by the first generation in calculating how to build its new world. The educational message that it had transmitted to its children betrayed it; it turned out that the lovely poetic expression of its worldview, "Man is nothing but the shape of his native land," imbued as it was with true feeling, had missed a prior truth, whose absence left it no more than a line of empty rhetoric. A man can be shaped by his native landscape if he has a native land, and if that land has a shape—that is, if a man has truly wished to bind himself to that land, and has molded its image out of a sense of identity with the culture of his people. Those who undertook to realize the Zionist goal could at least have learned from their own experience that a man can be born in a particular country, and even love it, without it being his homeland; and that a man may even consider a land to be his home without ever having seen it except in his imagination. Love for one's native scenery is, of course, an important aspect of the experience of living in one's homeland, and a person exiled from his own country feels the lack of it. But it is not the determinative factor in his relationship to his land. What determines this is his own consciousness and will. It is a sense of commitment formed on the basis of his identification with his people. A person is not born of his land, but of his people. The Hebrew expression *moledet,* which we have translated as "homeland," itself refers in its original, biblical sense to one's family, tribe, and people. Only by way of these does it relate to the land in which the people lives. Moreover, there is more to the "shape" of the land than the configurations of its landscape; rather, it is molded by the creative activity of the imagination, and human feeling plays an important part in it. It is thus as correct to say that a land is no more than the shape of the soul of its people as it is to say that a man is shaped by his native landscape.

It would thus seem that the way the Zionist movement in the land of Israel educated its young towards love of their land had had its foundation knocked out from under it. This foundation was, indeed, still present in the background in a dim, abstract way, barely hinted at in studies of the Bible and of history, barely evident in the activity and way of life of those who labored to make Zionism's aspirations a reality. The generation that grew up in the land could sense that something essential had not been handed down to them, and that something was missing from their lives. But this is a poor comfort, for a gaping hole cannot be filled by one's sense of its emptiness.

To correct this error, a bridge must be found to connect the present with the past, and the internal sources within the Jewish heritage from which Zionism drew its driving force must be rediscovered. There must be a return, first of all, to the Bible, not only as evidence of the way the people once lived in its land, but also as a mold in which to cast the image of the land in keeping with the vision of the people. The Bible, so far from us in time, is yet very close to us in that it has to do with the way the people lived in the land to which it has returned. On the other hand, however, a national movement must keep in mind that it is most directly sustained by the works that its culture has produced closest to it in time. It cannot simply skip over the intermediate links in the chain; it must relate to the entire historical continuity.

This may appear a simple matter, but in fact it is not. The proper image of the homeland cannot be formulated through learning alone. It takes its shape from the people's way of life, and from the whole cultural pattern that is gradually worked together in the land; and it is here that the really big question arises. The founders had concealed the positive wellsprings of Zionism that lay within the Jewish heritage because of their rebellion against the exile, which demanded that they transform the image of the land that had crystallized over the centuries while the people languished abroad. A return to the image that can be gathered from the sources will oblige us to reorient ourselves in this respect. While this does not necessarily mean a total affirmation of the vision that guided the exile, it does require an affirmation of the "religious" motif that stems from the biblical concept of the promised land. This would signal a far-reaching change in the world view of secular Zionism and in the way it has been realized until now. The fact that it is hard to imagine Zionism continuing into the next generation if no such change should occur does not suffice to make it come to pass. Rather, the present generation must actively recognize the intrinsic value of the image welling up from our heritage. In other words, a positive choice must be made, and the considerations upon which it must be based lie beyond the realm of Zionist ideology. While the continuation of the Zionist endeavor may depend upon this happening, it is only by dealing directly with the spiritual values of Judaism that this transformation can be brought about.

Our path has led us from the biblical vision of a homeland which was at the same time the people's land of destiny to the exilic dream of a land of destiny which was not then a homeland, and thence to the Zionist vision of a homeland which is no land of destiny. We have now arrived at a fateful juncture. Has our people the spiritual and material resources necessary for completing the two-pronged endeavor demanded of it, and to reconcile the divergent elements comprising its vision as well? Will it prove capable of reviving and fulfilling the dual ideal of Scripture—that of the homeland which is a land of destiny? These are the fundamental questions which must be answered through the way we continue to rebuild the land of Israel, socially and physically, in thought, creative work, and education.

Notes

Part I. National Home or Land of Destiny

Chapter 1. The Biblical View

1. Rabbi Yehezkel Abramsky, *Eretz Yisrael Nahalat Am Yisrael* (Jerusalem: privately published, n.d.).
2. A. D. Gordon, "Mikhtavim LaGolah," in *HaUmah Veha'Avodah (Collected Works of A. D. Gordon,* ed. Hasifriyu Hazionit) (Jerusalem, 1952), pp. 517–63.
3. P. Rosenzweig, *Achdut HaMikra* (Naharaim, Jerusalem: Bialik Institute 1961), pp. 26–31.
4. Gen. 15:18–20; Exod. 23:31.
5. Deut. 8:7–10.
6. Deut. 11:9–12.
7. Num. 34:1–3.
8. Amos 2:10.
9. Exod. 3:8. Also, the land in which the "seven peoples" dwell, Deut. 7:1.
10. Gen. 23:4.
11. Gen. 12:5–9.
12. *Sifrei* on Numbers, Deuteronomy, and Joshua.
13. *Sifrei* on Judges and Samuel.
14. *Sifrei* on Kings and Jeremiah.
15. Deut. 12:29–31.
16. Gen. 15:16.
17. Gen. 9:20–27.
18. Many times, beginning with Exod. 23:22–33.
19. Deut. 11:17.
20. Gen. 13:14–18; 15:7–18; 17:7–8; 26:2–4; 28:13–16; and many other places.
21. Jer. 11.
22. As in note 18; see also my essay, "The Destruction of Amalek and the expulsion of the Amorites," in The Journal of Hebrew Writers' Association (Tel Aviv), *Mozniam,* vol. 33, nos. 3 and 4 (1971).
23. The clearest theoretical expression of the nature of this purified ritual, too, is to be found in Solomon's prayer on the occasion of the dedication of the Temple, in 1 Kings 8.
24. Leviticus 25; Exodus 23:11; Deuteronomy 15.
25. On *terumah* and tithing: Lev. 22, 27; Num. 18; Deut. 14, 18. On first fruits: Deut. 16. On *hallah:* Num. 15, 18. On *leket, shikhechah* and *pe'ah:* Lev. 23:22; Deut. 24:19.
26. As in note 1.
27. Gen. 1:1.
28. Gen. 1:26–27.
29. Gen. 1:28–29; 2:15.
30. Gen. 2:18–25.
31. This is the point of the genealogies in the book of Genesis—to describe how the families developed into tribes and peoples, in order to populate the earth and to fill it.

32. The lineage of Adam, in Genesis, chap. 5, and later that of Noah, Gen. 9:18, and 10:1.

33. Gen. 10:2.

34. Gen. chap. 10, and the recurrent words: "after their families, after their tongues, in their lands, in their nations," verses 20 and 30. See also Deut. 32:7–9. A concise statement of all we have said up to now is found in Jer. 27, verse 5.

35. Amos 9:7–15.

36. Judg. 11:12–27.

37. Ibid. 11:24.

38. Gen. 15.

39. Deut. 29–30.

40. See my essay, "Eretz Yisrael KaMoledet Ha'Am HaYehudi," in *Leumiut Yehudit,* ed. E. Schweid (Jerusalem: S. Zack & Co., 1972), pp. 90–108.

41. Exod. 19:5; Deut. 7:6–8; Deut. 26:17–19.

42. Gen. 12:10; 13:1.

43. Ps. 48.

44. "and [thou] didst water it with thy foot. . . ," Deut. 11:10.

45. This is one of the motifs appearing in the story of the Tower of Babel, and in the story of Joseph in Egypt.

46. Especially according to the story of Joseph in Egypt.

47. *Encyclopedia Mikrait,* s.v. "Ba'al."

48. I Kings 18.

49. This is the recurrent motif of the book of Deuteronomy, from chapter 9 onwards.

50. Martin Buber, *Torat HaNevi'im, HaMifneh el HeAtid* (Tel Aviv: Bialik Institute, 1950), pp. 91–143.

51. Jer. 27.

52. An outstanding representative of this stream of thought is Rabbi Yehuda Halevi, in the *Kuzari.* See also my essay, "Am Yisrael veArtzo BaMishnat Rabbi Yehuda Halevi," in *Emunat Am Yisrael veTarbuto* (Jerusalem: S. Zack Co., 1977).

53. An outstanding representative of this stream is Maimonides.

54. Deut. 12:5.

55. This idea began to develop already with the establishment of the Tabernacle in the desert. The Tabernacle symbolizes the presence of God in the midst of the people. See also the *Encyclopedia Mikrait,* s.v. "Mishkan HaShem."

56. Jer. 2:7.

57. This is true particularly of the prophecies of Jeremiah.

58. Isa. 1.

59. Amos 9:11–15; Mic. 4; et al.

60. Hos. 2:18–25.

61. Isa. 11, 12.

62. Isa. 2:1–12.

Part II. From the Exile

Chapter 1. The Homeland Destroyed

1. From the beginning of the "Hibbat Zion" movement onwards, a great deal of literature has been written about the land of Israel, especially in light of Scripture and the works of the Sages. A good number of these books are anthologies of texts drawn from the sources. The following list includes but a few of this number. The following discussion is based upon these anthologies. The reader will find his way eased especially by using the *Sefer HaAgadah* compiled by Bialik and Ravnitzky.

a. I. M. Gutman, "Eretz Yisrael baMidrash uvaTalmud," in *Festschrift zum 75 jährigen Bestehen des jüdisch Theologischen Seminars.* Breslau, 1921.

b. Yehuda Zisling, *Yalkut Eretz Yisrael.*

c. I. Bernstein, *MiPi Rishonim veAcharonim.*

d. C. N. Bialik and I. C. Ravnitzky, comps., *Sefer HaAgadah,* pt. 3, 2.

2. *Encyclopedia Talmudlt,* s.v. "Eretz Yisrael."

3. *Encyclopedia Ivrit,* s.v. "Galut (Golah)."

4. G. Alon, *Toldot HaYehudim beEretz Yisrael baTkufat haMishnah vehaTalmud,* vol. I, introduction (Tel Aviv: Hakibbuz Hameuchad, 1952), pp. 3–25.

5. A. H. Weiss, *Dor Dor veDorshav,* bk. 11, chap. 4.

6. A. G. Horowitz, *Zikaron LiYrushalayim.*

7. For example, "Rabbi Shimon ben Yohai said . . . that regarding all the other lands, the one has what the other has not, and the other has what this has not; but the land of Israel lacks for nothing, as Scripture states, 'thou shalt not lack any thing in it' (Deut. 8:9)." (*Sifrei* to the *sedra* of *Ekev*).

8. For example, " '. . . and [I would] give thee a pleasant land, the goodliest heritage of the hosts of the nations." (Jer. 3:19) What is meant by 'the hosts of the nations'? That all the nations gather there in their hosts and want it for themselves." (*Midrash Shochar Tov, Mizmor*).

9. For example, " 'then shalt thou arise, and get thee up unto the place which the Lord thy God shall choose.' (Deut. 17:8) This teaches us that the Temple is higher than all the rest of the land of Israel, and the land of Israel is higher than all of the other lands." (*Zebachim* 54b)

10. For example, " 'it is not as the land of Egypt.' The land of Egypt drinks of its own waters, while the land of Israel drinks rainwater. In the land of Egypt, the low-lying places are watered, but the high places are not; in the land of Israel, both low and high have water . . . In the land of Egypt, if one does not work the soil with mattock and axe far into the night, it will give him nothing, but not so the land of Israel; there the people sleep upon their beds, and God brings down the rain unto them." (*Sifrei* to the *sedra* of *Vezot HaBrachah*).

11. For example, "One ought always to dwell in the land of Israel, even in a town populated mainly by idolaters, and not abroad, even in a town populated mainly by Jews; for one who dwells in the land of Israel is like one who has a God, while if one lives abroad, it is as though he had no God." (*Ketubot* 110b).

12. For example, "The Holy One, Blessed be He, said to Moses, 'The land is dear to me, and the people of Israel is dear to me; I shall bring the people that is dear to Me into the land that is dear to Me.' " (Numbers Rabbah 23).

13. For example, "Three things were given us only conditionally, the land of Israel, the Temple and the Kingdom of David . . ." (*Mekhilta* to the *sedra* of *Yitro*).

14. For example, "Rami bar Yehezkel happened to come to Bnei Brak one day, and he saw goats eating under the fig trees, and honey was dripping down from the figs, and milk was flowing from the animals, and the two mixed with one another; and he said, 'That is what is meant by "flowing with milk and honey." ' " (*Ketubot* 111b).

15. *Sifrei* to the *sedra* of *Re'eh.*

16. *Ketubot* 110b.

Chapter 3. Judah Halevi

1. *Kuzari,* second essay, pars. 14–16.

2. Ibid., pars. 13–14.

3. Ibid., par. 22.

4. This work was, indeed, preserved as part of the literature of Christian thought, and only in the nineteenth century was the identity of its author discovered.

5. For the details of the historical background to this, see I. Baer, *Toldot HaYehudim beSepharad haNotzrit,* ch. 1 (Tel Aviv: Am Oved, 1959), pp. 23–45.

6. See E. Schweid, "Omanut HaDialog baSefer HaKuzari uMashma'utah HaIyyunit," in *Ta'am VeHakashah* (Tel Aviv: Massada Ltd., 1970), pp. 37–80.

7. The interested reader will find a complete analysis of this in the above essay.

8. *Kuzari,* first essay, introduction.

9. Aristotle sees curiosity, or the natural urge to know, as the motive for man's search for truth. This is a natural quality, for all that is potential seeks to become actual, and intellect is man's unique potential.

10. *Kuzari,* first essay, par. 1. The outstanding representative of this view in Jewish thought is Maimonides, who defines prophecy as an intellectual plenitude.

11. Ibid., introduction.

12. This idea is developed throughout the first and third essays.

13. For details of this, see the section dealing with the first essay in my article cited above, n. 6.

14. *Kuzari,* first essay, pars. 63–37.

15. Ibid., fourth essay, par. 3.

16. Ibid., first essay, par. 95.

17. This assumption is also implicit in the description of the pious man's way to perfection at the beginning of the third essay. He must first perfect himself as a man, by working on his human qualities.

18. *Kuzari,* second essay, pars. 17–20.

19. Ibid., first essay, pars. 41–43. Also the fourth essay, pars. 6–9.

20. Ibid., second essay, par. 23.

21. Ibid., second essay, par. 2.

22. Ibid., par. 11.

23. Ibid., pars. 30–44.

24. Ibid., par. 12.

25. Ibid., par. 24.

Chapter 4. Maimonides

1. *Kuzari,* first essay, pars. 63–67.

2. See my book, *Iyyunim beShmonah Perakim LaRambam* (Jerusalem: The Jewish Agency, 1965).

3. *Shmonah Perakim,* chap. 4.

4. What follows is based upon the *Sefer HaMitzvot* and the *Mishneh Torah.*

5. A full discussion of this matter would require the examination of a great many passages which are not confined to the concept of "holiness" but help to construct it. See, for example, *Hilkhot Yesodei HaTorah,* chapter 2. God, who is conceived as being utterly different from the created world, is holiness itself, and the spiritual bodies are close to Him in that they are spiritual; and this is the degree of their holiness.

6. This, again, may be concluded from the study of a great many passages. A statement appearing in *Hilkhot Beit HaBehirah,* chap. 7, par. 1, however, is characteristic: "To be in awe of the Temple is a positive commandment. But it is not of the Temple that one is in awe, but of Him who commanded this awe."

7. See the above note, and also *Hilkhot Klei HaMikdash,* chap. 1, par. 12: "And this does not continue down through the generations. Rather, the vessels all became sanctified because they were used in the Temple, through the service that war made of them, as Scripture states: '[the vessels of ministry,] wherewith they minister in the sanctuary.' By this ministry are they sanctified."

8. *Hilkhot Terumot,* chap. 1, pars. 1–10, and also *Hilkhot Beit HaBehirah,*" chap. 6, par. 16.

9. *Hilkhot Terumot,* chap. 1, par. 3.

10. This emphasis is found in the same place, ibid., par. 2.

11. *Hilkhot Melakhim,* chap. 5, pars. 6–12.

12. As in note 9.

13. *"Hilkhot Beit HaBehirah,"* chaps. 1, par. 3; chap. 2, par. 1; chap. 7, par. 7.

14. See E. Schweid, *IIuRambam veChug Hashpa'ato* (Akademon, 1968).

15. *Moreh Nevukhim,* pt. 2, chaps. 33, 34; pt. 3, 18.

16. Ibid.

17. *Mishneh Torah, "Hilkhot Avodat Kokhavim,"* chap. 1; *Iggeret Teimen.*

18. *Moreh Nevukhim,* pt. 3, chap. 17.

19. *Hilkhot Beit HaBehirah,* chap. 2, pars. 1–2.

20. *Moreh Nevukhim,* pt. 3, chap. 24.

21. *Kuzari,* second essay, pars. 18–20.

22. *Sefer HaMitzvot,* Positive Commandments, commandment no. 153.

Chapter 5. A Symbolic Entity

1. I. Baer, *Toldot HaYehudim BeSepharad HaNotzrit* (Tel Aviv: Am Oved), pt. 1, chap. 3, 64.

2. G. Scholem, *Major Trends in Jewish Mysticism* (New York: Schocken Books, 1941), lecture 7.

3. Ibid., lecture 8.

4. Haim Rivlin, "Ma'alat HaAretz," in *Eretz Yisrael BeFerush HaRamban LaTorah* (Jerusalem, 1969).

5. I. Tishbi, "Mavo LeMishnat HaZohar," chap. 4, section on "HaTopographia shel HaZohar," *Mishnat HaZohar,* vol. 1 (Jerusalem, 1949).

6. G. Scholem, *The Messianic Idea in Judaism* (New York: Schocken Books, 1971).

7. J. Ben Shlomo, Introduction to *Sha'arei Orah,* Sifriat Dorot edition (Jerusalem).

8. Scholem, *Major Trends,* lecture 1.

9. The aim of this work is explained at the beginning of chapter 1, and there, too, the way the names and appellations are to be understood symbolically is described. The mystery of the divine emanations and of the *sefirot* is set down without any explanation with the mention of the first name, which responds to the *sefirah* of *malkhut* and becomes clearer and clearer as the book goes on, reaching full clarification in chapter 5.

10. The chapters of the book are arranged according to this number, one chapter for each attribute or *sefirah,* from *malkhut* to *keter.* We shall not here enter into the complex question of the distinction between the first *sefirah* and the *Einsof,* or how they are to be identified separately.

11. This function of the last *sefirah* is to be found at the beginning of the explanation of the first name, in chapter 1.

12. The special status of the people of Israel is discussed in the explanation of the name *"Shekhinah"* in chapter 1, and after this in all the chapters of the book.

13. Chapter 2, in the section dealing with the appellation *"Abir Ya'akov,"* and again in chapter 5, at the beginning of the chapter.

14. End of chapter 1: "And chief of all the principles that we have related to you, we must relate the tradition that in every place where our Sages mention *Knesset Israel,* they are referring to the attribute that is called *Adonai* or *Shekhinah,* or any of the other names we have discussed, and it is this that sustains the community of Israel; by its means are they gathered together, and by it is the Jewish people distinguished from all other peoples."

15. This idea recurs in almost every chapter of the book and receives a particularly full explanation in chapter 5.

16. End of chapter 1: "And since this attribute draws supernal blessings and various kinds of

abundance and emanations down from the tree of life, it is called the Land of Life, and the dead who are buried in the land of Israel, which is its particular province, will be the first to be revived." Further on, in chapter 2, the author devotes a lengthy discussion to the identity of the *sefirah* of *Yesod* with "Mount Zion," and to that of the *sefirah* of *malkhut* with Jerusalem and Mount Moriah.

17. A special discussion is devoted to this issue in chapter 8.

18. Introduction to chapter 1.

19. Middle of chapter 5.

20. These relationships are described at length in chapter 5.

21. These relationships are described at length in chapter 2.

22. These relationships are described at length in chapter 5.

23. These relationships are described at length in chapter 8.

24. Middle of chapter 5, in the explanation of the mystery of the phrase, *"ve'arastikh li le'olam."*

25. Chapter 8.

26. End of chapter 2.

27. End of chapter 8.

28. G. Scholem, *Shabbatai Tzvi,* vol. 1, (Tel Aviv: Am Oved, 1957), chap. 1, 4.

29. A typical example is that of the Ba'al Shem Tov, who wanted to go to the land of Israel all his life but was never able to do so.

30. A particularly strong expression of this experience appears in the book *"Nahalat Yisrael,"* by Rabbi Israel Ze'ev Hurvitz.

Part III. Regaining the Land of Destiny

Chapter 1. Nachman of Bratslav

1. Solomon Schechter, *Safed in the Sixteenth Century,* Studies in Judaism, Second Series.

2. G. Scholem, *Shabbatai Tzvi,* vol. 1 (Tel Aviv, 1957), pp. 1–82. chap. 1.

3. A. Kariv, *"Shitato shel HaMaHaRaL,"* introduction to *Kitvei MaHaRaL MiPrag* (Jerusalem, 1960).

4. Rabbi Judah Loew (the MaHaRaL of Prague), *Gur Arieh,* Sedra Lekh Lekha, "Or Chadash Le'Esther," I, 1.

5. Rav Nachman of Bratslav's comments about the land of Israel are brought together in the *Sefer Eretz Yisrael,* which was printed on its own (Jerusalem, 1941), and also at the beginning of the book *Zimrat Ha'Aretz* (Jerusalem, 1968). "Seder Nesi'ato la'Aretz HaKedoshah" is appended to *Shivchei HaRaN* (Jerusalem, 1944).

On Rabbi Nachman's ideas concerning the land of Israel, see I. K. Miklishinsky, "Eretz Yisrael BeMishnat MoHaRaN MiBraslav," in *HaHasidut veZion* (Jerusalem: Mosad Harav Kook, 1963), and M. Buber, *Bein Am LeArtzo* (Jerusalem).

6. The allusion from which this may be understood occurs at the very beginning of the report of Rabbi Nachman's journey: "Before our late Rabbi travelled to the land of Israel, he was in Kamenitz, and his journey to Kamenitz was very wondrous . . . Our Rabbi said: 'Whosoever knows why the land of Israel was at first in the hands of the Canaanites and later was handed over to the people of Israel, that person will know why he was first in Kamenitz and from there went to the land of Israel.'" Kamenitz was a Frankist center, and from this analogy it would appear that he identified the Frankists as the Canaanites of his day. In reference to this, see Ben Halperin's article on Zion in modern Herbrew literature. On Rabbi Nachman's attitude towards Sabbateanism and Frankism in general, see, in the anthology *Zion in Jewish Literature,* A. Halkin, ed. (New York, 1961), the article by Yosef Weiss: "Tachanot Chaim Rishonot veTechilat HaMachloket" (*Mechkarim BeChasidut Breslav,* Jerusalem, 1978).

7. Ben Zion Dinur, "She'elat HaGeulah veDerakheiha BaReishit HaHaskalah uFulmus HaEmantsipatsia HaRishonah," in *BaMifneh HaDorot* (Jerusalem, 1955).

8. G. Scholem, *Major Trends in Jewish Mysticism,* lecture 8.

9. On this and on "the attractive power of the limit" in Rabbi Nachman's thought, see Yosef Weisse, *Mechkarim BaChasidut Breslav* (Jerusalem: Mossad Bialik, 1975) chap. 7.

10. *Sefer Eretz-Yisrael* 14, 19, 31 et al.

11. Ibid., p. 17.

12. Ibid., pp. 24, 31.

13. Ibid., introduction.

14. Ibid., Sihot HaRaN MeEretz Yisrael, in *Likkutei Tinayna,* 116.

15. Ibid., p. 15.

16. Ibid., Mahadura Batra, 9.

17. Ibid., foreword.

18. Ibid., p. 16.

19. Ibid., Mahadura Batra, 11.

20. Ibid., Mahadura Batra, 11

21. Ibid., introduction.

22. Ibid., p. 31.

23. Ibid., p. 42: "And not only can we restore its holiness to the land of Israel, but we also have the power, by virtue of the effect of undeserved grace and that secret Torah of which we spoke above, to imbue any place outside of the land (to which we come) with the holiness of the land of Israel." Similarly, p. 44, and also pp. 70, 71, 72.

24. Ibid., pp. 20, 32, 49. And regarding the special status accorded the power of the imagination in Rabbi Nachman's thought, see Hillel Zeitlin, *Rabbi Nachman MiBrasley,* section 11.

25. Ibid., p. 64.

Chapter 2. The People Redeems Itself

1. Ben Zion Dinur, "HaYesodot HaIdeologiim Shel HaAliot BaShenot 5500–5600," in *BaMifneh HaDorot* (Jerusalem, 1955); Rabbi Y. L. HaCohen Maimon, "HaTzionut HaDatit veHitpatchutach," in *LaSha'ah velaDor* (Jerusalem: Mossad Bialik, 1965).

2. Ben Zion Dinburg, *Hibbat Zion* (Tel Aviv: Mosad Harav Kook, 1932–34).

3. *Kitvei HaRav Yehuda H. Alkalay,* brought out and interpreted by Dr. Yitzhak Rafael (Jerusalem, 1975); Ya'akov Katz, "Meshichiut veLeumiut baMishnato shel HaRav Yehuda Alkalay," in *Measef Shivat Zion,* vol. 4 (Jerusalem, 1956).

4. Rabbi Tzvi Hirsch Kalischer, *Drishat Zion,* brought out and annotated by Dr. Israel Klausner (Jerusalem: Mosad Harav Kook, 1965); Ya'akov Katz, "Demuto HaHistorit shel HaRav Tzvi Hirsch Kalischer," in *Measef Shivat Zion,* vols. 2–3, (Jerusalem, 1953).

5. Mordecai Levin, *Erkei Hevrah veKalkalah BaIdeologiah Shel Tekufat HaHaskalah* (Jerusalem: Mossad Bialik, 1976); Israel Klausner, "Shivah LeAvodat Ha'Adamah voleEretz Yisrael," in *Sinai,* no. 246 (Jerusalem, 1957).

6. A typical example of this type of reasoning: Chaim Ya'akov Kramer, *Doresh LeTzion* (1886).

7. Meshullam Natan Brozer, *Tzidkat Zion* (Berditchev, 1903); I. Don Yichieh, *HaTzionut* (Vilna, 1903); Avraham Ya'akov Slotzki, ed., *Shivat Tzion* (Warsaw, 1892).

8. Yonah Dov Blumberg, *Kuntres Mitzvat Yeshivat Eretz Yisrael* (Vilna, 1898), 6.

9. P. Lachover, *Toldot HaSifrut HaIvrit HaChadashah,* chap. 17.

10. For example, Eliezer Ben-Yehuda, *Sefer Eretz-Yisrael* (Jerusalem, 1883).

11. For example, Yehuda Edel Zisling, *Yalkut Eretz-Yisrael* (Vilna, 1890).

12. For example, Eliyakum, Getzel Hurvitz, *Zikkaron Yerushalayim* (Warsaw, 1912).

13. For example, Yonah Dov Blumberg, n. 8.

14. HaRav Yitzhak Nissenbaum, *HaYahadut HaLeumit* (Warsaw, no date), 47–50.

Chapter 3. Why the Land of Israel

1. An instructive example of this is to be found further on in Ber Borochov's essay, "LeShe'elat Tzion veTeritoria," in B. Borochov, *Katavim Nivcharim,* vol. 1 (Am Oved, 1944).
2. *Kol Kitvei Achad HaAm beKerekh Echad,* Dvir, p. 337.
3. Ibid., 339.
4. A typical expression of this appears in the essay "Shalosh Madregot," Ibid., 150–53.
5. "HaBokhim," beginning of the essay.
6. "Kol Bnei HaNe'urim," appeared in *HaMelitz,* Nisan 5642. Also printed in *Darkei HaNo'ar,* G. Hanoch, ed. (Tel Aviv, 1937).
7. Dr. Yitzhak Rielf, "Arukat Bat-Ami," in *Mivchar Ma'amarim,* Hebrew translation, A. Levinson, ed. (Tel Aviv, 1946).
8. A characteristic example appears in Eliezer Ben-Yehuda's pamphlet, *Medinat Ha-Yehudim.*
9. M. L. Lilienblum, *Al Techiat Yisrael Al Admat Avotav* (Jerusalem: Zionist Federation, 1953).
10. Borochov, "LeShe'elat Tzion ve Teritoria," as note 1 above.
11. Borochov, "LeShe'elot HaTeoria HaTzionit," in *Katavim Nivcharim,* vol. 1, as above.
12. A. M. Berakhyahu, "HaMedinah vehaMasoret," in *Nekhasim veArakhin* (Dvir, 1938), pp. 93–116.
13. Ibid., p. 115.

Part IV. Building the Homeland

Chapter 1. Confronting the Real Land

1. "Hoi Artzi, Horati," *Shirat Rahel* (Tel Aviv: Davar Publishing, 1939), 94.
2. I. Lamdan, "BaHamsin," *Massada* (Tel Aviv: Hedim, 1927), chap. 4, 4.
3. S. Y. Agnon, *Tmol Shilshom* (Jerusalem), p. 7.
4. C. N. Bialik, "Megillat HaEsh," verse 6.
5. C. N. Bialik, "Zohar," "HaBreikhah," "Echad Echad uv'Eyn Ro'eh."
6. Rahel "Hoi Artzi, Horati," as note 1 above.
7. E. Schweid, "Kelev Huzot veAdam," in the book *Shalosh Ashmorot* (Tel Aviv: Am Oved, 1964).
8. Israel Ze'ev Hurvitz, *Nachalah LeYisrael* (Jerusalem, 1881)).
9. Z. S. Levontin, *LeEretz Avoteinu,* pt. 1, chap. 19.
10. E. Ben-Yehuda, *Sefer Eretz-Yisrael* (Jerusalem, 1883), foreword.
11. E. Ya'ari, *Zikhronot Eretz-Yisrael* (Tel Aviv: Massada Co., 1946).
12. A. D. Gordon, "HaUmah vehaAvodah," letter written from the land of Israel (Jerusalem: Hasifria Hazionith, 1952), p. 77.
13. Ibid.
14. A. D. Gordon, *Mikhtavim veReshimot*(Jerusalem: Hasifria Hazionith, 1952), p. 91.
15. Ibid., 196.
16. A. D. Gordon, "HaUmah vehaAvodah," *Mikhtav SheLo Nishlach BeZmano,* 493.

Chapter 2. What Should the Homeland Be Like

1. A. Shlonsky, "BeReishit LiYizrael," *Shirim* (Tel Aviv: Sifriath Poalim, 1961), 2:263.
2. A. Shlonsky, "Mul Giv'ah Lo B'nuiah," ibid., 265.
3. A. Shlonsky, "Amal," ibid., 1:165.

4. Contrast E. Schweid, "HaYahadut KeTarbut," in *Emunat Yisrael veTarbuto* (Jerusalem: Zack Co., 1976).

5. Contrast V. K. Laudermilek, *Eretz Yisrael HaAretz HaYe'udah* (Tel Aviv: Massada Co., 1945). What he had to say about the relationship between a people and its soil drew an interested response among contemporary secular Zionist thinkers in the *yishuv*.

6. Rabbi Yehezkel Abramsky, *Eretz Yisrael Nahalat Am Yisrael*, Preface (Jerusalem: Abramsky, n.d.).

7. Ibid.

8. Ibid.

9. Contrast E. Luz, *Dat veLeumiut BaTnu'ah HaTzionit beReishitah* (Ph.D. diss., Brandeis University), chap. 3.

10. E. Schweid, *Demokratia veHalakhah: Studies in the Thought of Rabbi Haim Hirschenson* (Jerusalem: Magnes Press, 1978).

Chapter 3. A. D. Gordon

1. A. D. Gordon to Dubnov, in *Asufot* 7:197–200.

2. E. Schweid, "LeBe'ayat HaMekorot Shel Mishnat A. D. Gordon," in the Proceedings of the World Congress on Jewish Studies, pp. 345–51.

3. Gordon, *Mikhtavim veReshimot,* 196.

4. This subject is treated systematically in Gordon's comprehensive essay, "HaAdam vehaTeva," in his volume on *HaAdam vehaTeva* (Jerusalem: Hasifria Hazionith, 1951). I have dealt with this subject systematically in my book, *HaYehid, Olamo shel A. D. Gordon* (Am Oved, 1970), pt. 3.

5. "Am Adam," *Ketavim,* volume on *HaUmah vehaAvodah,* 258–263.

6. For further discussion of this issue, see my above book, pt. 4, sec. 3.

7. For further discussion of this issue, see my above book, pt. 2, sec. 3.

8. As above, pt. 2, sec. 1.

9. Gordon's writings on this subject are compiled in my booklet, *HaHe'azah LaUtopi—Iyyon bePerakim Aktuali'im MiMishnato shel A. D. Gordon,* (Jerusalem: Ministry of Education and Culture, 1972), 38–41.

10. Gordon, "LeBeirur HaHevdel Bein HaYahadut vehaNotzrut," *Ketavim,* volume on *HaAdam vehaTeva,* 284–85.

11. "Mikhtav Shelo Nishlach beZmano," *Ketavim,* volume on *HaUmah vehaAvodah,* 497.

12. Ibid., 494–95.

13. Ibid., 496.

14. Ibid., 496–97.

15. Gordon, "Mikhtavim LaGolah," *Ketavim,* volume on *HaUmah vehaAvodah,* 560.

16. For further discussion of this issue, see my above book, pt. 5.

17. As above, pt. 6.

18. Gordon, "Mikhtavim LaGolah," as above.

Chapter 4. Rav Kook

1. A. I. Kook, *Orot HaKodesh* (Jerusalem: Mosad Harav Kook, 1963), pt. 2, 423–24.

2. To develop an understanding of this line of thought, see Gershom Scholem, *Shabbatai Tzvi,* vol. 1, chap. 1, sec. 4: "The Lurianic Kabbalah and its Mythology of Exile and Redemption."

3. What follows is based on Rav Kook's essay, "LeMahalakh HaIdeot BeYisrael," in *Orot,* 102–18.

4. Kook, "Orot HaTechiah," in *Orot,* 86–87.
5. The same idea appears in Rabbi Joseph Gikatilla's *Sha'arei Orah,* chap. 2.
6. Kook, "Eretz Yisrael," in *Orot,* 9.
7. Ibid., 9–10.
8. The same idea appears in *Sha'arei Orah,* as above, chap. 1.
9. See Kook, "Zer'onim," sec. 3, in *Orot,* 121–23.
10. Kook, "Orot HaTechiah," in *Orot,* 57–60.
11. "Orot Yisrael," in *Orot,* 171–72.

Chapter 5. The Right of the People

1. A very characteristic example of this way of thinking is to be found in the writings of Ber Borochov. See his "LeShe'elat Tzion veTerritoria," in *Ketavim Nivacharim* (Tel Aviv: Am Oved, 1944), 141. The reader would do well to contrast this with Ahad HaAm's "Perek Zik-hronot," in the "Appendices" to *Al Parashat Derakhim* (Tel Aviv: Dirr, 1947).
2. A well-thought-out summary of this position is to be found in M. Beilinson's essay, "Lemi HaAretz?" (in *Kitvei M. Beilinson*). See the collection *Am veMoledet* (Jerusalem: Histadrat Zionit, 1949), edited by H. Merhavia. The view of H. Arlozorov is most interesting in this connection, for its signals the turning point. Arlozorov criticizes the native, apolitical position of the Jewish *yishuv* on this issue. At the same time, however, he further develops these basic arguments. See his articles, "Me'oraot Mai," "Va'adat HaMandatim vehaTzionut," and "HaYesod HaKalkali shel HaProblema HaAravit," in his *Ketavim* (Stibel, 1933–34), vols. 1 and 2.
3. A characteristic example appears in the above-noted book by Rabbi Yehezkel Abramsky, *Eretz Yisrael Nahalat Am Yisrael.*
4. A. D. Gordon, "HaKongress," in *Ketavim,* volume on *HaUmah vehaAvodah,* 203; "Avodatenu MeAtah," ibid., 243–46; "Mikhtavim LaGolah," ibid., 560.
5. M. Buber, "Mikhtav Galui LeMahatma Gandi," in *Te'udah veYe'ud,* vol. 2 (Jerusalem: Hasifria Hazionith, 1964), pp. 163–75.
6. See E. Simon's book on the "Kav HaTichum" in Buber's thought (Merkaz Lelimudim Arviyim Givat Haviva, 1971).
7. A comprehensive discussion of this issue from a legal and ethical point of view appears in the book *Zekhutenu HaHistorit HaMishpatit Al Eretz Yisrael* by Reuven Gafni (Jerusalem: privately published, 1933).
8. These arguments are to be found in their most complete, systematic form in the following essays: Ben-Zion Dinur, "Zekhutenu al Eretz Yisrael"; Yitzhak Tabenkin, "Iyyunim beShe'elat Zekhutenu al HaAretz"; Dr. A. Heller, "LeMi HaZekhut al HaAretz HaZot?". These are collected in *Tik Mekorot,* no. 5, *Zekhuto Shel Am Yisrael LeEretz Yisrael,* in the *Sidrat Iyyunim BeTorat HaTzionut* (Jerusalem: Zionist Federation, n.d.).
9. As in Z. Jabotinsky's view.
10. As in A. Ya'ari's view.
11. As in D. Ben-Gurion's view.
12. As in Rabbi I. D. Soloveitchik's view.

Conclusion

1. A first discussion of this issue appears in the *Sefer HaMadrikh* by Rav Mordecai Ben HaRav Shmuel Prahlikh (Warsaw, 1876); contrast this with Dr. S. Rubin's notebook, *Eretz HaIvrim* (1884).
2. David Ben-Gurion, "Kadmut Yisrael beArtzo," in *Iyyunim BaTanakh* (Am Oved, 1970).

3. Yosef Azariahu, "Yesod HaMoledet BaChinukh uvaHora'ah," in his *Ketavim,* vol. 2 (Tel Aviv: Histadrut Hamorim, 1946–54).

4. E. Schweid, "No'ar Yisraeli BeAspeklariah Kefulah," in *Shalosh Ashmorot* (Tel Aviv: Am Oved, 1964), pp. 185–202.

5. E. Schweid, "Lifnei Sha'arim Ne'ulim," in *S. Yizhar—Mivhar Ma'amarim al Yetzirato,* ed. ch. Wagid (Tel Aviv: Am Oved, 1972), p. 140–54.

Index